A ROSE VEILED IN BLACK

WESTERN ESOTERICISM IN CONTEXT II

A Rose Veiled in Black

Arcana and Art of Our Lady Babalon

Edited by

ROBERT FITZGERALD & DANIEL A. SCHULKE

THREE HANDS PRESS
2025

 First Three Hands Press paperback edition, February 2025.

Cover image: *The Kisses of the Stars Rain Hard Upon Her Body* by Linda MacFarlane, © 2018.
Original Babalon Henna motifs and Frontispiece Photo by Nicole DiMucci Potts.
Gosses Bluff satellite image in "Nuit and Babalon in Liber Nu" courtesy NASA.
Interior book design and dust jacket design by Joseph Uccello.
Deluxe edition designed by Daniel A. Schulke and James Dunk.

THREE HANDS PRESS
www.threehandspress.com

CONTENTS

Dedicated with Love and Admiration to

Leila Ida Nerissa Bathurst Waddell

MOTHER OF PAIN. MITCHELL NOLTE, 2014. DIGITAL PEN.

INTRODUCTION

The Saints Are Dead:

BABALON IN FUTURITY

And because there is no life therein, the guardians of the abyss shall bid the angels of the winds pass by. And the angels shall lay thy dust in the City of the Pyramids, and the name thereof shall be no more.

Liber Cheth Vel Vallum Abiegni Sub Figura CLVI, v. 6

THE LADY BABALON is one of the more enigmatic figures in the Cult of Thelema. She is a manifold deity in the sense that She is a divine harlot, an initiatrix, a creator and a destroyer. In representative form, the letters of Her name encompass an heptogrammic star; yet She lies beyond mere representation, and Her star signifies only the powers of Her train and not the station of Her immanence. She is the unsignified, a cipher conveying manifestation, and yet the veritable seal of the invisible Order of Illuminated Adepti guiding the course of our spiritual and planetary evolution. In Her subtle and etheric anatomy flows the life-blood of the Saints—the All-Living—and in this is Her deepest mystery, for, as it is written, in the Gospels, and in *Liber 418*, 'The Blood is the Life.' What does this mean and portend?

A saint is defined by his or her utmost faith and devotion unto God, or by the focus of their piety, on whichever deity or spirit is named as such. Usually, they live lives of austerity and ordeal, lives which provide examples of genuine spiritual practice and fealty to the letters of the Law. In Thelema, this Law is represented as Love, and Love under Will. It is a theurgy of union. But, union with what?

With one's Holy Guardian Angel. This is accomplished in a variety of ways, but what these ways have in common, in Thelema as a Cult of Love, is Babalon. For union with one's Holy Guardian Angel may only be had once one has crossed the Abyss, and first achieved union with Her. Those who succeed become the veritable Sainted Ones; known unto each other, yet nameless piles of dust in eternity. This union is perfected only once one has given every last drop of one's blood unto Her. In this is the Mystery of Her name, and the ordeal called the 'Abomination of Desolation.' The Path to Her is a lonely one, and fraught with many setbacks and ordeals. Finally one comes through the Abyss, and the final test is given. One gives all, and one's all is one's very life-blood.

The Mystery of the Blood is an ancient one, perhaps the most archaic mystery pertaining to physical incarnation. In Thelema, the 'drops' of one's blood are every thought, every seed, every womb, every soul that one has been, is and ever shall be. It is a concept that appears on the surface to be metaphorical, yet is anything but. For it is the *only reality* that exists. As a concept permeating the Holy Books of Thelema, it is, like Babalon Herself, expressed in a type of mystical and hypostatic language. It cannot be otherwise, but what is so expressed is a very real thing. This reality is given form in the Gnostic Mass, in the Rite of the Phoenix, and in all rituals dedicated unto Our Lady Babalon. Blood, suffused with the *numena* of one's will and LVX, is freely offered unto Her and the Gods.

Nothing is held back, for to do so would be to profane the very Mystery one is seeking to celebrate. In everything, one must give one's all. For the life of the flesh and the life of the Light, is the blood so given and so taken by the Mother of us all, Lady Babalon.

This aspect illuminates her capacious and dynamic qualities, for inasmuch as Babalon stands squarely within Thelemic tradition, she is neither a force of sequestration of power, nor of orthodoxy. She is, rather, a quintessential power of disruption of these modalities, a position entirely consistent with her appearance in the spirit workings of Dee and Kelley, and Crowley's *The Vision and the Voice*. This creative and disruptive quality shines through also in Parsons' *Liber 49*, despite its controversial status in the Thelemic canon. The embrace of All thus implies the Cup overflowing, a stance of embodiment that cannot be achieved by magical stasis or pure Mind. As such, her very nature demands embrace of the work, the *practice* of the Art of Magick.

Finally, the Saints are those whose lives are dedicated unto Her. Thus, they are the 'Dead'. But they are only dead to us who claim to be the living. In the Body of Our Lady Babalon, they live on, as dust, as sparks of the inmost fire, as examples to us all of their given life-blood and aspiration. May their lives serve as lamps to illuminate and fortify our own love and aspiration unto the Mother of Abomination, the Mother of All-Living.

Ultimately the nature of Babalon cannot be expressed, only experienced. It is our hope that this volume expresses the experience of Her through the art and words of its contributors and devotees.

—Robert Fitzgerald and Daniel A. Schulke

Babalon in the Aethyrs:

A CHRONOLOGY OF MANIFESTATION

Robert Fitzgerald

Though an angel in white robes leadeth me,
who shall ride upon me but the Woman of Abominations?

25th Aethyr, *Liber 418*

SO ASKS THE Lion-Serpent, the Great Beast 666, in the midst of a vision wherein Babalon, albeit veiled, makes Her initial appearance in the then very young Thelemic canon of works. The Angel who leads the Beast is an avatar of the Sphere of Binah, thus an 'Opener of the Way' for Babalon's ingress into the soul-sheaths of the Adept, and the aethyric envelope of the Earth. Earlier in the vision, Babalon remains solely in Biblical attire and metaphor, not yet fully manifest in the passage:

> *The first angel goes to the lion and closes his mouth...And the angel says: Blow, all ye trumpets, for I will loose my hands from the mouth of the lion, and his roaring shall enkindle the worlds.*

Thus, complete with revelatory trumpeting, Our Lady Babalon prepares the Beast to utter His word, and by water and fire usher in the New Aeon.[1]

1 This is both elemental and esoteric in meaning, for the water and fire is both the mode of aeonic transformation and an implicit reference to IX° sexual congress, in which the water is the 'menstruum' and the fire is the 'seed'. For a deeper understanding of the matter, the reader is referred to *Agape vel Liber C vel Azoth*, by the Master Therion.

Comparisons between Babalon in Thelemic cosmogony and the Whore of Babylon in the *Book of Revelations* have been dealt with at length by others, but needless to say the apocalyptic biblical work was very influential upon Therion's mind and outlook. In essence, the Whore of Babylon was, over time, and most especially in the visionary work contained within *Liber 418*, robed and transmogrified into Our Lady, the central mysterium of Thelema as a whole. A fact that should be noted concerning this relation is that Babylon spelt as 'Babalon' numerates cabalistically as 156, which is also the number of the holy mountain of the Semites, Zion, as well as the City of Pyramids within the Sphere of Binah. Each angelic tablet received by John Dee and Edward Kelley in their spirit workings also contains 156 squares, or pyramids (according to the Golden Dawn recension of the material). 156 reduces to 12, and it is within the 12th Aethyr that Babalon firmly establishes Herself. 12 is also the number of the Banners of God, a relation not to be overlooked when operating within the angelic system of evocation.

The following essay is an overview and a chronology of Babalon's appearances and designs within the rubric of *Liber 418: The Vision and the Voice*. It is intended to suggest further and deeper study upon a very complex subject, by no means exhausted herein. *The Vision and the Voice* is a record of Aleister Crowley and Victor Neuberg's exploration of a part of John Dee and Edward Kelley's so-called 'Enochian System of Magic.' Neither Dee nor Kelley ever labeled what they received from various angelic intelligences as 'Enochian'; a nomenclature given the material centuries later by initiates of the Order of the Golden Dawn. For the sake of historical accuracy then, all reference to this 'system' will herein be described merely as 'angelic'. *The Vision and the Voice* are transcriptions of the visions of the 30 Aethyrs as received by the two magicians, with Crowley taking the role of the Seer and Neuberg that of Scribe. The manner in which the aethyrs were opened and recorded is described by Crowley in his *Confessions*:

> *My method of obtaining 'The Vision and the Voice' was as follows: I had with me a great golden topaz (set in a Calvary cross of six squares, made of wood, painted vermilion), engraved with a Greek cross of five squares charged with the Rose of forty-nine petals. I held this as a rule in my hand. After choosing a spot where I was not likely to be disturbed, I would take this stone and recite the Enochian Key, and, after satisfying myself that the invoked forces were actually present, made the topaz play a part not unlike that of the looking-glass in the case of Alice…I would describe what I saw and repeat*

> *what I heard and Frater O.V. would write down my words and incidentally observe any phenomena which struck him as peculiar.*[2]

This is interesting on several levels, but chiefly on account of its simplicity. It almost entirely neglects the methodology that Crowley no doubt learned himself as a member of the Golden Dawn, in which many more steps are followed prior to the 'calling' or 'opening' of any given aethyr. Most important to our examination however, is the use of the dual crosses of both six and five squares, respectively, and bound by the Rose of 49, a number of Babalon. In a sense, perhaps unknown to Crowley at the time, his choice of scrying tool was one wholly consecrated unto Our Lady Babalon, and perhaps played an important role in the type and quality of the visions he received, especially those wherein Babalon communicates and is revealed. It should be remembered that Babalon's initial appearance within Thelema occurs not in *The Book of the Law*, but within the visions of *Liber 418*, exclusively.

28 Aethyrs (the 30th and the 29th were opened in 1900 by Crowley alone in Mexico) were scryed by Crowley and Neuberg in the Saharan desert, Algeria, from November 23rd to December 19th, 1909. The original manuscript of these operations survives in the Harry Ransom Humanities Research Center, University of Texas at Austin. It was first published in *The Equinox* I, Volume 5, in 1911, followed by a second edition, Thelema Publishing Co., in 1952, edited by Crowley's successor, Karl Germer. A third edition, and the one consulted herein was published by the Sangreal Foundation, in 1972, edited by Israel Regardie. A fourth (and so far final) edition was published within *The Equinox* IV, Volume 2, in 1998, edited by William Breeze. All four editions are valuable for material both left in and edited out of the original manuscript by the various editors. In consulting these editions and comparing them with the original manuscript, I have found Regardie's edition to be the most reliable, in terms of presenting relatively intact the wording of the original manuscript. It is however, flawed in its presentation of notes and footnotes, where Regardie mixes his own comments with those of the Master Therion, a deception notable for its egotism, regardless of whether intentional or not.

While Babalon (in an actual form) does not appear until the 25th Aethyr, She is briefly foreshadowed in a passage from the 28th Aethyr, relating to Saturn, and hence to the Sphere of Binah:

2 *The Confessions of Aleister Crowley*. Hill and Wang. New York. 1969, p. 616.

> *Time is not, save in the darkness of Her womb by whom evil came.*

Here Saturn is portrayed as the darkness existent in the womb of the Mother (within the aethyr referenced to Eve), and the vulgar association with evil it implies, both with the Whore of Babylon and later with the first mother of humanity. The territory and the imagery contained in this aethyr is chiefly Aeon of Osiris, for Babalon remains merely an attribute of Saturn. Hope for redemption is given, even this early on in the cosmogony by a later passage which states:

> *Verily the light is hidden, therefore he who hideth himself is like unto the light; but thou openest thyself; thou art like unto the darkness that bindeth the belly of the great goddess.*

It is a mystery of Thelema, and of the Ordeals of the Abyss, that one finds the Light in the Darkness and the Darkness in the Light, and this mystery may only be resolved in each individual star, as is significant to their orbit and incarnation. It hints at the dwelling place of the Adepts in the City of Pyramids, and to what such symbolism refers.

The formula of Babalon concerning the mystery of blood is revealed outright in the 27th Aethyr:

> *O Mother, wilt thou never have compassion on the children of earth? Was it not enough that the Rose should be red with the blood of thine heart, and that its petals should be 7 and by 7?*

The Rose here represents all of the created, i.e., *manifest* universe, of which Our Lady Babalon is its veritable heart. The formula is the number of the rose's petals, being 7 by 7, or 49 in numeration. The number and the formula of the Rose are further explicated in the 15th Aethyr, for which see below.

In the 25th Aethyr is described the arrival of the Great Beast of Revelations. His attributes, weapons and powers are listed. One sentence relating to these is particularly important in regards to Babalon:

> *...and his eight heads are as the charioteer of the West.*

Seven of these heads are given in *The Book of Lies*, Chapter 49: an angel, a saint, a poet, an adulterous woman, a man of valour, a satyr and a Lion-

Serpent. The eighth head is invisible, as the Head of the Order of the Silver Star, but in tandem all become the driver of the Chariot, whose tarot trump is governed by the letter Cheth, which, of course, is the number 8 and the number of the Holy Book dedicated to Babalon (*Liber Cheth Vel Vallum Abiegni Sub Figura CLVI*). Further in the record of the vision it is stated:

> *Yet in him is the woman that devoureth with her water all the fire of God.*

The Charioteer bears the Graal of Immortality, the Cup of Babalon. It is within Her cup that the Elixir is distilled, and every last drop of the Blood of the Adepts freely given. Babalon in the 25th aethyr is the woman who rides the Great Beast, preparing him for the utterance of the Word of the Aeon. Her appearance is implicit, symbolic and residing within him, as the forthcoming Lord of the New Aeon.

Babalon, as a force of initiation, is now preparing the adept, Therion, the Great Beast 666, to cross the Abyss and become one with Her. In the 24th aethyr this initiation is described by a Latin phrase which reads, *tres annos regimen oraculi*. The approximate time period to become a Master of the Temple is three years, which is 156 weeks. Babalon is declaring Her name in time, and the name of the aethyr, NIA, reflects this process. She remains, however, as AIN, *above* the Abyss. Her influence, from the Supernal Spheres, is descending. Therion writes: "*I am the soul of the Aethyr.*" He has achieved his first union with Our Lady Babalon, and like the force of Coph Nia, is duly *crushed*. The perfection of the Adept's vehicles for a complete crossing of the Abyss has not yet occurred and thus the vision remains enigmatic and symbolic in nature and expression. However, within the text of the 24th Aethyr is given a magical formula of four letters in whose combinations anything can be accomplished. Explicitly these letters are T.A.R.O. Esoterically they are Daleth, Teth, Pe and Ayin. Another formula, representing Babalon and the Beast conjoined is given in the name 'Elyon', which numerates to 156.

The manifestation of Our Lady continues in the 22nd Aethyr, still largely in symbolic form, though the symbolism is cosmic in scope. The aethyr appears to Therion in the form of a 'mysterious table of forty-nine squares.' This is the Holy Sevenfold Table received in the Angelic Workings of Dee and Kelley. It contains the names of the Angels of the Seven Planetary Spheres: Sabathiel, Tzadquiel, Madimiel, Shemashiel, Nogahel, Kikabiel and Levaniel. These names are read upon the table in a peculiar fashion, mostly diagonal. The name of Babalon can also be found on the table, albeit in a rather non-linear manner. If the letters are read horizontally in each column from left to right, magical formulas are given, each for the grounding of planetary energies within the body of the Adept and upon the earth. The table manifests in the vision amongst globules of dew, the

S	A	A	$^{21}_{8}$	E	M	E$_{8}$
B	T	Z	K	A	S	E$_{30}$
H	E	I	D	E	N	E
D	E	I	M	O	L$_{30}$	A
I$_{26}$	M	E	G	C	B	E
I	L	A	O	I$^{21}_{8}$	V	N
I	H	R	L	A	A	L$^{21}_{8}$

exudation of the Lion-Serpent, who governs the aethyr after a secret fashion. Yet it is ultimately Babalon who generates both the energy and the visionary array of the aethyr, for the Sevenfold Table is also Her Name and Her Sigil, in its relation to the Silver Star. The mystery of the aethyr is given as follows:

> *As there are 49 letters in the tablet, so are there 49 kinds of cosmos in every thought of God. And there are 49 interpretations of every cosmos, and each interpretation is manifested in 49 ways. Thus also are the calls 49, but to each call there are 49 visions. And each vision is composed of 49 elements...*

In the Angelic System of Dee and Kelley, there are 19 calls that open the Aethyrs, and summon the sub-elemental tabular spirits. The 49 calls referenced in the vision of the 22nd Aethyr correlate to calls found in an angelic transmission called *Liber Logaeth*, and the reader is referred thereuto. There exist no English translation of these calls, but in the present author's experience they serve chiefly to open astral gates belonging to and governed over by, Our Lady Babalon. An examination of *Liber Logaeth* and its relationship with Babalon is presently being conducted and written by the author, and will be published in due time. The vision and the table introduce Babalon as the Initiatrix of the New Aeon. The mystery of it remains unfathomable, yet Her angel declares:

> *For though thou art joined to the inmost mystery of the heaven, thou must accomplish the sevenfold task of the earth, even as thou sawest the Angels from the greatest unto the least.*

This 'sevenfold task' refers to working with the Planetary Angels of the tablet and to the utilization of the formula, ARARITA, in which all things are resumed into One. Of this, the reader is advised to consult Therion's *Liber 813 vel Ararita*, in which the complete formulary is given.

It is not until the 16th Aethyr is reached that Babalon makes a personal appearance, so to speak, and She is accompanied by the Angels of the Holy Sevenfold Table. She appears as a '*crowned virgin riding upon a bull*', thus illustrating the primeval archetype of Woman and Animal, and she '*lusts ever to mate myself with some beast*.' Here is the Mystery of Babalon made flesh, for upon the earth Her duty is to ride the Beast and draw forth his power and his seed, to give birth to mighty generations of abominable beings, those who understand the lust of the Goat and Snake. This concept is cognate with all heathen forms of worship, and reveals the lie that became 'civilization'. For it is only through the chaos of multiple types of breeding that the New Aeon may come to pass, and in myriads of genetic combinations. The ancients understood this in their very *blood*. And so it is that the Aeon shall be proceeded by great fire and great shedding of blood.

She continues, saying, '*And this is the salvation of the world...*' As the vision of the aethyr unfolds, the ministers and powers of the Beast are described. At its conclusion, Babalon as Virgin continues to ride upon the bull and is

> *...led by all those Angels of the Holy Sevenfold Table, and they are dancing around her with garlands and sheaves of flowers, loose robes and hair dancing in the wind.*

Then she reveals the Mystery of Union unto the Beast. Therion returns to earth on the wings of an eagle, and the mystery is sealed and seen by those with eyes to see. For the Angel of the Aethyr earlier declares: *Blessing and Worship to the Prophet of the Lovely Star*! It should be noted that the name of the 16th Aethyr is LEA, one of many revealed names of Our Lady Babalon.

Babalon's dance continues as the opening vision of the 15th Aethyr, in which as a column of fire She is '*...the lust of the spirit that eateth up the soul of man. I have prepared a feast for the adepts, and they that partake thereof shall see God.*' Her dance then becomes a '*Crimson Rose of 49 Petals*' in which She enters into its center. The Rose transforms into a huge amphitheater. Inside is a table that is a mystery '*...known only to the Angels and the Holy Sevenfold Table.*' This is the twelvefold table known as OIT. It is in totality the Angel known as HUA, who rules over the mysteries of the Supernals in the aethyrs as a whole. The table contains names of God that each invoke one of the elements. When read diagonally the letters form names of demons. It is through the revelation of both the Seven and the Twelvefold tables that Babalon declares and serves the God whose Name is concealed. The 15th Aethyr shows Babalon as both symbol (fire and rose) and as the feminine minister of the Rosy Cross. The entire aethyr and its message was foreshadowed by the metamorphoses of the girl-angel Madimi in the Angelic Records of Dee and Kelley over five hundred years ago. The (literal) groundwork is being laid for the final initiations of the Seer into the mysteries of the grade of Master of the Temple.

It is not until Therion scryed the 12th Aethyr that Babalon fully manifested. He writes:

> *The twelfth Aethyr describes the City of the Pyramids, whose queen is called BABALON, the Scarlet Woman, in whose hand is a cup filled with the blood of the saints. Her ecstasy is nourished by the desires which the Masters of the Temple have poured from their hearts for her sake. In this symbolism are many mysteries concealed. One is that if a single drop of blood be withheld from her cup it putrefies the being below the Abyss and vitiates the whole course of the adept's career.*[3]

The Mystery of Her Cup and the Blood of the Saints is the prime mysterium of Her cult, and the imagery witnessed by Therion in the 12th Aethyr demonstrates it amply. The aethyr opens to reveal a chariot of white fire.

3 *The Confessions of Aleister Crowley*, p. 622.

The charioteer clasps the chalice of Babalon. The chalice emanates a perfumed glow like that of Abramelin oil. The smell of human blood is especially prominent. The charioteer speaks:

> *Let him look upon the cup whose blood is mingled therein, for the wine of the cup is the blood of the saints. Glory unto the Scarlet Woman, Babalon the Mother of Abominations, that rideth upon the Beast, for she hath spilt their blood in every corner of the earth, and lo! She hath mingled it in the cup of her whoredom. With the breath of her kisses hath she fermented it, and it hath become the wine of the Sacrament, the wine of the Sabbath; and in the Holy Assembly hath she poured it out for her worshippers, and they have become drunken thereon, so that face to face they have beheld my Father. Thus are they made worthy to become partakers of the mystery of this holy vessel, for the blood is the life.*

In this speech the angel-charioteer reveals the Mystery of the Cup and the Blood. All adepts, in order to become Masters of the Temple, must give every last drop of their blood into Her cup, or else be lost in the eternal horrors of the Abyss. In other words, they must undergo and pass through *every* ordeal that the Abyss throws their way. For it is the Ordeals of the Path towards the Supernals that are their 'drops of blood.' One cannot cheat the Watcher and the Dweller at the Threshold. And, as the angel later discloses in the vision of the 12th Aethyr, one cannot hold back a single drop or substitute the blood of another, be it human or animal, in its stead, as shown in the parable of Passover. The Angel of Death is but a hypostatic emanation of Our Lady Babalon, a mystery perpetually misunderstood by both Jews and Christians. The true meaning of sacrifice, for the Master of the Temple, is that *every* last drop of blood must be poured into Her cup, lest the Wine of the Sabbath become corrupted and a seething pool of qlippothic slime. In light of this mystery, the angel continues:

> *This is the Mystery of Babalon, the Mother of Abominations, and this is the mystery of her adulteries, for she hath yielded up herself to everything that liveth, and hath become a partaker in its mystery. And because she hath made herself the servant of each, therefore is she become the mistress of all. Not as yet canst thou comprehend her glory.*

Babalon gives herself to all, even to those who fail the Ordeal of the Abyss, for in the chance union with all may the Great Work be accomplished.

This is not merely a vulgar expression of whoredom, but the greatest and most honorable of Her gifts to the Adepti. But in Her sacrifice, our own is demanded: the Blood of the Saints, and not the only saints who were, but those who are, and shall ever exist. Thus is her glory defined and sealed, for as the angel also pronounces:

> *Blessed are the saints, that their blood is mingled in the cup, and can never be separate any more. For Babalon the Beautiful, the Mother of Abominations, hath sworn by her holy kteis, whereof every point is a pang, that she will not rest from her adulteries until the blood of everything that liveth is gathered therein, and the wine thereof laid up and matured and consecrated, and worthy to gladden the heart of my Father.*

Babalon continues to expand throughout the aethyr and expound upon the universal mysteries, and it is within the 12th Aethyr, LOE, that She reveals nearly All. Therion writes in a note, '...*the death or love of the saints is really increased life. The formula of 156 is constant copulation or Samadhi on everything.*' The great mystery of the Gate of God, ON, is given, and its numeration, 120. This name is one of the Keys of Thelema, and its magic is portrayed in the mystery-plays of the rituals of the O.T.O. It is the Word and Formula that opens all gates, and the study of its letters, Ayin and Nun, will prove elucidating. It is one of the formulas of the Beast and the Woman conjoined, and is central to the secret of the IX°.

The angel-charioteer as Babalon concludes the vision of the aethyr with a discourse upon the relationship of the spheres and paths of the Tree of Life with the aethyrs, of which each individual must divine on their own. But She says, without explanation, '...*that in the Aethyrs is the knowledge of the Aeons, and of Thelema,*' making their study essential for any interested in the magic of Babalon and the Angelic System of Dee and Kelley.

The name of Babalon is invoked and the 10th Aethyr—that of Choronzon—is passed through. Herein is revealed the nature of Restriction, which may only truly be understood by those who have nurtured a love of Our Lady and maintained control over their lesser desires. In this is Choronzon seen as one of the Initiators of Her Ordalium: Choronzon is the Dweller in the Abyss, and is the face of the Adept's adversary. It may only be reckoned with, never defeated, for Choronzon is a child of Babalon and *beyond* understanding.

Whether realizing it or not, the confrontation with Choronzon ushered Therion across the Abyss. At the heart of the 10th Aethyr dwells the angel

Paraoan, who also ministers the mysteries of the 22nd Aethyr, wherein the Holy Sevenfold Table is shown in its entirety. Paraoan remains to the present day one of the more enigmatic angelic figures within the framework of the Watchtowers. I believe the entity to be resonant with the energies of a universal holy guardian angel type of entity, and one that oversees not merely a single individual, but entire planetary spheres. The table upon which his name is derived is the 'Rose of Babalon' Herself. It remains the work of present and future Adepts to integrate Paraoan's identity and role within the system as a unity.

In the 9th Aethyr Therion is approached by an angel who asks him, '*Who is this that cometh forth from the Abyss from the place of rent garments, the habitation of him that is only a name?*" Thus begins a series of questions and refrains in which the glory of Babalon is sung, and the non-identity of Therion is established, since, by passing through the Abyss he has attained unto the City of the Pyramids, his blood gathered in Her cup, and is now little more than a pile of dust. This is where the Adepts go and this is what they ultimately become, when their ego and their life-blood is absorbed in the Rose-Heart of Babalon.

After being so questioned, the Seer is shown a vision of the Daughter of Babalon, who is Babalon herself, and is escorted to a small chamber that is a map room. Herein is the Map of the Aethyrs which is seen as a flaming sword that descends through the Tree of Life. In order that the map be properly seen and comprehended, the Seer must 'invoke the Highest'. The Seer is not prepared and thus is cast forth from the map room and from the aethyr. In the 9th Aethyr Babalon has become a type of guide in the form of Her daughter. The mystery of the daughter is that she is ever a virgin and yet is the Bride of the King, and returns him to his Throne in the Supernals. A further and deeper union between Babalon and the Seer is implicated, and in part revealed, but only enough that pertains to the grade, or level of the Adept in the throes of such a betrothal. Herein are veils upon veils, but also an exaltation of spirit best expressed by the Seer himself when he declares during the midst of the vision:

> *Holy, Holy, Holy art thou, and blessed be Thy name forever, unto whom the Aeons are but the pulsings of thy blood.*

Babalon takes Her most dramatic physical and psychical formation in the 7th Aethyr, known as DEO. Therion in his note on the name states that it numerates to the number 44, which is the number for 'blood'. Also the letters of the name equate to the Fates, all women, who spin the Wheel of Destiny, to Virgo, the eternal Virgin, and to Libra, who bears the Sword of Wisdom and the Scales of Justice. This triad (actually a double trinity, with the Fates being three in number) reveal Babalon to be manifest fully in the sensorium of the Seer, who made the magical link with his HGA in the previous (8th) Aethyr. She appears as an angel and begins to lecture the Seer on the mysteries of the Word and Formulas of the New Aeon. She reveals that Her name '*concealeth the holy word that is the key of the abyss.*'

Therion postulates that this word is N.O.X., a magical formula that does indeed contain Her name. Perhaps the most important revelation is a continuation of what She revealed earlier in Latin: That the word TARO is the formula to use when uttering the Word of the Aeon, which Therion believed was THELEMA, though I believe he was mistaken in this, and that BABALON under the rubric of Night as espoused in the N.O.X. formula and appertaining rites, is the true word. Yet all of these mysteries of the Word are Hers to give and his alone to receive, and She tells him that, '*...of this thou hast not even the first letter.*' Even the Prophet of the Lovely Star will not be assuaged or relieved from the Ordeal X!

Babalon proceeds to show the Seer a series of visions concerning the Universal Peacock, and She does this in, '*...the form of a woman like the woman in the Apocalypse, but her beauty and her radiance are such that one cannot look thereon, save with sidelong glances.*' This is a curious phenomenon of the aethyr experience in general. Most of the angels and spirits in these realms take forms and ideas from the minds of enfleshed mortals and use them to clothe themselves with, as it were. It is not surprising that Babalon appeared to Therion as the Whore of Babylon. She takes many forms and all forms and appears to each Seer in a manner through which they can apprehend her 'glory'. Yet even the Master Therion cannot look at her directly! This is because Babalon originates from the Supernal spheres. She is a form of Nuit, of infinite space. As an earthly avatar borne of the Father (Saturn) she is the Mistress of Ordeals on all physical planes of existence.

Babalon continues Her knowledge lecture unto the Seer, revealing how, as Eve, she gave birth via the Serpent. She shows him the nightmare of the Black Brothers who have locked up their blood and failed the Ordeal of the Abyss. As the Libran Consort, Babalon reveals unto the Seer her house of origin and that one may only truly utter Her name in one's heart, and not through speech. But the Seer possesses not the Key to the House of Love, and is thus returned to his body.

The key to understanding Babalon in the aethyr of DEO is through the N.O.X. formula, for which see Book 4, by the Master Therion. The formula cannot be understood with the intellect, but only through the higher vehicles of perception, once one has crossed the Abyss and come to the Night of Pan. These matters by necessity may only be spoken of in poetic terminology; hence the language not only found in *Liber 418*, but also throughout the Holy Books of Thelema.

In the 3rd Aethyr, the Seer receives all visions and information 'interiorly'. He is given a great deal of cabalistic lore and religious gnosis. Babalon only appears to him in this context, and in two vital passages. Here is the first:

> *And for this is BABALON under the power of the Magician, that she hath submitted herself unto the work; and she guardeth the Abyss. And in her is a perfect unity of that which is above; yet she is sent as the Redeemer to them that are below. For there is no other way into the Supernal Mystery but through her, and the Beast on which she rideth* ..

Therion saw Choronzon as an evil demon of dispersion, and in this he was correct, but only on a certain level. What he did not fathom was that Babalon *guardeth the Abyss.* One of her guardians was the Serpent, and Choronzon manifests in the vulgar idea of the Serpent as Tempter and Destroyer to all initiates at a specific interval of their journey towards the Supernal realms. He, as She, is the *Great Terror*, that is the offspring and ordeal of Her father, Saturn. The delusion of the Magician is insanity, and Choronzon unchecked, meaning, *un-equilibriated*, becomes a final obstacle that will ultimately destroy the Magician to the point where he or she will become a 'Black Brother', a thing of filth and corruption unable to withstand or behold the glory of the Vision of Babalon. One can only achieve the unity that is above the Abyss through Her in union with the Beast. This eternal copulation is thus the mystery of Incarnation, and one profaned by nearly every monotheistic and dualistic culture and religion on the earth. The Word of Sin is restriction and the denial of the Flesh that *redeems* through the blood that is Her sacrament.

The second passage runs:

> *...for BABALON is thy fortress against the iniquity of the Abyss, of the iniquity of that which bindeth her unto the Crown, and barreth her from the Crown; for not until thou art made one with CHAOS canst thou begin that*

> *last, that most terrible projection, the three-fold Regimen which alone constitutes the Great Work.*

This 'three-fold Regimen' is revealed by Babalon herself as BABALON, CHAOS and TARO. The formula is dual in exaction: Babalon and the Beast, or the work of Unity, and Taro, the building of the framework of the universe within one's soul. It should be noted that CHAOS numerates to 156. Combined with Babalon, also 156, is 312, or 6. 6 and 6 is 12, and 312 is 26 x 12, or, the Twelve Banners of God. These twelve rule over the entirety of the Aethyrs, and their interpenetration of each gives a superior understanding of the workings of the Universe beyond the map of the Sephiroth.

The 2nd Aethyr ARN is wholly saturated by Babalon, both in ideas and form. She is reflected throughout the entire matrix of the aethyr, and it could be said that She *is* the aethyr itself. Legends of the myth of creation, of the Serpent and Eve, of Cain and Abel, of brother and sister as husband and wife, of the progeny borne of woman and beast—all allegories relating the truths of these are recounted in the 2nd Aethyr. She gives the numbers of Her essence, being and form to the Seer. As a masculine angel she provides the New Aeonic translation of the First Angelic Call. Within it, life is celebrated as the play between CHAOS and BABALON, which is quite transgressive when compared to the original received by Dee and Kelley. The rest of the aethyr is comprised of information relevant only to a Master of the Temple. In Babalon 'all power is given.' She is the Flaming Sword that is the soul of Libra, the Balance of the Universe. The profundity of the record is truly beyond further commentary.

In the 1st Aethyr, LIL, Babalon takes on full manifestation as the Crowned and Conquering Child, Horus. She is ever the 'Babe in the Egg'.

By reading the records of the Aethyrs, as scryed by the Master Therion, one is brought into subtle and overwhelming contact with the Body and Spirit of Our Lady Babalon. Her nature and formulas are both implicitly and explicitly revealed, yet only after a fashion peculiar to the soul of the Great Beast 666. Through their study, and through constant meditation upon Her holy book, *Liber Cheth*, may the Student and Seeker of the Mysteries of Thelema come to a comprehension, both small and large, of the meaning of *Understanding*, which resides solely in the City of the Pyramids.

THE UNVEILING OF BABALON WITHIN THE VISIONS OF *LIBER 418*

Uti, 25th aethyr: Babalon appears as the Great Mother Isis. Her mystery is portrayed wholly symbolically, and according to the mythic imagery of past aeons. Herein is the first appearance of Babalon as the literal Seal of the A∴A∴.

Nia, 24th aethyr: Babalon appears as Venus, and is clothed with the finery of the Scarlet Woman. The initial formula of Her essence and word is tabulated. The symbolic sheaths begin to wear thin.

Lin, 22nd aethyr: The formula becomes fixed in the Holy Sevenfold Table, which demonstrates the power of Her Seal. The Rosy Cross appears.

Oxo, 15th aethyr: The Rosy Cross becomes established in the Void as the means of Manifestation. The Word of the Aeon is uttered in silence, and its Name is BABALON.

Loe, 12th aethyr: The Mystery of Babalon is revealed and She takes flesh, the Glory of Her Holy Kteis exalted.

Zax, 10th aethyr: The Horror of the Abyss is shewn to be the Babe of Babalon, the demon Choronzon. In the Abyss resides the Heart of Her Rose. Her Name resounds as the only sound heard by those still possessing sense.

Zip, 9th aethyr: The Song of Our Lady Babalon resounds throughout the Universe and establishes at the Beginning the Four Watchtowers of Creation. She manifests as her daughter, a mystery of Generation.

Deo, 7th aethyr: Babalon becomes the Wheel and Her formulas are given forth unto the Seer. The Joy of All is given to those strong enough to feel it.

Zon, 3rd aethyr: The Mysteries of the Magician reveal the formulas of Babalon in light of ancient sacraments and identities, particularly those of Lilith. Note that Lilith is herein described in a most abased manner and form, a blind hiding the fact that She is, indeed, the Queen of Night. Let there not be confusion however: Lilith is NOT Babalon as many have declared. Babalon IS Lilith, as She is ALL THINGS. Therion adhered to many Old Aeonic ideas; he was never able to fully escape the 'Wisdom' of the Patriarchs.

Arn, 2nd aethyr: Babalon fully manifests as the Woman riding the Beast. The mysteries of Her nature give rise to an accurate English translation of the 19th Key, in which She is clearly identified with the Mountain of Abiegnus. Thus, is She finally 'unveiled.'

Our Lady Babalon and Her Cup of Fornications:

APPROACHES TO A THELEMIC GODDESS

Gordan Djurdjevic

Gods are dangerous when they manifest themselves clearly.

—Homer, *The Iliad*

THELEMA, GREEK FOR 'Will', is a religio-philosophical system inaugurated by the British poet, practitioner of magical arts, and prolific writer of esoteric literature, Aleister Crowley (1875–1947). According to his own account, in the Spring of 1904 Crowley received, via direct-voice transmission, the text of *The Book of the Law*, the fundamental source of the Thelemic doctrine, and the year 1904 is in consequence considered the inception of the New Aeon announced by this prophetic text. *The Book of the Law* or *Liber AL vel Legis* (subsequently cited as *AL*) is a difficult text to summarize and Crowley himself firmly believed that its meaning is to be left for individual Thelemites (persons accepting the law of Thelema) to determine for themselves. The following few remarks should nevertheless suffice in order to provide the necessary context for the subsequent exposition of the subject matter that forms the focus of this paper.

The three chapters that comprise *The Book of the Law* are related to the three main *dramatis personae* of the text; these are the principal divine figures of Thelema: the Goddess Nuit (first chapter), her counterpart Hadit (second chapter), and their 'child', Heru-Ra-Ha (third chapter). Heru-Ra-Ha has a dual aspect: in his active form, he is referred to as Ra-Hoor-Khuit, while his passive form is known as Hoor-Par-Kraat. (From one point of view, this Thelemic Trinity consists of the Mother, Father, and Child, while from another, gendered perspective, it consists of Woman, Man, and Androgyne.) Nuit is related to 'Infinite Space, and the Infinite Stars thereof' (*AL* I: 22). She is the Lady of the Stars and represents the totality of the universe, without and within, in its unlimited potential. Hadit, her counterpart, is somewhat analogous to the Hindu Upanishadic concept of Ātman. Nuit is circumference without borders and Hadit is the center, which is everywhere, 'in every heart of man, and in the core of every star' (*AL* II: 6). The relationship between Nuit and Hadit is compared by Crowley to the relationship between Śiva and Śakti in Tantra, or between Tao and Teh in Lao Tzu's Taoism. Heru-Ra-Ha, an aspect of god Horus, is considered to be the Lord of the present historical cycle, which Crowley also designates as the Aeon of the Crowned and Conquering Child.

According to Crowley's exegesis, the central message of *The Book of the Law* is broadly speaking encapsulated in three sentences from the text. These are: 'Do what thou wilt shall be the whole of the Law' (*AL* I: 40); 'Love is the law, love under will' (*AL* I: 57); and, 'Every man and every woman is a star' (*AL* I: 3). Crowley consistently and robustly rejected the 'do as you like' interpretation of the import of the first quoted maxim. Instead, he argued that every individual has a unique will, which needs to be discovered and pursued with utmost determination. In a similar vein, the nature of this will is by the second maxim explained to be love. Crowley understands love as a drive towards union between any two elements, such as subject and object for example, but which can take infinite number of forms, and which drive in many respects carries similarity with the Hindu concept of Yoga (etymologically, 'union'). The third maxim is self-explanatory but it merits remarking that its import is that the source of light, for each individual, lies within him or her. It is, in a sense, simply a rephrasing of the statement 'The kingdom of God is within you' (Luke 17: 21).

The above considerations were necessary in order to contextualize the basic background of the discussion that follows. The context is the arrival of the New Aeon (of the Crowned and Conquering Child, Horus), the new religion or ideology (Thelema), and its Prophet (Crowley as the solar Beast). The Beast, however, is not the sole representative of the new dispensation: he functions together with his magical partner who is also designated with reference to the Book of Revelation as the Scarlet Woman, who rides upon the Beast and holds up her cup of fornication. The text of the Book of Revelation (17: 5) refers to her as Babylon but Crowley (1998, p. 152), as a result of information delivered in a particular vision, adopts a variant title and calls her Babalon, translating her name as 'the Gate of the God On [Sun].'[1] Babalon is thus one of the fundamental theomorphic concepts in Thelema, endowed with an array of qualifying determinants. It will become evident in due course that Babalon relates to Nuit, to a kabbalistic Sephira on the Tree of Life, to a particular spiritual experience, to a mode of meditation, to a form of sexual practice, and to an attitude towards reality and one's fate. All of these complex elements are perhaps most pointedly unified in a particular symbolic image of Babalon, and that is the image of the Whore. The rest of this essay will be devoted to exploration of the above set of notions with an emphasis on sexual aspects inherent in the idea of Babalon.

BABALON IN *THE BOOK OF THE LAW* AND *THE VISION AND THE VOICE*

The principal textual source of Crowley's prophetic claim is *The Book of the Law*. A relevant verse from the first chapter of the book announces: 'Now ye shall know that the chosen priest & apostle of the infinite space is the prince-priest the Beast; and in his woman called the Scarlet Woman is all power given' (*AL* I: 15). Crowley argued that these two, the Beast and the Scarlet Woman, are two principal officers of the New Aeon. Throughout his life, Crowley searched for a magical partner who would satisfactorily perform the role of the Scarlet Woman and a number of his mistresses assumed the mantle, often for only a short span of time. The nature of the office will be discussed subsequently but it is important at this stage to underscore what was already mentioned in connection with Crowley's identification with the Beast: the nature of these archetypes (the Beast and the Scarlet Woman) was re-interpreted as indicative of the new ideological orientation provided by the system of Thelema and the intention was emphatically not to side with the forces of evil but to provide a novel model of service to humanity.[2] It is thus utterly out of place to consider Crowley

1 See Aleister Crowley et al., *The Vision and the Voice: With Commentaries and Other Papers*, Weiser, 1999, p. 152. This text was first published as a 'Special Supplement' in Aleister Crowley et al., *The Equinox: A Review of Scientific Illuminism*, Vol. I, no. 5, 1911, pp. 1–176.

2 'My mortal part was to help humanity by Jupiterian work, such as governing, teaching, creating, exhorting men to aspire to become nobler, holier, worthier, kinglier, kindlier and more generous'. Aleister Crowley, *The Confessions of Aleister Crowley*, Arkana,

and Thelema 'Satanic', and the pervasive endurance of this gross misconception is lamentable.

The Book of the Law does not specifically mention Babalon. A verse spoken by the Goddess Nuit in the first chapter of the text relates to her prophet that she has 'a secret name which I will give him when at last he knoweth me' (*AL* I: 22). Crowley later argued that this secret name is in fact Babalon. The name and the character of Babalon are revealed in a visionary text of considerable complexity known as *The Vision and the Voice*. This text is in fact a magical record, detailing the results of Crowley's work with the system of Enochian magick, based on the Golden Dawn elaboration of the material originally complied by the Elizabethan scholarly magus John Dee and his collaborator Edward Kelley. Crowley's magical partner in this instance was the British poet Victor Neuburg and the work consisted of ritual invocations conducted while traveling on foot in the Algerian part of the Sahara desert in 1909. As a result of these invocations, Crowley received a significant body of teachings that, he was convinced, both elaborated upon and provided further confirmation of the fundamentals of Thelema initially presented in *The Book of the Law*. The whole episode, which took about a month of daily work, assumed for Crowley also the character and formal aspect of initiation and he claimed that as a result of these experiences he managed to cross the Abyss—a technical term denoting the annihilation of personality—and thus became a Master of the Temple—another technical term, in this case referring to a person who has successfully crossed the Abyss.

The Vision and the Voice provides a significant elaboration of the Thelemic world-view and is 'a principal scriptural source for the Theogony of the Supernal Triad of the Crowned and Conquering Child, Chaos, and Babalon'.[3] The Supernal Triad mentioned in the quote refers to the three highest *sephiroth* on the kabbalistic Tree of Life (Kether, Chokmah, and Binah); in a more simplified terms, it may be considered a Thelemic equivalent of the Holy Trinity, replacing the Christian Father-Son-Holy Ghost with the Child-Father-Mother. From a certain point of view, the role of Babalon is paramount in this initiatic context, for it is through her agency that a candidate, in this case Crowley, is able to cross the Abyss and achieve an understanding of the universe from an ego-less point of view. It emerges from the text that Babalon is both a theophany and a symbolic

1979, p. 622.

3 V.V., in Crowley, *Vision and Voice*, p. X.

reference for a particular attitude towards trans-subjective reality. Babalon is referred to as a Harlot and as such she stands in stark opposition to the symbol of the Virgin Mary in Christianity, who is here considered as representative of the formula of shutting oneself up, expressed through her continence. This is a sensitive and highly controversial subject and as such it deserves further clarification.

At the outset, it is essential to consider the context: *The Vision and the Voice*, the principal source of the Thelemic ideas regarding Babalon, is a magical record documenting an attempt to transcend and annihilate one's ego in order to achieve the higher spiritual understanding of reality. This is a process that involves letting go and opening up and, in doing so, dissolving the habitual egocentric grip on identity boundaries. The opposite of that is the process of walling oneself in, of building up a 'fortress' of one's identity. Structurally and analogically, these two attitudes, the opening up as opposed to walling in, may be—and in the case of *The Vision and the Voice* actually are—symbolized by the Harlot and the Virgin. The content of the visionary and auditory experience and its subsequent exegesis convinced Crowley that these two, the Harlot and the Virgin, represent two opposing magical formulae, and he associated the latter with what he perceived as the imperfection in the Christian world-view. This imperfection ultimately consists of the fear of life expressed through the resistance to open oneself completely up to it, leading to the dichotomy of good versus evil, God versus Devil.

In his commentaries on *The Book of the Law*, Crowley (1996, p. 171) identifies the Scarlet Woman with the Hindu Tantric notion of *śakti* and correlates her further with the symbol of the 'magical door' that stands between the Tao and the material/manifested world. He expands: 'The great Obstacle then is if that Door be locked up. Therefore Our Lady must be symbolized as an Whore'.[4] Obviously, the opposite tendency is the gesture of shutting: 'Shutting the Door is preventing the Operation of Change, i.e. of Love'.[5] Citing the classic examples of Circe, Calypso, Kundry et al. as representatives of this negative tendency, and clarifying the associated danger that they present as a liability to be shut up 'in their Gardens', Crowley sets forward the conceptual implications to their final conclusion and in the process arrives at one of the cornerstones of Thelemic worldview. He argues that the ultimate danger inherent in the process of shut-

4 Aleister Crowley, *The Law is For All*, New Falcon, 1996, p. 171.

5 Ibid.

ting oneself up against the forces of change amounts to the idea of *nirvāṇa* (Pali, *nibbana*) understood as the 'eternal rest', which he robustly rejects. 'This nibbana-idea is the coward "Mother's Boy" idea; one ought to take a refreshing dip in the *tao*, no more. I think this must be brought forward as the Cardinal Point of Our Holy Law.'[6]

The symbol of the Harlot obviously contains a strong sexual element. It is characteristic of the notion of Babalon that the correlation between symbolic and literal interpretation of its meaning is tight, as hinted by the intimate connection between *sephirot* Binah and Malkuth on the Tree of Life, standing among other correlates for the Mother and the Daughter. There are also clear indications that Crowley considered what he terms the 'formula of Babalon' as an expression of both the general attitude towards life and as a specific method of meditation. In his commentary to a chapter from *The Book of Lies*, Crowley writes: 'The chapter is a counsel to accept all impressions; it is the formula of the Scarlet Woman'.[7] One could argue that there is a trace of his former Buddhist meditation training in the cited instruction 'to accept all impressions'. As an overall indication for one's orientation towards world and life, this is an embracing gesture. That this is symbolized by the image of the Harlot, who similarly accepts everybody without picking and choosing, is somewhat unexpected but not necessarily out of place, as it is somewhat unexpected to express one's relationship towards the field of one's perceptual experience by stating that 'the formula of 156 [the numerical value of Babalon] is constant copulation or *samādhi* on Everything.'[8] But the symbolic and meditational application of the formula of the Scarlet Woman/Babalon is only a part of the picture, the other component being its employment as a sexual formula. This latter aspect is best contextualized through an example of one of Crowley's lovers.

LEAH HIRSIG AND BABALON

Crowley considered his major magical and sexual partners as Scarlet Women. He composed an oath that such partners were to take upon formal acceptance of their office, based on the instructions from *The Book of the Law*. Arguably, the most noteworthy of these women was the American high

6 Ibid.

7 Aleister Crowley, *The Book of Lies*, Weiser, 1981, p.19.

8 Crowley, *Vision and the Voice*, p.152, n.1.

school teacher of Swiss extraction, Leah Hirsig (1883–1975). They met in New York City and later moved to Italy where Crowley and his disciples rented a villa in Cefalù, which they transformed into an Abbey of Thelema. Leah assisted Crowley in some of his major magical activities and initiations, assuming herself the role of Alostrael, the 'Virgin Guardian of the Sangraal'. One aspect of their common practice had to do with their mutual agreement to give their bodies freely to whoever desired it. In addition, magical activities in the Abbey were spiced with the regular and copious consumption of a variety of intoxicants.

It is relatively easy to understand Crowley's activities in Cefalù as example of his unrestrained hedonism at the best and of his utter depravity at the worst. But there is a room for an alternative interpretation. I suggest that both Crowley and Hirsig underwent an extreme phase of devotional self-abandonment while in Cefalù. They experienced and engaged with what Julia Kristeva calls abjection: an uncanny power resulting from the collapse of social order that relates to transgression, humiliation, and filth and which she significantly interprets as an attitude towards Mother.[9] More specifically, their mutual and consensual immersion in sexual and substance-use excesses could be read as an attempt to implement some of the injunctions contained in *Liber AL* as well as in *Liber CLVI*, a short inspired text focused on the explorations of the 'mysteries of the Holy Grail'. At the obvious level of the meaning of this text, it seems apparent that the devotion towards Babalon, which leads to the Grail, consists in renouncing everything that one is and has. In many respects, the events at the Abbey of Thelema fit this scenario.

The most tragic event that occurred during the Cefalù period was without doubt the death of Crowley's and Hirsig's daughter Poupée. Crowley's diaries testify to the extent of his suffering at the time. A curious remark brings the episode into specific light related to the subject matter at hand. Crowley asks a rhetorical question: Why wasn't he able to save the life of his child using his magical powers, which he was apparently persuaded of? His response is that the *whole* of humanity is his child and that it would have been inappropriate for him to single out one specific person as worthy of salvation. In other words, despite the personal feeling of tragic loss, Crowley approached even this episode by the gesture of acceptance, which is in the final reckoning characteristic of the formula of Babalon.

9 Kristeva, Julia. *Powers of Horror: An Essay on Abjection*, Columbia University Press, 1982.

As far as Leah Hirsig is concerned, her own magical diaries chronicle the depth of her own struggle with the role of the Scarlet Woman, which assumes increasingly distressing features after her splitting up with Crowley. We read of her depression, poverty, alcohol and drugs, and of her will to die. She would eventually renounce her role and distance herself from both Crowley and Thelema but those few years during which she identified with her magical persona of Alostrael are significant as a testimony of an attempt to transcend the boundaries of the 'human, all too human' condition.

On September 22, 1924, while in Paris, after her recent breakup with Crowley, Hirsig makes an entry into her journal stating: 'This diary is the beginning of a Magical career of one who knows herself as Babalon.'[10] Transcribing from the scraps of paper what she wrote the day before, she lays bare the state of a person in deep anguish, at the age of nervous breakdown, contemplating her own death. At 2:30 AM she returns into her hotel room and notes: 'I could not sleep and not having any more nails to bite I had to have some cigarettes. I also got a bottle of white wine and I intend to drink as much as I can keep down.'[11] What happened during the previous day consisted of her attempts to get in touch with various acquaintances, mostly without success. Some events that Hirsig mentions are depressingly ugly: 'The concierge's wife kicked me in the back and the man beat my face. I reported the matter to the police who could do nothing. They called a second police to the tenement and he insisted that I get out. I did.'[12]

Recollecting her recent experiences, Hirsig expresses her dissatisfaction with the man Crowley but states her continuing loyalty to his magical persona as the Prophet of Thelema. This inner contradiction and conflict that often obtains between secular and sacral aspects of one's personality and one's actions is a well-known element in the biography of many religious figures. This is particularly the case in those instances when a person claims to be incarnating religious archetypes and this remark applies as much to Crowley as the Beast as it does to Hirsig (and other Scarlet Women) as Babalon. The ability to incarnate such archetypes obviously implies the obliteration of one's habitual sense of the ego, otherwise its own inflation is the result, spelling failure to the project. It should be noted that the

10 Leah Hirsig, 'Diary of Babalon', in Hirsig, *Three Chapters in My Life*, unpublished MS, p. 4.

11 Ibid., p. 5.

12 Ibid.

assumption of such divine archetypes is a common practice in Vajrayāna Buddhism, however, precisely for the reason of potential danger inherent in the method, the practice is not attempted unless the student has had some insight into the ontological emptiness of phenomena, including one's personality. The understanding of emptiness, relativity, contingency, or constructed nature of one's person and every other phenomenon without exception on the one hand prevents the inflation of the ego while on the other hand it simultaneously makes possible the transformation of one's ordinary personal identity into the identity of a Buddha or a bodhisattva.

To return to Hirsig and her Diary of Babalon: on the same day she wrote to Crowley as follows: 'I hereby renounce the title The Scarlet Woman and pass it on to the "Scarlet Concubine of his desire" [*AL* III: 14], the daughter of Babalon.'[13] She significantly signs the note as Babalon. The text of her resignation letter similarly suggests that her successor as the Scarlet Woman (Dorothy Olsen) is her daughter, while she herself is Babalon. Her other journal entries in this period display simultaneously expressions of despair ('My beloved Beast...I am going to die tonight'—Sept. 26[14]) and the continuing conviction that she is indeed Babalon and as such reconciled with and accepting of her fate ('I am Babalon, the Great Mother, the Mother of the Children of the New Aeon, the Aeon of Horus! I die in giving-birth to my children. But I shall live again!'—Sept. 24/5[15]). One of the most revealing statements is expressed in her intended farewell letter to Crowley, where she writes: 'Remember that Alostrael, Babalon...—The Scarlet Woman lives forever. Leah Hirsig dies but then *I never knew her*' (Sept. 26; emphasis added).[16]

INTERPRETATIONS AND CONCLUSIONS

As already mentioned, Leah Hirsig eventually renounced both her role of a Scarlet Woman and Thelema itself. Nevertheless, her importance as a representative of a particular type of a devotee within the context of a nascent religious movement is significant and deserving of consideration. It

13 Ibid. p. 8.
14 Ibid. p. 46.
15 Ibid. p. 43.
16 Ibid. p. 46.

would be relatively easy, but fundamentally out of place, to psychoanalyze the above described fragment of her biography and interpret it as merely indicative of a nervous breakdown or maybe even as a psychotic episode. This *was* a nervous breakdown, maybe even a psychotic episode, but this, in and of itself, does not sufficiently or adequately explain the situation at its fundamental core. Both Hirsig and Crowley were engaged in a spiritual quest and their activities and experiences need to be interpreted within the religious framework of exegesis: other explanations are naturally possible but ultimately reductive in this context. Crowley's and Hirsig's mutual and interpersonal amorous and sexual relationships were driven by a conscious attempt to embody and manifest magical personas of the Beast and Babalon. In a sense, my interpretation is an instance of turning the classical psychoanalytical perspective upside-down: instead of reducing the mystical to the sexual, I am arguing that, within the framework of their self-proclaimed and self-conscious intent, to properly understand Crowley and Hirsig in this context, we need to approach the sexual as the mystical.[17] This accords with Crowley's statement, rebuffing the proposal that 'religion is nothing but a morbid manifestation of the sexual instinct' (which is, by the way, a typical Freudian perspective) by an elegant postulation: 'When you have proved that God is merely a name for the sex instinct, it appears to me not far to the perception that the sex instinct is God.'[18] Expressed somewhat differently, an interpretative model best suited to understand the subject under scrutiny suggests that in attempting to fulfill their roles, Crowley and Hirsig approached sex as something numinous, as a hierophany and a *mysterium tremendum*.

The implication of this model of analysis lies in the following: by telescoping the religious quest into a sexual frame of reference, the sexuality is detached from its secular connotations and transformed into a force capable of dissolving the boundaries of one's secular, egocentric identity. The historian of religions Mircea Eliade argued that any and every form and aspect of phenomenal reality might be capable of serving the role of hierophany: the sacred must needs manifests in the profane but once this happens, the profane loses its former character and becomes, to those who

17 Among scholarly literature on this subject, see in particular the work of Jeffrey Kripal. This subject forms a red thread observable in all his output but for what is perhaps the most clear elaboration see Kripal, *Kālī's Child: The Mystical and the Erotic in the Life and Teachings of Ramakrishna*, University of Chicago Press, 1995.

18 Aleister Crowley et al., *The Equinox*, Vol. III, no. 1, 1919, p. 280.

adhere to the relevant religious worldview, something special, singled out from the rest of secular environment. This leads to a paradox, however: by participating in both the sacred and the profane realms of reality, the object or person that serves the hierophanic role becomes the site of a *coincidentia oppositorum*. This is precisely, I suggest, what happened to Crowley and Hirsig in the context under investigation: both their personalities and their chosen method of religious practice—the sexual magick—were simultaneously profane (by nature of their manifest existence) *and* sacred (by virtue of their assumed value). Stated somewhat conversely: while the signifiers were profane (Crowley—Hirsig—sexual acts), the signifieds were sacral (Beast—Babalon—magical rituals).

Crowley's identification with the Beast commenced already in his childhood but this intuitive premonition of his future role assumed formalized (and ideologically altered) features upon his acceptance of the mantle of the Prophet of Thelema. Leah Hirsig acted as his Scarlet Woman, taking upon herself the magical persona of Alostrael, the 'Guardian of the Sangraal', and eventually, as we have seen above, she fully identified with Babalon. The willing assumption of these mystical personas was an extension of the practice of the assumption of God forms, as observed in the Hermetic Order of the Golden Dawn and in Crowley's A∴A∴.[19] Both the Beast and Babalon possess strong sexual connotations and in one symbolic register they also stand for *lingam* and *yoni*. Acceptance of the following requires a grain of salt, but in order for Crowley and Hirsig to fulfill their chosen roles and to abandon their habitual secular personas, they had to shift identity to their sexual functions, symbolized by their respective organs. Sex instinct was the indication of the presence of gods and their avatars were *lingam* (the Beast) and *yoni* (Babalon). This meant and implied, in the final reckoning, self-abandonment, and ultimately self-annihilation. In such a context, sex was not, properly speaking, an instrument of pleasure: it was a terrifying force that led through the Chapel Perilous into the 'Night of Pan' and the 'City of Pyramids', where one becomes a pile of dust in a Pyramid that is as much one's tomb as it is the place of initiation.

There are many indications in Crowley's vast literary opus that corroborate, to a lesser or larger degree, this mode of analysis. It is commonly assumed that most of his practice of sexual magick was conducted under the aegis of O.T.O. methods, which while not completely incorrect overlooks the fact of the sexual component in the offices of the Beast and Scarlet

19 See 'Liber O vel Manus et Sagittae' for a description of the practice.

Woman, both of which concern the matter pertaining to A∴A∴, not to mention the general appreciation of the sanctity of sex in Thelema. As an example, a brief look at Crowley's *Book of Lies*, originally composed prior to his involvement with the O.T.O., should illustrate the relevance of spiritualized approach to sexual issues within the background of A∴A∴ teachings. In the chapter called 'Dewdrops', Crowley elaborates on the properties of what he calls the 'Dew of Immortality'—which may safely be understood as a reference to the metaphysical aspect of semen—as containing the quintessence and every tendency of one's soul and body, and concludes with a directive: 'Let this go free, even as It will; thou art not its master, but a vehicle of It.'[20] The commentary stipulates that the man is only the guardian and servant of this elixir, the nature of which is otherwise in accordance with the Cosmic Will. Similarly, in the ritual of the Gnostic Mass ('Liber XV'), one way of looking at the rite is to see it as an interplay between two principal magical 'weapons': the Cup (Priestess) and the Lance (Priest). The eidolon of Priest and his main function is represented by the Lance and the eidolon of Priestess and her main function is exemplified by the Cup: the human persons are just the carriers and assistants.

The ultimate relevance of all of this may become clearer if we consider the role that religious symbols and religion itself exert onto society. In his essay on 'Religion as System', the Romanian scholar Ioan Couliano writes cogently on the issue: 'If indeed religion acts like "software" or a "program" within human society, then it may only be to the message of religion that society is able to respond; thus, there is hope that by transformations in the sphere of religion the impending future of societies or social groups might be reprogrammed'.[21] Considered in such light, Thelema does not only introduce a (relatively) new set of religious symbols but perhaps more importantly, with some of them, it turns the old ones upside down and in the process effects the Nietzschean transvaluation of the traditional values: the meek Lamb is replaced by the solar Beast and the Virgin is replaced by the symbol of the Whore. There is a liberating force behind this—at least to those who feel constrained by the dominant culture—comparable to what Mikhail Bakhtin theorized about as the 'carnivalesque': the social

20 Crowley, *Book of Lies*, p.46.

21 Couliano, Ioan. 'Introduction: Religion as System', in Mircea Eliade, Ioan Couliano, and Hillary Wiesner, *The HarperCollins Guide to the World Religions*, 1991: p. 7.

condition brought about by reversing the established order through a free exercise and celebration of the 'material bodily lower stratum.'[22]

This liberation through transvaluation and reversal of traditional cultural codes is, outside the magical context, in particular observable among some strands of feminist movement in their choice of role-models for self-identification such as Lilith, Kali, and, for some, Babalon (as a matter of fact, from the Thelemic point of view, they can all be seen as aspects of Babalon). At the level of popular culture, the embrace and celebration of what the patriarchy rejected, maligned, and marginalized is also noticeable, among other things, in the choice of names ('nomen est omen'): of music festivals such as Lilith Fair, magazines such as *Bitch*, websites such as Jezebel.com, and books such as Inga Muscio's *Cunt*. So when, for example, the last mentioned book devotes a chapter on Whores and calls for their appreciation, it is possible to recognize in thusly expressed Zeitgeist an indication of the fact that Babalon—an alternative model of women's self-identification—is indeed alive and growing in importance and popularity. Katon Shual even went so far as to state that 'Babalon has become a new magical archetype for the nineties sexual woman.'[23]

If, however, Babalon indeed stands for an archetypal power behind specific configurations of contemporary Zeitgeist, it is to be expected that her manifestations would exceed the limitations of conscious affiliation and self-chosen identification. The psychologists C. G. Jung and James Hillman suggested that in our secular societies gods manifest as diseases. In other words, there is a certain 'personality' to one's neuroses and ills that may be placed in a mythical context and identified with appropriate divine figures.[24] If one is allowed to speculate, it could be said that sexual neuroses of various types are among the most typical malaises of contemporary society. What they manifest are the sexual gods and goddesses, such as, in the present context, Babalon. Within the parameters of the preceding discussion, the issue, the 'disease', lies in the profanation of sex. An aspect of this profanation consists of the trivialization of sexual magick through its conflation with sex as such, without concomitant obliteration of egotistical involvement in the act on one hand, and its subsequent mischaracterization as a ritual on the other. I would venture to suggest that we all too often witness a confusion between knowing and acting in this—as in many

22 Bakhtin, Mikhail. *Rabelais and His World*, Indiana University Press, 1984.
23 Shual, Katon. *Sexual Magick*, Mandrake, 1995, p.29.
24 See, for example, James Hillman, ed., *Facing the Gods*, Spring, 1980.

another—form of spirituality: everyone seems to know what the 'secret' of sexual magick is, but the point is that the secret does not consist in the knowledge of, but in the ability to do, what is involved. In the vocabulary of Hindu Tantra, the manner of discourse and behaviour displayed towards the subject reveals that so many are simply *paśus* in this regard. As Trungpa Rinpoche would have said, here, as elsewhere, we see so many instances of spiritual materialism, which is probably nothing to marvel at, for as the Goddess Nuit, whose other name is Babalon, states in *The Book of the Law*, her servants are 'few and secret' (*AL*, I: 10).

Introductory Theoria

ON PROGRESSIVE FORMULAS OF THE BABALON PRIESTESSHOOD

Amodali

I will open my garments, and stand naked before you, that your love may be more enflamed toward me.[1]

THE PERCEPTION OF the role of the Scarlet Woman has evolved from Aleister Crowley's position that magical partners need not be initiated magicians and preferably chosen for suitability by male practitioners through the unconscious agency of phallic desire, to one in which female practitioners now consciously adopt the role of the Babalon priestess as a fiercely independent statement of sexual liberation. The political and sociological reform implicit in the archetype of Babalon is thus incredibly important. However, many practitioners, myself included, perceive that there is much left to be magically expressed and fulfilled within Babalon's magic, in theory, and practice. The legacy of 'old aeon' magical models of femininity still cast a shadow, and this seems to be responsible for reductive attitudes, and a lack of expectation often encountered in response to female practitioners, as if their function is somehow fully established and set in stone. The fundamental disequilibrium within the current is rooted in the inner planes, and arguably the greatest challenge for contemporary practitioners

1 Speech of the Daughter of Fortitude. Dee, John and Causabon, M. *A True and Faithful Relation*. Golem Media, 2008 p. 25.

is to examine the higher magical formulas to clarify and reform the epistemological foundation of the current. Kenneth Grant believed that the vehicles of the future priestesshood were gathering on the astral planes and not likely to emerge until the far future.[2] My belief is that this radical shift within human consciousness is happening now in response to a very deep and powerful collective longing for the unveiling of the goddess and reconnection to a primal unity that nurtures a greater understanding of our place within the cosmos. The nature of this primal unity is understood to be deeply and fundamentally erotic within the 156 Current. However, the revelation or apokatastasis of the Babalon current requires the deeper mysteries to be embodied—and bestowed—by an independent priestesshood with initiatory determination. A process of *magical* liberation for women is essential for the progression of the 156 Current and the removal of what Grant identified as 'veiling particles'[3] which has hindered its full manifestation.

The initiatic imperative of the feminine sexual gnosis identified with Babalon's magic is clear from the definitive position of the 'Daughter of Fortitude', who declares 'I sanctify and am not sanctified'.[4] The technical means to embody this position fully and generate the magical quintessence or *pneuma* cognate with this powerful archetype has not been fully identified within the primary sources of the current. The embodied practices that began to formulate and manifest aspects of sacred sexuality in the West only began to emerge during the Occult Revival.

However, the ongoing momentum has yet to influence some of the more deeply ingrained prejudicial biases regarding feminine position. These imbalances have prevented the formulation of cohesive, progressive development within Babalon's sexual mysteries. The higher magical formulas concerned with embodiment that are central to her magic have been elusive. I propose that this is due to fundamental core misinterpretations and structural distortions of the archetypes and formulas key to Babalon's magic.

2 'The ancient rites of Isis veiled certain signs or Chakras which are only now beginning to revolve in the psycho-astral vehicles of the new priestesses. *Within the next few centuries many such priestesses will enter the stream of the human life-wave which animates this planet.*' Grant, Kenneth. *Aleister Crowley and the Hidden God.* Muller, 1973 p. 161.

3 Grant, Kenneth. *Aleister Crowley and the Hidden God.* Muller, 1973 p. 162.

4 Dee, John and Causabon, M. *A True and Faithful Relation*, p. *25.

The emergence of Babalon, initially within the so-called Enochian corpus of John Dee, through to the work of Crowley, marks an incredibly important watershed within the sexual mysteries of the Western Mystery Tradition. During this period, the female sex-magical current began to emerge from the inner planes into manifestation in the West, marked by the subliminal incubation of a distinctively female, Venusian, spirit. However, the 156 Current remained partially veiled throughout the Occult Revival, and the lack of an unbroken, initiatic, primordial tradition of female sex magical praxis in the West has been extremely problematical. The only solution to this unacceptable void is a long process of gnostic retrieval. As Babalon is an Enochian word/intelligence[5], it makes sense for female practitioners in particular to re-examine the Enochian corpus as a primary source in relationship to sex magical praxis as part of a reforming movement from which the revolutionary sexual formulas of Babalon will emerge.

The communications recorded in Dee's diaries, from Galvah/I AM, the 'Daughter of Fortitude', and Crowley's encounters with Babalon in *The Vision and the Voice*, all seem to emanate from a vividly erotic sexual arcanum. It seems clear that the 156 Current and the harlotry of Babalon is concerned with the manifestation of the secrets of Nature and magical understanding as transmitted through a vast arcanum of female sexual intelligence and embodied sex magical gnosis. As one penetrates to the essence of the current, the veneer of Biblical/Christian interpretations of the harlotry of Babylon dissolves, to reveal a profoundly occult mysterium of magical whoredom that draws upon hidden aspects of a primordial, sex-magical egregore within the Western Mystery Tradition. The formulas that are the source of embodiment practices can be found within the corpus of Babalon herself, the wider egregore of the 156 Current and mysteries of Isis/Sophia. It is important to acknowledge the influence that the Isisian mysteries had upon Dee's work. The goddess Isis and The Sophia (wisdom) represented the world soul and secrets of Nature that Dee and the mystics and alchemists of his era sought to penetrate. Dee was particularly fascinated with fragments contained in the alchemical document, *Codex Marcianus*[6] attributed to Zosimos, in which Isis gains knowledge of the secrets of Alchemy by engaging with the Angel Amnael, thus in theory equating Isis with Alchemical sex magic in Dee's imagination. The female

5 Laycock, D. *The Complete Enochian Dictionary*. Weiser, 2001 p. 83.
6 Von Franz, M. L. *Alchemy*. Inner City Books, 1980 p. 43.

Enochian intelligences have many correspondences with archetypes of Isis/Sophia in practice.

The work of John Dee and Aleister Crowley provides the primary gateway into the 156 Current. However, Babalon's ophidian magic immerses aspirants into a vast feminine, sexual gnosis that is a specialist discipline in itself, and is as complex and sophisticated as the greater corpora of Enochian/Thelemic magical practices. The *pneuma* of the Babalon priestess is extracted from a dynamic liminal space that is magically evoked from the bio-etheric architecture and erotic phenomenology of the female body. The training process is one of autopoesis and does not require operation within conventional polarity formulas. Although the approaches introduced here may be considered unorthodox by traditional Thelemic/Enochian practitioners, it is arguably only through innovation and the challenging of consensus conceptual boundaries, that an authentic pathway to reform can be achieved.

In practice, it has been found that key correspondences exist that affirm a fundamental syzygy between Babalon's septenary occult anatomy and the female body. Further correlations are found that reveal insights into embodiment practices within many of the central magical formulations of Dee's extended 'Angelic' corpus and Crowley's Enochian legacy. Through these correspondences, a progressive system of the female mysteries of Babalon can be formulated, that are based upon configurations of the female subtle body, particular to the 156 Current. Some of the concepts and formulas that inform the development of this very specific 'magical body' are herein introduced. The intention is to elevate the role of the Scarlet Woman to one in which her magical adepthood is fully established and reflected in theory and praxis. Within research briefly introduced here, some of Babalon's core symbolic archetypes and formulas are deconstructed and replaced with formulations that are authentic to the magical phenomenology of embodiment practice. Babalon is reaffirmed here as the spearhead of a sexually dynamic, initiatory arcana the Enochian wisdom goddesses, analogous with the Isis/Sophia of Western tradition and an explosive Icon and magical torch-bearer of the new sexuality.

THE GRAAL AND THE PNEUMA 156

My garments are from the beginning, and my dwelling place is in myself.[7]

The opening line of *Liber Cheth* delivers the emphatic message, 'This is the secret of the Holy Graal.'[8] The subsequent passages establish the process of dissolution and abnegation of ego and worldly attachment necessary to attain union with Babalon. 'Thou shalt mingle thy life with the universal life. Thou shalt not keep back one drop.'[9] *Liber Cheth* delivers the formula of the aspirant and when correctly performed prepares and cleanses the vessel of the devotee for the higher mysteries of the current. However, in terms of the secrets of the Graal it delivers only a partial formula. The mysteries of the substance of the 'wine', the means to the attainment of union with Babalon and the supernal mysteries of the crossing of the Abyss, are diffused through the wider Thelemic corpus and ritual formulas. However aspects of the higher magical formulation concerned with the formula of the Graal seem to be missing or distorted from the female practitioner's perspective. The harlotry of Babalon is a highly complex metaphysical concept that signifies an active process of magical, copulatory engagement with the ALL, rather than one of a simple, passive receptivity. The magical role of cup-bearer requires a lengthy training process and techniques that deliver active transubstantiation of the 'wine'. The incorporation of this aspect of Babalon as Wisdom Goddess or one that bestows magical 'Understanding' is paramount to the efficacy of the elixirs.

This assertion is contrary to the given wisdom on elixir work within many traditions and in Thelema. The concept of a female alchemist or Adept that works consciously with the elixirs produced by sex magic is largely alien as a concept in orthodox theory and practice. The potent stance taken by the female voices in the Enochian corpus defies the reductive archetypes ascribed to the female position within the Western Mystery Tradition. They provide an authentic source of what could be described as the *prima materia* of an empowering feminine epistemology. A textual and magical foundation from which the magical science of the 'Pneuma 156' and the substance of the 'wine' and fleshly garments of wisdom may accordingly be developed.

7 Dee and Causabon. *A True and Faithful Relation*, p. *25.

8 Crowley, Aleister. *Liber Cheth. Gems from the Equinox* V1. Falcon Press, 1982. p. 603.

9 Ibid.

A symbolic and practical system can be derived from this fertile ground that enfleshes and extends concepts such as Irigary's 'sensible, transcendental' archetype of the divine woman.[10] This supports a position in which the female has an asymmetrical relationship to male, and is in being and substance 'radically and positively other'.[11] The position is established by the opening quotation of this section by the 'Daughter of Fortitude' which affirms the primordial integrity of the feminine spirit. This concept of asymmetry and inviolability is incredibly important to the development of initiatic magical formulas within the 156 Current. The adherence to Old Aeon orthodoxies within the highest Thelemic mysteries creates barriers to the creation of new more balanced formulas and negate the development of the dynamic, asymmetrical, fluidic gnosis that I believe the Babalon current must generate.

For example, although Lady Frieda Harris's image and Crowley's conceptualisation of Babalon astride Therion in the 'Lust' tarot card of the Thoth Tarot Deck, vividly portrays the turbulent and highly charged nature of the mysteries of 'Teth' and 156 Current, it can be suggested that the formula as shown is flawed. If we compare the Crowley card with the Rider-Waite version, we can see that the lemniscate above the head of the woman is missing from Crowley's rendering. Thus in the Waite version, a mercurial, magical element of will is being imposed by the female figure and this can be interpreted as representing an authoritative role for a female magician, which comes through the mediating/taming of the powerful, leonine, serpent fire. The red lion, identified by Wang as 'the force of nature under perfect control,'[12] is in alchemical symbolism defined as the directing power of the philosophic mercury. This observation contrasts starkly with Crowley's commentary on his version of the card in which he states, '*there is in this card no attempt to direct the course of the operation*'.[13] The unsealing of the force of TETH requires a relinquishment of ego and openness to the abandonment and entrancement of erotic synaesthesia. However, Babalon's magic reveals an initiatory intelligence of female magical will that operates on the mercurial level, implied by the lemniscate. Blending the symbolism of both cards by merging the sexual frenzy of an ecstatically unfettered priestess with the lion-serpent tamed under the

10 Burke, C., Schor, N. and M. Whitford. *Engaging with Irigary*. p.124.

11 Ibid, p. 121.

12 Wang, R. *The Qabalistic Tarot*. Weiser, 1983 p. 207.

13 Crowley, Aleister. *The Book of Thoth*. Weiser, 1984 p. 93.

lemniscate, gives a more complete understanding of the pathway of Teth, which reforms the position of the priestess to one bearing an active, directing force.

Grant did challenge some aspects of Crowley's beliefs that distorted perceptions of the elixirs, even if the counterbalancing research he presented on the 'Kalas' did not entirely resolve these problems. However, he did correctly acknowledge that the magical will of the priestess 'can be applied effectively without any physical intervention on the part of the priest'[14] and that the Scarlet Woman 'embraces both the inwardly directed or mystical current and the magical or outwardly directed current of consciousness.'[15] In de-constructing some of the core symbolism associated with Babalon such as that of the Graal, the mysteries of a feminine process of 'mercurial' transubstantiation begin to emerge. The membrane where the cup touches the upper realm is often alluded to as the 'Veil of Isis' in Hermetic Qabalistic Tradition. Isis is revered within freemasonry as mistress of alchemy and magic, and she is considered to be the directing intelligence within such operations. The 'directing intelligence' of the role of the Babalon priestess is further enhanced by the development of inner symbioses with the firesnake or 'lion serpent' or beast. This crucial aspect of training is of profound import and changes the nature of polarity work as displayed in the 'Lust' card beyond recognition.

The formulas of Babalon constitute a very particular spiritual challenge to the western psyche and one that addresses a schism at the heart of the Western Mystery Tradition. The Enochian magical corpus creates a framework that must be literally fleshed out by the female sexual formulas: without this living, corporeal substrate, vital keys are missing that hinder the very precise and technical production of the elixirs necessary to create the 'Body of Babalon'. The priestess possesses the holy wine, yet this is not the raw menstruum of Nature. The 'Lust' card clearly demonstrates that the Graal touches the veil of the supernal realm and thus has been uplifted and transmuted by the Scarlet Woman to create the Chrysopoeia, the ultimate salve that unlocks the entrance to the City of Pyramids. The magical gnosis contained within the 'garments', referred to in the opening quotes also have particular relevance within the current and the initiatic formulas. It is by restoring the mysteries of the dynamic garments, active elixirs and techniques of transmission, that the current will move forward.

14 Grant, Kenneth. *Aleister Crowley and the Hidden God*. Muller, 1973 p. 43.
15 Ibid., p. 45.

The magnum opus of the Adept priestess is thus one not only of return to a primal unity, but a progressive formulation of a priestesshood that upholds the feminine *pneuma* in radical new permutations.

THE BODY OF BABALON

True wisdom is always painted with a woman's garment.[16]

The following material is derived from over twenty-five years of magical practice. The work has required a cohesive and precise formulation of the occult anatomy of the Babalon priestess, which I have termed the 'Body of Babalon.'[17] This concept is defined as 'the fully activated sex magical body of the priestess'. This definition requires the reformation of concepts of gender relationships and female subtle corpora in relation to magical formulas within the current, and the cultivation of a specific *pneuma* produced by female practitioners.

The practices and formulas are derived from immersion within states of extreme *ecstasis* and entranced possession.[18] Over time, a system has emerged which possessed an inner integrity that has produced a progressive Post-Thelemic formulation of Babalon's sex magical current.[19] The system has also confirmed that the *Heptarchia Mystica* of Babalon—as alluded to from Crowley's corpus, and rooted in Dee's work—has a set of magical correspondences that relate specifically to the occult anatomy of the priestess. The work has also informed modern perceptions of Babalon as the contemporary western correlate of the Tantric 'Shakti' force. This force manifests through the magical female intelligences associated with the 156 Current such as Nuit, Isis, Venus and the female Enochian spirits, Galvah, I AM, and the 'Daughter of Fortitude'. These goddess-forms have been revealed as holding initiatory, sexual formulas that exist within a complex interrelationship. Magical research into the interpolation of the *Heptarchia Mystica* of Babalon with the Enochian corpus is ongoing and a vast undertaking. The highly technical practices derived from the 'Body of

16 Dee and Causabon. *A True and Faithful Relation*. p. 13; and Leitch, A. *The Angelical Language. Vol. 1.* Llewellyn Publications, 2010. p. 66.

17 www.threehandspress.com/amodali_interview. August 2014.

18 http://www.amodali.com/babalon-ritual-phenomenolgy/

19 Amodali. *The Marks of Teth*. Three Hands Press, forthcoming 2016.

Babalon' enflesh the Enochian formulas and tables with a substrate of specific feminine arcana encoded within flesh, through the sexual, Ophidian gnosis—the 'Marks of Teth'.

The practices have a training stage, during which the 'Body of Babalon' is forged. There are also further advanced formulas that extend beyond the preparatory practices that are concerned with the wider evolutionary remit of the current. Initiation is open to all, but the practices vary according to how one orientates one's physical vehicle to the process. However, by the necessity of determining the female initiatic formulas of the current, the focus has been upon female practices.

In brief, what is the nature of the 'Body of Babalon'? Construction of a Magic Square (Fig. 1.) using the name of Babalon is a basic device that is useful for creating rites devoted to Our Lady. The simplicity of the table condenses very profoundly, the many fundamental formulas of Babalon's magic in relationship to the priestess's magical body. These connections are not immediately obvious unless one is working with the practical process and thus the square is an excellent starting point for exploring the occult anatomy of Babalon.

Within the square, key numbers associated with the 156 current—4, 7, 28, 49 and 156—are resolved. The name 'Babalon' is equivalent to 156 in Hebrew Gematria. The seven is fundamental and is represented by the name of Babalon and has multiple correspondences within the theorems. The arrangement of the seven letters in the square generates the number 49, a crucial extension of the formula that is featured throughout the Enochian corpus. This generates further significance when translated into Enochian (Fig. 2) and presented in the schema (Fig. 3). The table also contains the Venusian formulas of 4×7 (The four being derived from the sides of the table) that Crowley refers to in the *The Vision and the Voice.*[20] The formula of 4×7 when employed in Babalon's magic is concerned with interpolation of the dynamic, serpentine heptarchy that is activated in the fleshly zones of the priestess, which together with the four layers of the 'Garments' of Wisdom, forms a dynamic architecture within the subtle anatomy. The four sides of the square can be likened to the base of the pyramid, creating a structural form that holds the quaternary aspects of

20 'Each plume of the peacock is full of eyes, that are at the same time 4×7. And for this is the number 28 reflected down into Netzach; and that 28 is Kaph Cheth (Kach) power. For she is Sakti, the eternal energy of the Concealed One.' Crowley, Aleister. *The Vision and the Voice. Gems from the Equinox.* Falcon Press. DEO. 7th Aethyr, p. 540.

her occult anatomy, which when extruded to the central point generates the pyramidal planes that create the supernal architecture of the 'City of Pyramids'.

B	A	B	A	L	O	N
A	B	A	L	O	N	B
B	A	L	O	N	B	A
A	L	O	N	B	A	B
L	O	N	B	A	B	A
O	N	B	A	B	A	L
N	B	A	B	A	L	O

Fig 1. Magic Square of Babalon. Cubing the 4 (4×4×4), also interestingly generates the number of the emanations of the Yogini Sequence within the kaula Tantric system.

Sixty Four is also the number of DNA codons, thus equating the magic of Babalon in this sigil with alchemical secrets of nature, embedded within the Serpent DNA. The horizontal and vertical rows and columns generate seven permutations of the word Babalon, each obviously 156 by Gematria, which are aligned with the seven magical zones of the Priestess's body.

The formula of the 4×7 as mentioned previously is completed in embodiment practices with the dynamic interaction of the seven magical zones with the quaternary 'garments'.[21] This mechanism has profound magical implications that reveal the wisdom body of Babalon as embodying the secrets of nature and the holy garment of Galvah/I AM, the primal mother of the angels in all her glory. The opening quote from Galvah reinforces the corporeal nature of female wisdom or magic. The garments are

21 'But the key into this gate is the balance of the seven and the four'. *The Vision and the Voice* Op. cit, p. 538.

the true ritual garb of the Babalon priestess that signify the completion of her magical training and the establishment of the orgonic, sensoria that is the occult field of action of 156. The garment of wisdom defines the architecture of a highly complex, magical, phenomenological space through which the priestess directs her magic. When the table is translated into Enochian (Fig. 2), the seven permutations of Babalon's name can be intoned as one word and aligned with the corporeal heptarchic zones within appropriate workings or broken down into separate letters, which when arranged onto a circular schema (Fig. 3), signify the 49 tinctures from which the holy elixirs of Babalon are derived. The training process is lengthy and complex and will be explored fully in a forthcoming publication.[22]

THE ELIXIR 49

For behold I am understanding and science dwelleth in me...[23]

The mysterium of the 'Body of Babalon' deepens when examining the formula of 49 shown in Fig. 2. The importance of the formula of 49 within Babalon's magic is revealed in Crowley's description of the dancer clothed in scarlet fire and the 49-petalled crimson rose in the 15th aethyr[24], and throughout the *Vision and the Voice*. In practice, this is not a mystery confined to OXO, but has been found to have a set of correspondences that relate to the subtle anatomy of the Babalon priestess and the formulation of the elixirs. The magic square (fig. 2) generates the schema (fig. 3), which is a variant on the Star of Babalon. The image delineates the series of emanations cultivated through the magical training of the priestess. The Pneuma 156 requires a lengthy incubation and active generation via the magical will of the priestess. The diagram shows the spectrum of elixirs extrapolated from a 7×7 highly complex set of circulations that transmute the substance of the priestess within Babalon's *Heptarchia Mystica*. The diagram (Fig. 3), mirrors the structure of the training of the Babalon priest-

22 Amodali. *The Marks of Teth*. Three Hands Press, forthcoming 2016.

23 The Daughter of Fortitude. Dee and Causabon. *A True and Faithful Relation*, p. *25.

24 'Now it is clear what she has woven in her dance; it is the Crimson Rose of 49 petals, and the pillars are the cross with which it is conjoined. And between the pillars shoot out rays of pure green fire; and now all the pillars are golden. She ceases to dance and dwindles, gathering herself into the centre of the rose'. *The Vision and the Voice*, p. 491.

esshood. The heads of the serpentine emanations are embossed with the Enochian letters that relate to the position of the names of Babalon on the magic square and the subtle body of the priestess. Each of the 49 serpents is collared with a lemniscate, as each serpent must be birthed through a process of active cultivation of the magic of Babalon. The 49 serpents create a magico-physical dynamo that interpolate with the cultivation of the 'Garments' of the priestess, a quaternary, etheric cocoon that sheaths the body.

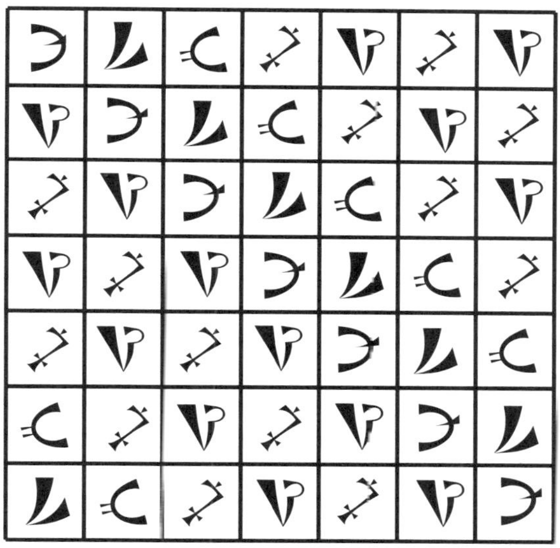

Fig 2. ENOCHIAN TABLE OF BABALON.

The deities associated with the 156 egregore predominate at different stages of the work. The premise within this research is that within the Enochian system, Galvah corresponds to the primal mother, who holds the templates of the cosmic sexual intelligence on the inner planes, and Babalon represents the physical manifestation of these garments of wisdom in the form of the embodied magic of the priestess. The process generates lost initiatic keys that can only be accessed through the female body, as the opening quote from Galvah/I AM in the previous section expresses. The practice culminates with the development of the 'solar raiment', which signifies the completion of the training stage and the blending of an elixir that pierces the veil of Isis, the sublime tincture that opens the Temple of Babalon in the City of Pyramids. The creation of this elixir has some equivalence with Grant's 'Secret Kala' and is the 49th elixir or petal of the rose. Thus the schema encompasses the full spectra of the copulative gnosis that generates the true substance of Babalon's cup, culminating with the creation of this 49th elixir, the Chrysopoeia. This has been found in practice to be an accurate representation of Babalon's Graal.

FIG 3. SCHEMA OF THE ELIXIR 49.

The process outlined here is in contrast to Grant's appraisal of the ultimate female quintessence, the 'kala'[25] or 'Goddess 15.'[26] Grant popularised the concept of the 'kalas' through his influential publications, and this had

25 Sanskrit = 'Time'
26 Grant, Kenneth. *Aleister Crowley and the Hidden God*. Muller,1973 p. 120.

an important role in highlighting Tantric sex magical concepts and practices that have become a keystone of modern interpretations of female occult anatomy and sex magic. The 'Kalas' are magical elixirs and emanations that are generated within the female secretions through a complex system in which the 'Tithis' of the lunar month are represented and aligned with an array of bright and dark goddesses. According to Grant, this practice culminates with the generation of a mysterious 15th elixir, that is produced at a specified juncture of the female lunar cycle. Within Babalon's magic the uterus and menstrual cycle is also the Alembic from which the sacred elixirs emanate. However it has been found in practice that the lunar circulation forms just one aspect of a complex multi-dimensional system of 49 emanations.

The angel Raphael dictated to Dee that 'Every element hath 49 manner of understandings.'[27] The generation of the 49th elixir within Babalon's *Heptarchia Mystica* is a practice that conforms to the pattern of 49 layers of unfolding gnosis that is outlined within the Enochian practice of 'Gebofal'.[28] The practice of Gebofal unlocks understanding of the 49 parts of the book of life, 'Liber Loageth'. The angel Nalvage comments on the creation of the book that "These tables are to be written, not by men, but by the finger of her which is the mother of virtue..."[29] *Liber Loageth* contains knowledge of all the mysteries of creation. However, the language and mysteries of Nature have many levels of which speech and written organization is just one aspect.

The path of Babalon is one in which a matrix of the physical and subtle forces of Nature are embodied and sublimated within the living flesh, to create an erotically-charged, corporeal 'language' and physical quintessence.[30] From this sex magical substrate, the Ophidian gnosis is communicated through the living body of the priestess. The Harlotry of Babalon unseals the sexual gnosis embedded within the 49 petals of the rose, through a process of ecstatic trance, in which the priestess copulates with the ALL. The Primal mother Galvah/I AM is the ineffable source of the

27 Dee, John. *Five Books of Mystery*, pp. 296–97.

28 Leitch, A. *The Angelical Language. Vol.1.* Llewellyn Publications, 2010, p. 173. An excellent overview on the primary textual sources and practices relating to Gebofal can be found here.

29 Dee and Causabon. *A True and Faithful Relation*, p. 64.

30 'And this is because she transmitteth the word to the understanding, and therefore she hath many forms, and each goddess of love is but a letter of the alphabet of love.' *The Vision and the Voice*, pg. 539.

process. Babalon is the sevenfold sexual mystery, and her priestesses are the Graal of her manifestation. The syzygy of flesh and *pneuma*, generated by the priestess through invocation of Babalon and the female Enochian spirits, creates the matrix from which the complex phenomenological field of Babalon's magic is generated. The process in its entirety produces a subtle but important distinction from Grant's position which delineates a dichotomy between the formulas of the 'child' and the formula of the 'virgin priestess.'[31] The training process of the Babalon priestess encompasses both formulas into a coherent whole. This is as stated earlier, a process of autopoesis, in which the priestess creates a magical simulacrum of Babalon within her own flesh.

To conclude, the premise in this research is that a foundational epistemology of the Babalon current and the substance of the Pneuma 156 must be derived from multidimensional formulas contained within the magical corpus of Babalon in name and spirit. It is important to awaken and develop this complex gnosis within the framework of the original Enochian sources of the current and the 156 egregore within the Western Mystery Tradition. The wisdom aspect of the female sexual mysteries, the Alchemical Secrets of Isis have been veiled within the current. Through the 'Body of Babalon' these complex arcana find a route into manifestation and this supports the cultivation of the lemniscate, the higher magical will of the priestess. Steiner insisted that 'We must speak of the lost Isis, the divine Sophia. We must set out in search of the dead body of the new Isis.'[32] However, the unfolding momentum of the 156 current that this 'new Isis' which Isis which can be understood by deeper examination of the Enochian Corpus, will be found in the living bodies of a Babalon Priestesshood and the higher mysteries of the Graal.

31 *Aleister Crowley and the Hidden God.* Op. cit., p. 45.

32 wn.rsarchive.org/lectures/19201224p01.html

Nuit and Babalon in Liber Nu:

THE AUSTRALIA WORKING

Robert C. Stein

THE CLASS A LIBER, *Liber CLVI vel Cheth vel Vallum Abiegni* begins with verses that extol many aspects of Babalon/Nuit and union at different levels.

> 1. *This is the secret of the Holy Grail, that is the sacred vessel of our Lady the Scarlet Woman, Babalon, the Mother of Abominations, the bride of Chaos, that rideth upon our Lord the Beast.*
>
> 2. *Thou shalt drain out thy blood that is thy life into the golden cup of her fornication.*
>
> 3. *Thou shalt mingle thy life with the universal life [Nuit]. Thou shalt keep not back one drop.*

As the result, the text describes the dead man in Binah as follows:

> 6. *And because there is no life therein, the guardians of the abyss shall bid the angels of the winds pass by. And the angels shall lay thy dust in the City of the Pyramids, and the name thereof shall be no more.*

Thus the Aspirant becomes Nothing with Nuit, the dark silence. She is the focus of Liber Nu. In some senses, Nuit compares to Hoor-Paar-Kraat as Babalon compares to Ra-Hoor-Khuit. They contrast principle and action. Nuit is silence, the inexpressible ultimate, the unknown source, the infinite without. She expresses the essence of the Ain Soph, the limitless, dark light. Babalon is a voice of that silence, a revealer, an initiator.

Liber Nu, *Liber XI*, has many facets and levels. It is a specific application of Bhakti Yoga, *Liber CLXXV vel Astarte*. It includes multiple levels of mystery, mysticism and magick. It has analogs in *Liber XV*, the public Gnostic Mass. It applies the Soldier and the Hunchback (!+?) from *The Book of Lies*—asking questions, making hypotheses, testing them and seeking truth. It reifies *Solve et Coagula*.

Liber Nu is a magical experiment. It uses the four powers of the Sphinx and *Chapter I* of *Liber XXXI vel AL*. It teaches, through action, the structure of ritual and how to manifest it. The ritual and its preparation are microcosmic. The setting also represents the greater temple, the universe, the macrocosm. Above all, it is a love ritual—a marriage ritual between Had (as Hadit) and Nuit (as Nu). Success comes from the union of both—Abrahadabra!

In doing the ritual of Liber Nu, the aspirant's aim is to achieve ecstasy of union within the Microcosm; and to incorporate the counterpart in the Macrocosm.

Liber Nu and Liber Had are distinctive among those published in *Equinox I*. 7. They are both in Class D, and addressed to the winners of Ordeal x. Each has its imprimatur with Three Neteru, V.V.V.V.V., N. Fra A∴A∴, and O. M 7°=4□. They share this with *Liber CCXX* in *Equinox I*, 10.

In the Old Commentary, Crowley (1974) says about *Liber XXXI*, III: 22: "The Ordeal 'X' will be dealt with in private." His New Comment has Nuith and Hadit as incommensurables and absolutes (≈stellar). It is solar/phallic when it involves Babalon. He alludes to achieving the perfect man of alchemy, the union of conscious and unconscious of Jung. The interpretation here has Ordeal x uniting the aspirant, the Infinite within, to the Infinite without—transcendent.

Other libers, regardless of class designation have only the imprimatur N[emo]. Fra A∴A∴,. The *Liber AL* imprimatur differs in the Centennial Edition. It omits the Neteru. Clearly, these rituals are high magic. They inspire perfection of execution in a pristine environment. They emphasize importance of detail and correspondence for achieving success.

The Glow Worm, Chapter 11 of *Liber CCCXXXIII, The Book of Lies,* describes the nature of that book. It starts with four lines relating to that which is above the Abyss:

> *Concerning the Holy Three-in-Naught. Nuit, Hadit, Ra-Hoor-Khuit, are only to be understood*
> *by the Master of the Temple.*
> *They are above The Abyss, and contain all contradictions*
> *In themselves.*
> *Below them is a seeming duality of Chaos and Babalon;*
> *these are called Father and Mother,*
> *but it is not so.*
> *They are called Brother and Sister,*
> *but it is not so.*
> *They are called Husband and Wife,*
> *but it is not so.*
> *The reflection of All is Pan: the Night of Pan is the Annihilation of the All.*

Night represents the three "its", dark and unknown, possibly the Ain Soph, where form is not expressed. Three-in-Naught suggests Ain Soph and Ain. This contrasts with the first trigram of *Liber XXVII vel Trigrammaton*, which text begins:

> *Here is Nothing under its three forms. It is not, yet informeth all things.*

Chaos and Babalon occur in *The Book of Lies,* Chapter 25 version of The Star Ruby. This version opened the active Ritual of Liber Nu, reported below. In the Dover edition (1976) of *Magick in Theory and Practice*, Teth connects the Beast in Chesed to Babalon in Geburah. There, Babalon is more akin to a microcosmic Venus in Netzach on the Tree of Life. Crowley's commentary says:

> *The first part of this chapter describes the universe in its highest sense, down to Tiphareth; it is the new and perfect cosmogony of Liber Legis.*

Crowley interprets the Holy Three to be in the Upper Triad of the Tree of Life. Chaos and Babalon are Chokmah and Binah respectively. They are one; the essential unity of the supernal Triad is here insisted upon.

(Here, I interpret the Holy Three—Nuit, Hadit, Hru-Ra-Ha—complete within the Veils of Negative Existence, in Ain Soph. I put Ra-Hoor-Khuit in Tiphareth, with Chaos and Babalon completing the Upper Triad in the Briatic Phase of the three-dimensional Quantum Tree of Life. *q.v.*)

TO KNOW

Before undertaking the ritual itself, it is necessary to know the cast. Each first verse of the three Liber AL chapters define them. The text creates questions, observations and relationships about their cosmogony.

Chapter I: p. 1,≈v. 1: Had! The manifestation of Nuit.

[Quotations from Liber AL refer to the 1904 manuscript page or facsimile, *Liber XXXI*. Subsequent typescript verse citations follow from Crowley's revised interpretation in *Equinox I,* 10 in 1913.]

The differentiation between manifest and non-manifest occurs at the Abyss, between Briah and Yetzirah in qabalistic understanding. Had is manifest, below the Abyss. Hadit is non-manifest, above the Abyss. In the ritual Hadit appears manifest, but at a higher level of awareness (Yetzirah vs. Assiah) than Had (*sensu stricto*). The aspirant is more an Adept. The aspirant to Ordeal x assumes a microcosmic view toward unity with Nu.

Chapter I: p. 22,≈v. 66. The Manifestation of Nuit is at an end.

Success occurs when Had (≈the aspirant) unites with Nuit. Had is destroyed—he becomes Hadit.

Chapter II: p. 1, v. 1: Nu! The hiding of Hadit.

Nu is manifest—below the Abyss. Nuit is non-manifest—above the Abyss. At various levels, Nuit is expressed in other than her stellar identity. On the Path of Teth in *The Book of Thoth,* she rides a Seven-headed Beast , the Serpent, on the path between Chesed and Geburah. Then she is Babalon, or the Scarlet Woman.

Chapter II: p. 1, v. 3:

> *In the sphere I [Hadit] am everywhere the center, as she [Nuit], the circumference is nowhere found.*

"The Blue-lidded daughter of Sunset" and "the naked Brilliance of the voluptuous night sky" describe stellar Nuit. In *The Book of Thoth*, Crowley notes the universe is an expansion of the number four. In a timeless three-dimensional cube, this is 43=64=Tetragrammaton, יהוה. It includes the mercuric and qliphothic, light and dark aspects shown in *Liber CCXXXI* plus the Veils of Negative Existence.

Chapter II: 79 is a counterpart to Chapter I: p. 22:

> *The end of the hiding of Hadit [Nu]; and blessing+worship to the prophet of the lovely Star [Hadit]!*
>
> *In success, Hadit destroys Nu by union. Nu, when with Hadit, becomes Nuit.*

Chapter III: p. 1, v. 1: Ahaahadabra! The reward of Ra Hoor Khuit.

Parallel to the previous first verses, Ra Hoor Khut (with the T) is the non-manifest union of Nuit and Hadit. A bit of gematria shows how Ra Hoor Khu(i)t becomes manifest in the Aeon of Horus, the Child:

Ahaahadabra (אהאאהאדאברא)=222=209+13

(Not Abrahadabra, as interpreted by Crowley in *Liber CCXX* in 1913. Compare the first four and last four letters of the word in the manuscript and the two instances of Abrahadabra in this chapter. They are not the same!)

Half of Hru Ra Ha (הרו רא הא, 418)=Ra Hoor Khut=209

Liber XXXI, III: page 9, verse 35:

The half of the word of Heru-ra-ha,
called Hoor-pa-kraat and Ra-Hoor-Khuit.

Liber 777
209=Chief Seer or Prophet (אבראה)
=Reward (אגרה)

13 = Beloved (אהבה);
Unity (אטר); He shall come (יבא)

Ra-Hoor-Khuit hath taken his seat in the East at the Equinox of the Gods; and let Asar be with Isa, who also are one. But they are not of me. Let Asar be the adorant, Isa the sufferer; Hoor in his secret name and splendour is the Lord initiating *Liber XXXI*, I, p. 13, ≈ v. 49.

Chapter III: p. 21, v. 74–75 follows the pattern of earlier chapters:

> *There is splendour in my name hidden and glorious, as the sun of midnight [Nuit] is ever the son [Ra Hoor Khut]. The ending of the words is the Word Abrahadabra. The Book of the Law is Written and Concealed. Aum. Ha.*

The reward (≈ manifestation) of Ra Hoor Khut is as Chief Seer and Prophet of the new Æon of Horus. His silent authority is Hoor-paar-Kraat revealed by Aiwass in *Liber XXXI*, I: p. 1, ≈ v. 7.

In Chapter 49, Waratah Blossoms, in *The Book of Lies*, Crowley reveals Babalon (=156) as the secret name in *XXXI*, Chapter I: p. 4, ≈ v. 22. He gives cross-references to Chapters 28 and 29. There he identifies Laylah (his Australian Scarlet Woman/Babalon), whose name means Night in Arabic with N.O.X. The reference chain then refers back to Chapter 11, The Glow-Worm, described earlier.

TO WILL

Every magical act should have an objective and express will, just as every scientific experiment states its hypothesis, and tests it. Will in Liber Nu is simple, direct and clear—unrestricted union of the aspirant with Nuit/Babalon. The aspirant must cross the Veil of Paroketh from the material World of Assiah (≈ becoming Had, an Adept), to the Formative World of Yetzirah (the foretaste of Hadit), which culminates at Tiphareth and Da'ath. This is Knowledge and Conversation with one's Holy Guardian Angel.

Beauty and Truth are Tiphareth and Da'ath. A qabalist recognizes this in the god name for Tiphareth in Assiah, יֱהוִה אליה ודעת Adonai Elohim vDa'ath, the God of Beauty and Knowledge. Keats echoed it in ending his *Ode on a Grecian Urn*:

> *Beauty is truth, truth beauty, that is all Ye know on earth, and all ye need to know.*

The Thelemic version says: "Seek beauty, for in beauty is eternal truth revealed." This expresses the view of the Liber Nu ritual. The view of the traditional Tree of Life has Tiphareth eclipsing Da'ath.

Crowley relates Will to the life of an Adept. The first and last lines of The Gun-Barrel in *The Book of Lies*, Chapter 15 read:

> *Mighty and erect is this Will of mine, this Pyramid of fire whose summit is lost in Heaven. Upon it have I burned the corpse of my desires.*

and

> *This is The Night wherein I am lost, the Love through which I am no longer I.*

This is the anticipated aim of Liber Nu. *Liber DCLXXI vel Pyramidos* identifies Will:

> *So life takes Fire from Death and runs whirling amid the Suns. Hail, Asi! Pace the Path. Bind on the girdle of the Starry One.*

This veil has the aspirant below the Abyss, the outer approach to the City of the Pyramids, to Babalon in Binah.

TO DARE

In essence, the ordeal is attaining to magical union through a microcosmic ritual reflecting the universal temple. The ritual tests truth garnered during the preparations. It challenges knowledge. It measures understanding and love. It measures commitment to Babalon/Nuit. It reveals beauty and truth. From N.O.X. comes L.V.X. into the world of the Adept. But the map is not the territory.

This is One Man's particular experience with *Liber XI*, Liber Nu, *The Book of the Cult of the Infinite Without*, and a commentary about its effect.

THE AUSTRALIA WORKING

> *But to love me is better than all things: if under the night stars in the desert thou presently burnest mine incense before me invoking me with a pure heart and the serpent flame therein, thou shalt come a little to lie in my bosom. For one kiss will thou then be willing to give all: but whoso gives one particle of dust shall lose all in that hour.*
>
> *Liber XXXI*, I: pp. 19, 20, ≈v. 61

This states the mystery of *Liber XI*, Liber Nu. It has parallels in *Liber XV* the Gnostic Mass.

THE LOCATION, THE TEMPLE

Tnorala, Gosse's Bluff, Northern Territory, Australia
23° 49' South Latitude; 132° 18' East Longitude

Gosse's Bluff, about 160 kilometers west of Alice Springs, stands up to 180 meters above the Missionary Plain. The Krichauff and West MacDonald Ranges limit the Plain on south and north. From above, the effect is an eye looking up from the Australian desert. A friend located it on a satellite photograph, and suggested its appropriateness for this working.

To native Western Aranda aboriginals, Tnorala is its name. According to local legend, it formed in Creation Time. A group of celestial women danced as stars along the Milky Way. Tired, one of them put her baby in a basket and set it down. The carrier fell from the dancing area and crashed to earth, forming the crater. The morning and evening stars are the baby's mother and father, still searching for it—as was Venus rising at the end of the actual ritual performance.

Gosse's Bluff formed some 142 million years ago. Now it is an eroded remnant of that 600 meter diameter comet/asteroid impact event recognized as the 25th largest crater known on earth. Originally, the crater was about 22 km in diameter. One to two kilometers of earth have since eroded from above it. The remaining, present ring of rock is three to four kilometers in diameter. A shallower circular rise forms a larger outer ring. The ritual was performed overnight on a rising knoll in the center of the circle.

Tnorala is a sacred site for the Arandas. Fires and overnight camping are no longer permitted. This protects its pristine condition. However, visitors do have access to an information kiosk inside the crater, and its surrounding areas.

GOSSE'S BLUFF, AERIAL VIEW, COURTESY NASA.

THE SKY
23 Sept. 1985, e.v. Equinox at 23:08
Sun enters Libra, the southern Vernal Equinox

The sky was clear. Pollution was minimized by isolation from human habitation and the rim of the Bluff itself. At arrival, near sunset, the Milky Way divided the sky into east and west halves. During the ritual, it had rotated to horizontal. The division disappeared. The light near the horizon comes through more atmosphere than that from above. It produces a slight haze with distinct circular upper limit, leaving a clear opening above. The aspirant looked at the dome into the universe as through the pupil of an eye with translucent iris.

Canopus is the bright southern star that marks the southern pole of the axis of rotation of the Galaxy, the Milky Way. The Moon entered Aquarius at 17:39, just after the time of arrival. During the ritual the Moon and Jupiter sank below the horizon. From then until the rising of Venus near morning, no planets were above the horizon. Looking up, the aspirant escaped the Solar System. His view expanded to fill the universe, unobstructed by either the Galaxy or Solar System. Hadit and Nu had direct contact.

Halley's Comet rose about 1 AM. It was on its latest inward journey to the sun. Though visible when using a telescope, it was not bright enough to see. (For several nights in mid-December, the Aspirant did see it, using binoculars, from Nauru and Fiji in the middle of the Great Sea, the Pacific Ocean. It moved along the bottom of the Great Square of Pegasus. Its perihelion occurred on 9 Feb 1986.)

THE ACTUAL RITE

The ritual of Liber Nu took place at night. Ultimately, all knowledge comes from the dark, chaotic unknown. The aspirant became conscious of the Veils of Negative Existence, the dark beyond the light.

A. The magical weapons are the possessions for the ritual. Their symbolism and meaning derive from focus and reinforcement within the consciousness of the aspirant. Careful preparation, realization and consecration empower them. Paragraphs 1–4, and 28 of Liber Nu describe them. Consecration occurred during the ritual.

The nemyss and robe were blue/yellow and red, respectively. The nemyss represented Nuit, the stellar night sky; the red robe, Hadit. The color symbolism repeated in the altar candles.

The compounded incense/perfume followed characteristics given in *Liber XXXI,* I: p. 18,≈v. 59. The appropriate resinous woods and gums symbolizing the rite were Benzoin (*Styrax*) for Scorpio and the Aspirant, and *Eucalyptus* and Tea Tree (*Melaleuca*) oils for Australia, and Galbanum (*Ferula*) for the Equinox in Libra. Each possesses healing, balancing properties. The oils and gums were absorbed into a blue maple dust matrix flecked with gold. The smoke from the incense symbolized will and aspiration ascending in search of union.

The pantacle design followed *Liber XXXI,* I: p. 19 (modified),≈v. 60. The individual red circle included a six-armed white star derived from the trigram in the last verse of *Liber XXVII vel Trigrammaton*. This focused understanding gained through preparation. It included details from *Liber DCLXXI vel Pyramidos* and *Liber DCCCXIII vel Ararita*, Chapter VII.

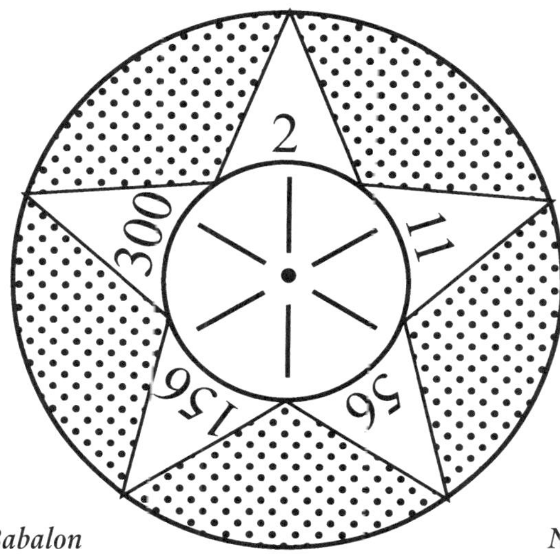

Babalon *Nu*

The preparatory meditations made the aspirant aware of attributes of Nuit/Babalon and beyond:

Divide:
2 = For I am divided for love's sake, for the chance of union. (*Liber XXXI*, I: p. 7, ≈ v. 29) = Unity is absolute. Interpretation has 0 = 1 and 1 = 2 expanded. 6 ÷ 50 = 0.12. A basic formula of the universe, nature, origin. 0 = 1 = 2 = ∞.

From division or contrast comes all knowledge.

Every number is infinite, there is no difference (*Liber XXXI*, I: p.1, ≈ v. 4).

Add: 11 = 5 + 6. Pentagram ★ and Hexagram ✡ united, Abrahadabra.

56=50+6=NU=נאה Beautiful—particularly describing Nuit and Babalon.

Multiply:
156=100 (10×10)+50+6=באבאלע Babalon, ≈The bosom of Nu

10=אש Enchanter, גבה Exalted, טב Bosom

=12×13. 12=דגה. Multiply 13=אטד Unity. *Solve et Coagula*

300=50×6=אור בפאהה Khabs am Pekht, Light in Extension

=פירוד Separation

=רוט אלהימ Ruach Elohim, Spirit of God in בראית (*Gen.* I: 3)

=Elohim spelled in full, אלה למד הי יוד מנ [≈Ain Soph]

Understand:
67=בינה Binah, Understanding, The Great Sea, City of the Pyramids, The Abode of Babalon. A prime number.

The Six-pointed Star and the Dot
61=אין Negative, Non-existence, Not, the Stainless Abode. The dark central dot.

...sixfold star of glory whereby they might see to return to the stainless Abode. (*Liber XXVII*, last trigram)

and

One and beyond One, beyond the Word and the Fool.
(*Liber DCCCXIII*, VII: 13)

Each expresses an exalted state, the universality and divinity of Nuit/Babalon. *The Vision and the Voice* (Crowley, 1911) further reveals much about them.

The text below is a condensed record of the rite performed. It includes hymns from *XXXI Hymns to the Star Goddess* by Frater Achad. This is his mystical and poetic interpretation of Liber Nu.

B. The above discussion summarizes the preparatory comprehension, meditation and ethical practices.

C. The Rite Performed.

000. This is a ritual of the Cult of the Infinite Without. (≈The Ain, Nothing without form).

The ritual occurred in a dark, silent, sublime and pristine temple. Perfection and isolation reflect Nothing and Everything.

00. The Aspirant is Hadit. Nuit is the infinite expansion of the Rose: Hadit is the infinite concentration of the Rood. The aspirant is the performer.

Hru Ra Ha completes the awareness of Ain Soph.

0. Memorize *The Book of the Law*, Chapter I.

Memorizing made the aspirant conscious of its content and subtlety. Through memorizing, the basic grimoire of the ritual, the aspirant, recognized related material elsewhere. This cannot be stressed too much. When one views *Liber XXXI* as a dark stellar revelation, analogy to the Qliphoth (≈the Ain Soph Aur) is possible.

The ritual started with writing the text of Chapter I into the diary by the light of the moon. This focused awareness on Nu/Babalon.

1. *Liber XXV*, The Star Ruby from *The Book of Lies*.

The ritual followed with banishing unwanted forces. It invoked Nuit and Hadit in universal and local (consciousness) aspects. The circular rim of the Bluff became the symbolic limit of the magical, microcosmic temple. The temple of Nuit is Space, the naked brilliance of the voluptuous night sky.

(South of the Tropic of Capricorn, invocation, deosil, is counterclockwise. Banishing, widdershins, is clockwise. Some parallels occur between the mercuric and qliphothic, the light and dark aspects. They are reflections of one another.)

The forces in the four quarters were invoked into the circle.

Chaos in the East—	Unorganized; Pregnant Dawn, Light and knowledge. Birth.
Babalon in the South—	Nuit; The Goddess—Light, life, love, liberty.
Eros in the West—	Babalon/Venus; Sunset, Light returns to darkness. Death. Union.
Psyche in the North—	Consciousness; Dark, Night —Transformation. Rebirth or Conception.

After defining the ritual circle, the aspirant moved to the center of its horizontal plane. Invoking Pan with the dark signs of N.O.X., he connected to the three-dimensional dome of the Macrocosm. Finally, he sealed this temple/universe with the pentagram and hexagram.

2. *Liber XXXVI,* The Star Sapphire from *The Book of Lies.*

This invoked (deosil) the family, symbolic of unity and division, life and death, dark and light, succession, Tetragrammaton. The signs of N.O.X. invoke origin from darkness. Ararita, the power of Unity, connects the manifest personae on the horizontal microcosmic plane to the Three-in-Naught on the vertical, macrocosmic plane. The Adept aspired to Hadit, rather than Had.

In the Star Sapphire, the aspirant faces the Abyss and invokes Da'ath, the sephira of Knowledge. P and K represent Phallus and Kteis (≈microcosmic), Power and Knowledge (≈macrocosmic), and aspiration and inspiration (opposites).

The "Omnia" is a core formula— $\infty+2+1+0$. Hadit, the Adept, armed with his Magick Rood, unites with his Mystic Rose, Nuit, the All. It reflects the earlier formula of the Universe, but is the same. The Point and the Circle join in death and life.

3. The Consecration of the elemental weapons—wand, incense, cup, and pantacle, representing fire, air, water, and earth—completed temple and altar preparations.

4. The Invocation began with Achad's Hymn #1:

> *Mother of the Sun, whose Body is White with the Milk of the Stars, bend upon thy servant and impart unto him Thy Secret Kiss!*

The incantation from Achad Hymn #9 continued:

> *In the Daylight I see not Thy Body of Stars, O beloved... I am but a tiny spermatozoon, but within me is the fiery and concentrated essence of life... and Draw me up into Thyself, O Sun! Project me into the Body of Our Lady Nuit!*
>
> *Then shall a new Star be born, and I shall see thee even in the Daylight, O Beloved.*

5. The Elixir.

The mystical union of Nuit and Hadit
The cup and the wand [≈Babalon and the Beast conjoined]

6. Consummation.

Absorption of the elixir.
The magical union of microcosm to macrocosm.

7. Falling into Nuit. Achad Hymn #29

> *Falling, falling, falling! Thus fall the Rays from the Body of Stars upon this tiny planet, O beloved!*
> *Innumerable streams of Light like Star-rain upon the black earth...I felt that I, too, was falling, falling, falling,*
> *in an ecstasy of fear and love into the void abyss of space. Then did I remember that Thou art continuous.*
> *Beneath, above, around me are Thou. And lo, from a falling star I became as a comet wheeling in infinite Circles, each at a different angle, till my course traced out the Infinite Sphere that is the Symbol of Thee, O Beloved.*

Then did I aspire to find the Centre of All. And even now I am falling, falling, falling.

This is surrender of Will—falling into Nuit, the night sky. The aspirant overcomes fear of falling (cremnophobia) and becomes One (1) with Nuit (0). He knows stopping is failure. Using the Sign of Apophis, he soars into Nuit, the void of space. The path of a comet symbolizes his flight.

TO BE SILENT

8. Meditation.

This modified outline is parallel to the original meditation. Above the Abyss is unity; below it is duality.

0. Universe
1. Galaxy
2. Zodiac
3. Solar System

THE ABYSS

4. Temple	4. Aspirant
5. Ritual Circle	5. Mind/Soul
6. Altar	6. Body
7. Candles	7. Gonads
8. Flame	8. Spermatozoon
9. Burning point	9. Gene
10. Atom	10. DNA

The meditation continued until the aspirant fell asleep. He awoke before dawn. Venus had risen in the east. The Milky Way was above the horizon, dividing the sky. Many shooting stars passed overhead during the night. Soon it was day.

9. The Result. Expressed through Achad's Hymn #31:

Three eternities are passed...I have outstripped a million Stars in my race across Thy Breast—The Milky Way. When shall I come to the Secret Centre of Thy Being?

> *Thus left I Time and Space and Circumstance, and every Star became as an atom in my Body, when it became Thy Body. Now never shall I be known, for it is I that go.*
> *But Thou, O Beloved, though Thou art infinitely Great, art Thou not energized by the Invisible Point—the Infinitely Small?*
> *A Million Eternities are Present. Deem not of Change; This is the Here and Now, and I am NOT.*

In the ecstasy of falling, the aspirant experienced enormity and intimacy with Nuit—Everywhere. He became at the center of it all—Nowhere.

10. Earthing.

Bury a small amount of incense. Return the Bluff to its pristine state! Banish—the last line of the Star Ruby. Clear the temple. Depart in mid-morning.

Only the aspirant can evaluate his specific and overall success. As with the details of the ritual, the results are individual and silent.

Specifically in Liber Nu, success is judged by the rewards. They include:

Appreciation of detail and symbol, importance of preparation
Appreciation of physical and magical environments
Awareness of the nature of the Infinite Sky and the Infinite Stars Ecstasy of Had with Babalon
Solve, Coagula, Solve = Coagula, Solve, Coagula
Expansion of Consciousness

> *And the sign shall be my ecstasy, the consciousness of the continuity of existence.*
>
> *Liber XXXI*, I: p. 6, ≈ v. 26.

CODA

Liber AL, Ch. I

I am the blue-lidded daughter of sunset: I am the naked brilliance of the voluptuous night sky. To me! To me! The manifestation of Nuit is at an end.

Liber Trigrammaton

Therefore was the end of it sorrow; yet in that sorrow a sixfold star of glory whereby they might see to return unto the stainless Abode; yea unto the Stainless Abode.

Liber Ararita, Ch. VII

11. And All and One and Naught were slain in the slaying of the Warrior 418. 12. In the slaying of the subtlety that expanded all these things into the Twelve Rays of the Crown. 13. That returned unto One, and beyond One, even unto the vision of the Fool in his folly that chanted the word Ararita, and beyond the Word and the Fool; yea, beyond the Word and the Fool.

Through the Liber Nu ritual, the aspirant experienced the pristine immensity of Nuit, the universe, the surrender and falling into her bosom. That instant of transcendence still remains. Initiation continues.

The mysteries of Nuit and Babalon occur throughout the Class A libers of Thelema. They continue to provide focus, inspiration and ecstasy. Special guides include Liber AL, Liber Trigrammaton, and Liber Ararita.

Tarot Atu VIII, Lust and Atu XXI, the Universe depict different levels of Nuit/Babalon. In each, the female is above the male, a view of Thelemic cosmogony.

Liber XXXI, I: p. 2–3, ≈ v. 15–17 [interpolated terms in brackets]:

Now yet [sic, t without crossbar, ? = at time of writing] shall know that the chosen priest + apostle [≈ the office] of infinite space [≈ Nuit] is the prince priest the Beast [≈ the man, a person in office] and in his woman [≈ the person], called the Scarlet Woman [≈ the office], is all power given. [italics added for emphasis] They shall gather my children into their fold: [≈ those in the New Æon] they shall bring the glory of the stars [≈ Nuit] into the hearts of men.

> *[≈ Had! The manifestation of Nuit. ≈ Universal Will expressed] For he is ever a sun, and she a moon [≈ alchemical symbols of sexual identity and contrast, Solve et Coagula, the process]. But to him is the winged secret flame [≈ Hadit nature] and to her the stooping starlight [≈ Nuit nature]. But ye are not so chosen [≈ ?yet, see above]*

On the Universe card, the central female [≈ Nuit, Sophia] presses her heel on the head of the serpent (≈ male]. She opens her arms like a cup—receptive to eternity—parallel to the Sign of Apophis used by the aspirant during his falling.

In contrast, the Lust card depicts a more mundane level, with Babalon riding the Beast and raising her cup of fornication. The snake and the seven-headed beast are cognate, as Nuit and Babalon are cognate.

In *The Book of Thoth*, p. 143ff Crowley quotes the Ninth Æthyr of *The Vision and the Voice* (*Equinox I*, V: p. 106):

> *And the ring of the horizon above her is a company of glorious Archangels with joined hands, that stand and sing: This is the daughter of BABALON the Beautiful, that she hath borne unto the Father of All. And unto all hath she borne her.*
> *This is the Daughter of the King. This is the Virgin of Eternity, the prize of them that have overcome Space. This is she that the Holy One hath wrested from the Giant Time, and the prize that have overcome Space. This is she that is set upon the Throne of Understanding.*

It ends:

> *Holy, Holy, Holy art thou, and blessed be thy name forever, unto whom the Æons are but the pulsings of thy blood.*

Twenty-eight years have passed. Saturn returns on 2 Mar. 2014. A new stage of understanding has evolved. A new comet, ISON, reached the sun at perihelion on 28 Nov. 2013. Only a portion survived. It is now returning to space. What arrived for the aspirant on one returning comet is leaving on another. Unlike the first, it is falling into the universe, and will not return.

Waiting for the Scarlet Apocalypse:

BABALON AS REVOLUTIONARY REAPER IN THE WRITINGS OF JACK PARSONS

Manon Hedenborg-White

> *After all, the other name of Armageddon will not be written until the morning of Ragnarok, when at last Her banner is unfolded before the armies. (...) I know that Babalon is incarnate upon earth at this moment, although I do not know where or as whom.*
>
> —John W. Parsons to Marjorie Cameron, October 5, 1949.

JOHN W. PARSONS, dubbed 'the Che Guevara of occultism' by one of his biographers, is one of the most legendary and least understood characters of the occult revival. Rocketeer, poet, and polyamorous proto-feminist, his turbulent life and magical career have been the subject of two biographies to date. However, less has been said about the contents of his religious beliefs, principally his work with the Thelemic goddess Babalon. Loosely derived from the Biblical Whore of Babylon,[1] Aleister Crowley interpreted Babalon as the gateway between the manifest and the numinous; a sacred harlot who receives any adept willing to sacrifice his or her ego in order to attain *unio mystica,* dissolution in the divine, and rebirth in the City of Pyra-

1 Rev. 17:1–18.

mids. Although Babalon is one of the principal deities in Crowley's pantheon, she is mostly silent in the Beast's writings; an initiatory passageway rather than a speaking subject in her own right. In Parsons' interpretation, coloured by his left-wing, proto-feminist leanings and passion for fantasy and mythology, Babalon instead becomes a blood-thirsty revolutionary, a living messiah, the quintessential New Woman. Although these aspects of Parsons' work have mostly been neglected, I would argue his writings have played a key role in enabling the post-Crowley Babalon to transcend her original function in Thelemic initiation, acquiring new levels of meaning and emerging as one of the most engaging and vibrant symbols in the contemporary esoteric *milieu.* I will here explore and discuss Babalon in the context of Parsons' works, with a focus on her transition from object to subject and the integration of Satanic elements and fictional, mythological, and anthropological themes and motifs, coming together to form a goddess who is not locked in time beyond the Abyss, but who has a history, a voice, and a destiny.

BACKGROUND

Jack Parsons was born on October 2, 1914. He was raised by his mother and grandparents, an only child who grew up precocious, spoilt, and something of a loner. An avid reader, he developed a love of fantasy and science fiction literature, which would last throughout his life. As a teenager, he befriended the considerably more popular Ed Forman, who shared Parsons' literary tastes. The two began experimenting with rockets together. Despite their lack of qualifications, Parsons and Forman eventually began working with Frank Malina, a graduate student at the California Institute of Technology (CALTECH), conducting unofficial experiments with the aim of developing functional rockets.[2]

Rocketry at this time was not a recognised science, and the notion of space travel was viewed as a scientifically impossible pipedream, a desperate vision sci-fi enthusiasts clung to rather than something recognised engineers would engage in. After initially being scorned by CALTECH, however, the trio gained the endorsement of legendary scientist Theodore von Karman (1881–1963), who allowed the slowly growing group of rocket

2 George Pendle, *Strange Angel: The Otherworldly Life of Rocket Scientist John Whiteside Parsons*, Mariner Books, 2006.

enthusiasts to conduct experiments on campus. Humorously dubbed the Suicide Squad, Parsons' merry band of rocketeers would eventually found the Jet Propulsion Laboratory (JPL), which would play a key role in the American space program. His contributions were essential to the development of the solid rocket fuel without which the moon landing would have been unfeasible. Parsons has a crater named after him on the dark side of the moon.

Parsons' contributions to the space program were not due to any formal qualifications, but rather to an intuitive knack for the science and an ability to see gateways where others saw barriers. A postmodern creative, he eschewed epistemological boundaries, drawing freely on fact and fiction; science and mythology, to inspire and enliven his work, spirituality, and relationships. The boy Parsons immersed himself in the realms of epic and romantic literature and mythology; the man Parsons recited Aleister Crowley's 'Hymn to Pan' during rocket launches and devoured works on comparative mythology and anthropology in his search for enchantment, magic, and transcendence. He found it, first through explosives and dreams of space travel, then through esotericism. Finally, it found him, through the voice of a goddess speaking to him in the desert.

INITIATION INTO OCCULTISM: THE EARLY YEARS WITH THE AGAPE LODGE

Southern California in the early twentieth century was a melting pot of alternative spirituality, in which the eccentric and romantic Parsons naturally became absorbed. He would approach magic in much the same way as he did rocketry, with unconventionality, zeal, and little patience for the rules of others. Having previously read Aleister Crowley's *Konx om Pax* (1907), he was invited in January 1939, to witness a performance of the Gnostic Mass, lead by Regina Kahl and Wilfred T. Smith at the O.T.O.'s Agape Lodge in Los Angeles. There, Parsons was also introduced to Jane Wolfe, who had lived with Crowley at his Abbey of Thelema in Sicily. Parsons' interest in Thelema and Crowley grew over time, and Smith would subsequently become a close friend and father figure to him. By the end of 1939, Parsons had assembled a sizeable collection of Crowley's books.[3]

On February 15, 1941, Jack and his wife Helen were formally initiated

3 Pendle, *Strange Angel*, pp. 132–136; 152–153.

into the O.T.O. Smith and Wolfe were both delighted to have recruited the young rocket scientist, and Parsons happily immersed himself in lodge activities. Still, relations within the Agape Lodge were not always uncomplicated, party due to the prevalence of polyamory among its membership. When Parsons started an affair with Helen's younger sister Sarah Northrup, alias Betty, a distraught Helen sought solace in the arms of Smith.[4]

At Parsons' suggestion, the lodge relocated to Pasadena in 1942. He found a suitable location in a stately mansion on 1003 Orange Grove Avenue, and the members moved in at once. In 1943, Parsons succeeded Smith as Lodge Master, after Crowley asked Smith to step down. Still, Parsons' enthusiasm for lodge life appeared to be dwindling. The strain of free sexual relations, feuding and incessant partying, as well as an on-going FBI investigation, took its toll on the community, and several of the older members tired and moved out, including Jane Wolfe. In early 1945, Regina Kahl died, and Parsons subsequently began turning 1003 into a secular bohemian community, mixing occultists with sci-fi enthusiasts and scientists.[5]

'FLAME IS OUR LADY, FLAME IS HER HAIR': THE BABALON WORKING

Lieutenant L. Ron Hubbard, prolific fantasy writer and future founder of the Church of Scientology, moved into 1003 in 1945. Although Parsons and Hubbard became instant friends, their camaraderie was complicated when Parsons' girlfriend Betty Northrup fell for Hubbard. Although Parsons prided himself on his immunity to jealousy, he was hurt by the intensity of Northrup's relationship with Hubbard. Parsons had considerable time to dwell on his emotions, as his career was similarly in a slump. Partly due to the pioneering discoveries of the old Suicide Squad, rocketry had become legitimate, and Parsons' unorthodox methods and lack of credentials made him seem increasingly like a liability. He had been phased out of JPL and impelled to sell his stock in the company he had co-founded.[6]

Thus, Parsons launched himself headfirst into more extraordinary forms of magic. He had been intrigued by witchcraft and darker magic since childhood, claiming to have invoked Satan successfully at the age of

4 Ibid., pp. 204–205.
5 Ibid., pp. 204–205; 207–214; 209; 243–245.
6 Ibid., pp. 239–241; 252–257.

13.[7] He was bored by the meticulous magical training programme Smith had advocated, and needed a distraction. In December 1945, Parsons began a series of conjurations to procure a female ritual partner or elemental mate, a concept first outlined in the teachings of Paracelsus. Convinced that Hubbard possessed particular magical sensitivity, Parsons soon invited the latter to partake in the proceedings. After two weeks, the two men travelled into the Mojave Desert together, adjourning at Parsons' favourite spot at the intersection of two large electrical power lines. At sunset, Parsons sensed that the work was completed, and returned home to discover a young woman at his doorstep, there in response to an advertisement for a new tenant.[8]

The woman, whom Parsons saw as his elemental, was 24-year-old Marjorie Cameron (1922–1995) of Belle Plaines, Iowa. Tall and striking with fiery red hair, the young woman likely reminded Parsons of April Bell, the sinister yet irresistible female protagonist of Jack Williamsons' fantasy novelette 'Darker Than You Think', which Parsons had read and loved.[9] First published in 1940 and released in extended novel form in 1948, the story centres on failed anthropologist and struggling newsman Will Barbee, who learns of the existence of an ancient, secret race of shape-shifting witches, waiting for a coming messiah known as the Child of Night.[10] As I will return to later in this text, the story's main motifs of a male seeker with a crucial role to play in the destiny of humanity and a red-haired, female initiatrix at his side appears to have entranced Parsons, and influenced his thinking in several ways.

Parsons was smitten with Cameron, and the pair immediately began performing a succession of sex magical rituals over the course of eight days. Through these magical operations, Parsons hoped to cause the goddess Babalon to be incarnated on earth in the shape of a human woman. This female Thelemic messiah would liberate the world and balance the energies of the Aeon of Horus, which Parsons saw as violent and chaotic, relating to 'power, violence, and energy'[11]. In contrast, he equated the force

7 John W. Parsons, *The Book of Anti-Christ*, n.d. ca 1948, Warburg Institute Library.

8 Martin P. Starr, *The Unknown God. W. T. Smith and the Thelemites*, Teitan Press, 2003, 313; John W. Parsons, *The Book of Babalon*, n.d. ca 1946, Warburg Institute Library; Pendle, *Strange Angel*, pp. 261–263.

9 Pendle, *Strange Angel*, 295.

10 Jack Williamson, *Darker Than You Think*, Fantasy Press, 1948.

11 Parsons, *Book of Babalon*.

of Babalon with 'love, understanding, and dionysian freedom'.[12] Thus, he perceived his own magical operation as a necessary counterbalance to the current Crowley had unleashed upon the world in 1904 with his reception of the supposedly divinely inspired *Liber AL vel Legis*, colloquially known as *The Book of the Law*. Unlike Crowley, who viewed himself as the key figure in the liberation of humanity through his religion of Thelema, Parsons ascribed this violently messianic and emancipatory force to the physical manifestation of the divine feminine. As will also become apparent, Parsons did not interpret Babalon merely as a sweet-natured female counterpart to Ra-Hoor-Khuit, but as a fierce and extremely powerful figure in her own right. In Parsons' portrayal of the single most important deity in his psycho-spiritual universe, Babalon largely replaces Horus as the divine embodiment of the New Aeon.

After eight days, Parsons returned to the desert, this time alone, to invoke Babalon. There, he heard a voice, identifying itself as the goddess and dictating in a similar fashion to Crowley's reception of *Liber AL* what came to be called *Liber 49*, described as 'the fourth chapter of the Book of the Law'.[13] An idiosyncratic blend of Thelemic and Biblical references, the text announces the coming manifestation of Babalon in the form of a human female, come to judge the nations and liberate mankind from bondage. The text instructs Parsons to prepare for her manifestation, and includes a number of more or less veiled hints to his own, imminent death. In *Liber 49*, the goddess also provides further ritual instructions for the next stage of the Babalon Working.

In large portions of this text, the goddess seemingly addresses her future, human daughter directly. The ways in which Babalon speaks to Parsons and her imminent corporeal manifestation differ quite significantly. While the former is addressed as 'fool', and told that he will be 'outcast and accursed', Babalon refers to her daughter as 'wise, and sure, and excellent', and says that 'all power, all hope, all future' will be in her hands.[14] In general, the passages in which Babalon speaks directly to Parsons are more commanding, and occasionally disdainful in tone, while those addressed to her daughter are phrased in loving and highly respectful language. This disparity is emphasised by the allusions to Parsons' demise, creating the image that he will pay with his life for Babalon's manifestation, while the

12 Ibid
13 Ibid.
14 Ibid.

force of the goddess will continue to bring liberation to the world through her human avatar. The motif of the male magician, in this case Parsons, as an ultimately dispensable sacrifice continues throughout the latter's record of the Babalon Working, and emphasises the impression of the divine feminine—and woman—as the primary, dynamic force in Parsons' vision.

Following his reception of *Liber 49*, Parsons proceeded to conduct the rituals outlined by the goddess, using a number of invocations both original and borrowed from Crowley. With Hubbard as medium, he received further communications from Babalon, which became progressively darker and more foreboding as the operations proceeded. In one communication, Hubbard states: 'She shall absorb thee, and thou shalt become living flame before She incarnates'.[15] Although Parsons is warned repeatedly not to concern himself with the time and place of Babalon's manifestation, he finally declared his Babalon Working a success and that the goddess was now incarnate on earth in 'some living woman'.[16] Although his original intention was for Cameron to become pregnant with Babalon's earthly daughter, he revised his vision when his mistress did not conceive. Throughout the remainder of his life his idea of the exact time and place of Babalon's manifestation varied, and he sometimes appears to have believed that Cameron was, in fact, Babalon. Cameron herself believed this later in life.[17]

The interpretation of the Whore of Babylon as the goddess Babalon, a figure with a crucial initiatory function and a strong connection to liberated sexuality, is first seen in Crowley's writings. Parsons was of course strongly inspired by Crowley's work, and links his own work with one of the principal Thelemic deities to the Thelemic canon. *Liber 49* as well as Parsons' magical diaries from the operations and transcripts of the communications from the goddess are collected in *The Book of Babalon*, which references several of Crowley's texts, including *Liber AL vel Legis* (The Book of the Law), 'Liber Astarte', *The Vision & the Voice*, his play *Tannhäuser*, and the Gnostic Catholic Mass. Academic research on Thelemic history has thus tended to treat Parsons merely as Crowley's ill-fated acolyte, and his interpretation of Babalon as an extension of that of his mentor. This, I would argue, is a mistake, as there are substantial differences between Parsons'

15 Ibid.

16 Ibid.

17 Spencer Kansa, *Wormwood Star: The Magickal Life of Marjorie Cameron*, Mandrake, 2010.

exploration of the Babalon symbol, which foreshadow later developments in the esoteric milieu at large. Having provided this brief introduction to Parsons' life and the Babalon Working, I will now discuss the goddess in Parsons' life and writings.

THE SPEAKING BABALON: BLOOD SACRIFICE AND THE GODDESS IN THE WORLD

The Vision & the Voice comprises detailed descriptions of Crowley's visions exploring the Enochian Aethyrs. It is the first of Crowley's works in which Babalon is mentioned explicitly by name, and her appearance is described in detail in several passages. She features especially prominently in the 15th, 9th, 4th, and 2nd Aethyrs. However, the goddess in this visionary text is largely silent, with the notable exception of the beginning of the 15th Aethyr, where she calls:

> *Lo! I gather up every spirit that is pure, and weave him into my vesture of flame. I lick up the lives of men, and their souls sparkle from mine eyes. I am the mighty sorceress, the lust of the spirit. And by my dancing I gather for my mother Nuit the heads of all them that are baptized in the waters of life. I am the lust of the spirit that eateth up the soul of man. I have prepared a feast for the adepts, and they that partake thereof shall see God.*[18]

By gathering the spirits of the adept who is prepared to sacrifice their individual ego to the goddess, Babalon allows them to be reborn as a Magister Templi beyond the Abyss. The goddess thus has the qualities of a redeemer in Crowley's work, but crucially only to those who are ready to cross the Abyss, and who are prepared to sacrifice themselves. Babalon's residence is ultimately beyond the great void between the manifest and the numinous, and she does not, in Crowley's writings, descend into the manifest world to take action herself.

In the 12th Aethyr, Babalon plays a central but non-vocal role, as she is explored first through the words of a mystical charioteer who describes her nature and function, then through Crowley's vision, and then that of the angel of the Aethyr.[19] Babalon continues to be described from a third-

18 Aleister Crowley, *The Vision & the Voice*, Samuel Weiser Inc., 1998, p. 131.
19 Ibid., pp. 149–152.

person perspective throughout the remainder of the Aethyrs, with the exception of the 2nd, which contains a mysterious song given by 'one of Her ministers'.[20] Thus, although Babalon is one of the most important figures introduced in *The Vision & the Voice,* she mostly remains elusive and silent. The same is true of Crowley's 'Liber Cheth', a mystical text instructing the adept in the formula of Babalon, in which the goddess is also viewed from a third-person perspective.[21] Thus, Crowley's Babalon, although central to his initiatory system, is throughout most of his writings not a speaking subject in her own right. Instead, Babalon is defined by being one of several stages in the adept's Thelemic initiation, more specifically as the gateway to the City of Pyramids.

In contrast, the revelations presented in *The Book of Babalon* are primarily verbal, and Parsons provides very little indication of Babalon's visual appearance. 'Liber 49', as noted above, constitutes Babalon's personal address to Parsons, her future daughter, and humanity at large. The goddess subsequently guides her male adept through the operations, which are aimed at producing further communications and, ultimately, her human incarnation. It is hinted repeatedly that Parsons will have to sacrifice his life. Put simply, it is mostly the scarlet goddess calling the shots throughout most of the Babalon Working, and it is Parsons rather than Babalon who appears as a means to an end in this narrative. It is hinted repeatedly that Parsons will have to sacrifice himself, but this appears to be in service of the goddess and her human daughter, rather than for the purposes of his own initiation.

Parsons' work on the goddess thus diverges quite significantly from Crowley's with respect to the relative function and importance of Babalon and her male adept. Although Crowley also writes of the office of the Scarlet Woman, who is sometimes interpreted as the earthly representative of the goddess, this figure is primarily defined by being in a relationship with the Beast. Crowley indeed referred to many of his most important female lovers as Scarlet Women. In a comment to the 16th Aethyr, Crowley writes that his mistresses are 'but avatars' of the goddess.[22] In a comment to *Liber AL,* he writes that the Scarlet Woman is 'any woman that receives and

20 Ibid., p. 241.

21 Aleister Crowley, 'Liber Cheth vel Vallum Abiegni sub figura CLVI', *Equinox* 1:6 (1911), pp. 23–27.

22 Aleister Crowley, *The Vision & the Voice,* p. 129.

transmits [his] Solar Word and Being'.[23] Thus, although Crowley also had ideas about the Babalon principle descending into the manifest universe, the role of Scarlet Woman in his writings is clearly subordinate to the goddess herself. Moreover, the main criterion for being a Scarlet Woman in Crowley's mind, as illustrated by the above quote, was being in a relationship with the Beast. Crowley also tends to present the Scarlet Woman more as a female sidekick to the Beast rather than the driving force in the establishment of a utopian society in her own right. Parsons' writings on the Babalon figure as an agent of change in the world are, in this respect, different. While the Beast's Scarlet Women ceased to be avatars of the goddess after they had filled their function in his magical advancement, Babalon's human incarnation in Parsons' vision clearly has a function stretching far beyond Parsons' initiation, and even his mortal life, as illustrated by the many references in *The Book of Babalon* to his death.

In Parsons' writings, Babalon emerges as a figure capable of moving into the material realm and giving orders, and who does so with a worldly agenda of her own. Although the relationship between Parsons and Babalon is sometimes couched in romantic language, the goddess is clearly the dominant party, and rather than being defined by her romantic engagement with a male priest-adept, it is stated that Parsons 'shalt become living flame before She incarnates'.[24] Thus, it is Parsons rather than the goddess who appears to be the helper or sidekick in their relationship. Through direct and indirect references to the Bible, Revelation in particular, *The Book of Babalon* also portrays Babalon as a harbinger of final judgment and war, a champion of violent revolution. Rather than receiving the magician's ego and birthing him into the City of Pyramids, Babalon moves into the world on her own initiative and commands him to take action.

Thus, Parsons' conceptualisation of Babalon provides a more active and demanding version of the divine feminine than that offered by Crowley. Throughout most of the working, Babalon is the one telling Parsons what to do, to the point where she asks him to relinquish mortal life in exchange for her physical manifestation. The relationship between Babalon and her male priest-sacrifice is constructed in erotic, partly sadomasochistic terms.

23 Aleister Crowley, 'AL—The Comment Called "D", the Djeridensis Working', first published in Aleister Crowley, *Magical and Philosophical Commentaries on the Book of the Law*, 93 Publishing, 1974, accessed May 31, 2015, from *Hermetic.com*, http://hermetic.com/legis/djeridensis/chapter-i.html.

24 Parsons, *Book of Babalon*.

In one of the few original Babalon invocations detailed in *The Book of Babalon*, Parsons exclaims:

> *O BABALON, BABALON beloved, come now, partake of the sacrament, possess this shrine. Take me now! Let me be drunken on the wine of your fornications; let your kisses wanton me to death. Accept thou this sacrifice willingly given!*[25]

A central theme of *The Book of Babalon* is of the goddess as a sort of divine reaper, requiring her male adept's blood in sacrifice. In Crowley's writings, the draining of the adept's blood appears purely metaphorical, and in fact the Beast disparages the sacrificial use of blood in the devotional manual colloquially known as 'Liber Astarte'.[26] In *The Book of Babalon*, however, Parsons physically sheds his blood for the goddess several times. Parsons uses blood repeatedly in the workings to procure his elemental, and again several times on Hubbard's instructions when attempting to communicate directly with the goddess. Ultimately, the goddess asks Babalon to give his mortal life in exchange for her incarnation, stating: 'Mortality We have not asked this of another, nor shall we ever. (...) Is this accepted, are you willing to proceed.'[27] Parsons responds: 'I am willing'.[28] Thus, the blood motif has a far more literal meaning in Parsons' depiction of Babalon, emphasising the gravity of the latter's vision.

Although Crowley's descriptions of Babalon also evoke images of human sacrifice, not least in 'Liber Cheth', it is once again important to stress that this and similar excerpts are primarily metaphorical. Although the motif of human sacrifice in *The Book of Babalon* has gone largely neglected in previous academic scholarship, it is arguably central to the accomplishment of Parsons' (and, allegedly, Babalon's) vision. The theme of a bloodthirsty mother goddess craving human offerings also points to some of the literary works seemingly influencing Parsons' ideas, as expressed both in *The Book of Babalon* and, more directly, in his later writings on witchcraft (to be discussed below). For instance, Margaret Murray in her works *The Witch-Cult of Western Europe* (1921) and *The God of the Witches* (1931) argues

25 Ibid.
26 Aleister Crowley, 'ASTARTE vel Liber BERYLLI sub figura CL XXV', *Equinox* 1:7 (1911).
27 Parsons, *Book of Babalon*.
28 Ibid.

that the witch trials were an attempt to eradicate a surviving lineage of pre-Christian paganism, in which blood sacrifice played a central role. Parsons writes in the introduction to the Babalon Working that its background can be found in a number of anthropological texts, and his later writings draw on Murray's ideas in such a clear way that it can hardly be disputed that he read her works. Similar notions are also put forth in Robert Graves' *The White Goddess* (1948), although this work was published two years after the Babalon Working.

'As a perilous flame and a devious song': Babalon as revolutionary

Thus far, I have pinpointed the idea of Babalon as a figure who is capable of, and willing to, descend into the physical world rather than waiting patiently beyond the Abyss, as well as the emphasis on actual blood sacrifice as two of the innovations Parsons brings to the Babalon discourse. However, it is perhaps the notion of Babalon as a revolutionary with her own utopian vision that is Parsons' most important, original contribution to the discourse around the goddess. This aspect of Babalon is emphasised even more strongly in the essay 'Freedom is a Two-Edged Sword', which Parsons wrote between 1946 and 1950 (see following sections).[29] *The Book of Babalon* appears implicitly to have prepared for Parsons' feminist vision, articulated clearly in 'Freedom' by presenting the divine feminine as a revolutionary force, and Babalon as an active subject in the world. The notion of Babalon as a sort of vindictive messiah, come to earth to bring judgment and retribution, is also emphasised by the veiled allusions to the Bible in 'Liber 49'. Among other things, Babalon says: 'There is threshing of wheat and a trampling of grapes that shall not cease until the truth be known unto the least of men. But you who do not accept, you who see beyond, reach out your hands my children and reap the world in the hour of your harvest'.[30] This passage is highly similar to several excerpts in the Bible where divine punishment is connected to threshing, harvesting and reaping.[31] There are also many allusions to a sort of final battle, in which

29 John W. Parsons, 'Freedom is a Two-Edged Sword', in John W. Parsons, *Freedom is a Two-Edged Sword and Other Essays*, New Falcon Publications, 2001, pp. 9–44.

30 Parsons, *Book of Babalon*.

31 See e.g. Jeremiah 51:33; Rev. 14:14–15; and Joel 3:13.

Babalon will lead the fight for liberation and justice. In the final line of *Liber 49*, she calls out: 'Set my star upon your banners and go forward in joy and victory. None shall deny you, and none shall stand before you...'[32]

The poem 'The Birth of Babalon', seemingly an original creation of Parsons' used as an invocation of the goddess, emphasises the revolutionary warrior aspect of Babalon further. It is written that Babalon 'has taken flesh, she is come to judge the thrones ye rule upon. Quail ye kings for an end is come in the birth of BABALON'.[33] The poem seems to position Babalon implicitly against patriarchal monotheism and worldly power, constructing Babalon as a female revolutionary force that will wreak havoc on kings, priests and god himself:

Now God has called for his judgement book
and seen his name therein
And the grace of God and the guilt of God
have spelt it out as sin

His bloody priests have clutched his robes
and stained his linen gown
And his victims swarm from his broken hell
to drag his kingdom down.[34]

Although *The Vision & the Voice* has strong apocalyptic components, Parsons' texts thus emphasises themes of worldly revolution and societal transformation that are largely absent from Crowley's writings on Babalon. To a greater degree than his mentor, Parsons stresses the goddess' ferocity and strength, and posits her as the leader of a violent, global revolution. It bears pointing out that this image, which dominates most of *The Book of Babalon*, is also decidedly different from the goddess of 'love, understanding, and dionysian freedom' Parsons describes in its introduction. The frequent references to swords, trumpets, banners, and armies throughout the transcripts of the different parts of the Babalon Working depict her as a goddess of war, and create an interesting paradox in relation to the dichotomy between Horus and Babalon that Parsons posits at the beginning of the text. In the rest of *The Book of Babalon*, as well as the other works Par-

32 Parsons, *Book of Babalon*.
33 Ibid.
34 Ibid.

sons produced concerning the goddess throughout the remainder of his life, Babalon bears little resemblance to this proposed female embodiment of benevolence and sensualism who balances and passively channels the aggressive, male energy of Horus. The divine gender polarity of Horus and Babalon, alluded to in the introduction to *The Book of Babalon* is completely absent in the rest of the work, and Babalon—who emerges as a goddess of death, war and revolution as much as of love—appears to take on much of the aggression and chaos Parsons originally attributes to Horus. Rather than being part of a divine couple, Babalon gradually emerges as the single most important deity in Parsons' personal cosmology and vision of global salvation.

The Babalon Working marked a turning point in Parsons' magical career. After concluding the operations, he began to distance himself from the O.T.O. In March 1946, he wrote a letter to the members of the order, alluding in veiled terms to the Babalon Working, announcing his plans to sell the house at 1003, and requesting that all tenants relocate promptly. After Hubbard and Betty Northrup disappeared with a significant part of Parsons' life savings, the latter submitted his resignation to Crowley. Parsons married Cameron later that year and gradually began to put his time in the Agape Lodge behind him, although he seemingly continued to identify himself as a Thelemite, and viewed Crowley as an authority throughout the remainder of his life.[35]

PARSONS GOES SOLO: THE BLACK PILGRIMAGE AND THE RISE OF THE ANTICHRIST

In 1948, Parsons' life had, once again, taken a turn for the worse: Cameron had left him and departed for Mexico, and Parsons lost his security clearance at the aviation company where he worked due to suspected communist leanings. Around Halloween that year, Parsons felt called by Babalon to resume his work with her, and he commenced a 17-day magical working that culminated in the appearance of the goddess in one of his dreams, ordering him to conduct an astral ritual. Parsons came to refer to what followed as the 'Black Pilgrimage'.[36] The black pilgrimage is one of the more confusing and elusive concepts in Parsons' writings, in which Babalon's

35 Pendle, *Strange Angel*, 266–270; 277; Starr, *Unknown God*, 313–314.
36 John W. Parsons, *The Book of Anti-Christ*.

role as a demanding magical instructor becomes particularly clear. Parsons' concept of the black pilgrimage incorporates elements of fiction, and adds an additional figure from Christian apocalyptics—the Antichrist—to the narrative around Babalon. It is also interesting as it is seemingly the first example of Satanic concepts being included in the Babalon discourse, through veiled references to the Devil. Although the black pilgrimage appears in Parsons' mind to be connected to—or even identical with—the crossing of the Abyss, what little is available of his writing on the subject demonstrates that Parsons did not merely copy Crowley's views on Babalon or her initiatory function.

In *The Book of Anti-Christ*, Parsons describes undertaking an astral journey on Babalon's orders. After having neglected his initiatory work for some time, the goddess commands him to resume his magic. He describes embarking by sunset, bearing her sign, 'into the night past accursed and desolate places and Cyclopean ruins'.[37] Finally, he arrives at the city of Chorazin, where he sees a castle of black basalt. Parsons receives fleeting glimpses of his former incarnations as various historical men, seemingly united by their having (in Parsons' mind) tried and failed at elevating their female partners to representatives of the divine feminine.[38] These visions culminate in a reliving of the time Parsons himself invoked Satan at the age of thirteen, and cowered when the Devil appeared. A mysterious, robed figure asks him whether he will falter in the same way again, to which Parsons responds in the negative. He is subsequently led into the castle where he meets a mysterious ruler described as 'the Prince', after which things are done to him that he is forbidden from disclosing. Parsons presents the experience as traumatic, and claims it to have marked his transformation from mere mortal into the Antichrist himself, charged with fulfilling the Beast Crowley's work on earth and paving the way for Babalon's manifestation.[39] In the companion piece *Manifesto of the Anti-Christ*, Parsons, among

37 Parsons, *Book of Anti-Christ*.

38 Ibid. Among other things, there is a reference to 'Francis Hepburne, Earl Bothwell, manipulating Gellis Duncan, that was an unworthy instrument'. Both are historical figures: Duncan was a woman tried on charges of witchcraft in Scotland, and Francis Hepburne a nobleman who was arrested on charges of witchcraft in the same period. Although there is little indication in the historical material that the two were ever connected, Margaret Murray argued that Duncan was part of an existing witch cult, centred around the worship of a Horned God figure embodied by Hepburne. See Margaret Murray, *The Witch-Cult in Western Europe. A Study in Anthropology*, Clarendon Press, 1962.

39 Parsons, *Book of Anti-Christ*.

other things, swears to bring about the downfall of Christian morals, 'guilt and sin', and 'restriction and inhibition'.[40] He proclaims that he as the Antichrist will bring about the widespread acceptance of Thelema, and that Babalon will manifest within seven years to finish this work. He signs the manifesto 'Belarion, Antichrist'.[41]

Although Babalon is not the explicit main focus of either of these texts, she is decidedly central to Parsons' conceptualisation of the Antichrist and the Black Pilgrimage. *The Book of Anti-Christ* adds a darker, more explicitly antinomian flair to Parsons' vision. Although *The Book of Babalon* also features critique of institutionalized religion (see for instance 'The Birth of Babalon'), *The Book of Anti-Christ*, as the name suggests, is more bitterly polemical towards Christianity. In a sense, this emphasises Babalon's connection to the Biblical Whore of Babylon, an apocalyptic villain threatening the Christian faith. Parsons undertakes the Black Pilgrimage at her behest: in 'Liber 49', Babalon tells Parsons twice that he is to undergo the Black Pilgrimage, and it is she who appears to him in Autumn 1948, commanding him to return to his initiatory work and undertake the ordeal.[42] Given Parsons' declaration in Chorazin that he has given all of his blood to Babalon and the fact that he proclaimed himself a Magister Templi shortly after returning, it appears that Parsons in some way identified the Black Pilgrimage with crossing the Abyss. However, the source material is not entirely clear in this regard, as will be discussed later in this section. Either way, Parsons brought his own, eclectic touch to this procedure, which I will now discuss.

As stated above, Parsons claims the destination of his pilgrimage to be the city of Chorazin. This site, which is now a ruin, is mentioned in the Bible as one of three cities cursed by Jesus for failing to accept his teachings.[43] Several medieval theologians believed the Antichrist might come to be born in Chorazin. This notion clearly influenced Parsons; the latter explicitly states that his journey to the ruined city marked his transition into the figure. The black pilgrimage, however, is not a Biblical concept, but appears to be derived from the writings of English author and medievalist scholar M. R. James, specifically the short story 'Count Magnus', published in *Ghost Stories of an Antiquary* (1904). Many of James' stories centre

40 John W. Parsons, *Manifesto of the Anti-Christ*, n.d. Warburg Institute Library.
41 Ibid.
42 Parsons, *Book of Babalon*; Parsons, 'Manifesto of the Anti-Christ'.
43 Luke 10:13.

(ABOVE) *DEVOTION.* HANA LEE, 2015. OIL ON PANEL.
(PREVIOUS PAGE) *OUR LADY BABALON.* MITCHELL NOLTE, 2014. DIGITAL PAINTING.

BABALON. TIMO KETOLA, 2015. PASTEL ON PAPER.

BABALON. LINDA MACFARLANE, 2014. ACRYLIC ON CANVAS.

BABALON RUSHNYK. SARAH LINDSAY, 2013. NEEDLEWORK ON WOVEN TEXTILE.

BABALON. LIV RAINEY-SMITH, 2014. WOODCUT PRINT WITH HAND APPLIED GARNET, PURPURITE, TIGERS EYE, BLOODSTONE, AND JADE.

LEILA IDA NERISSA BATHURST WADDELL (THE RITES OF ELEUSIS). MITCHELL NOLTE, 2018. DIGITAL PAINTING.

BABALON AND THE FOUR PRINCES. BARRY WILLIAM HALE, ANNO VI, 2015 EV. ACRYLIC ON CANVAS.

around old books or artefacts with magical power, and 'Count Magnus' is no exception. Central to the story is the legend of a 17th century Swedish count who allegedly dabbled in black magic and made a black pilgrimage to Chorazin in order to attain a sinister servitor spirit.[44] Given that James was also a scholar, and the prevalence of related motifs in Swedish folklore, there is some reason to believe that this fictional story has some foundation in popular tradition. In the instructions to the prospective pilgrim cited in the story, it is stated that the latter after arriving in Chorazin must salute 'the Prince of the air'.[45] This is in all likelihood a reference to Satan, referred to in the Bible as the 'prince of the power of the air'.[46] As noted above, Parsons also details meeting a mysterious prince in Chorazin.[47] M. R. James' work has been highly influential to the horror genre, and given Parsons' well-documented love of fantasy and sci-fi literature and association with many leading writers of the genre, it is highly likely that he was aware of the work. He was not the only appreciator of James in the Thelemic community, as Crowley's former Scarlet Woman and collaborator, the writer Mary D'Esti (1871–1931), was also a known admirer of the English author.[48]

As the Antichrist is not mentioned in 'Count Magnus', Parsons was in all likelihood either already familiar with the theological speculations regarding the site when reading James' story, or researched the meaning of the place after reading it. Thus, the idea of the black pilgrimage and Chorazin as the birthplace of the Antichrist appear to have become intertwined in his mind. Whether or not Parsons would have recognised James' prince of the air as a reference to Satan is difficult to know, but hardly unthinkable given the former's seeming familiarity with Biblical tradition. Either way, it is not difficult to see why the idea of a mysterious journey to a remote, desert castle with apocalyptic connotations, marking the rise to new heights of magical and spiritual power, would have appealed greatly to Parsons.

As noted above, Parsons associated the black pilgrimage with crossing the Abyss. The available sources do not lend themselves to any definitive conclusions regarding whether the black pilgrimage served as a sort of prelude to the Abyss, or whether the two were identical in Parsons'

44 M.R. James, 'Count Magnus', in *Ghost Stories of an Antiquary,* Edward Arnold, 1904.

45 Ibid.

46 Ephesians 2:2.

47 Parsons, *Book of Anti-Christ.*

48 Harold Bloom, *Modern Horror Writers,* Chelsea House Publishers, 1995.

mind. Nonetheless, the brief description of the pilgrimage, which mingles Parsons' ideas about Babalon and the Abyss with elements derived from 'Count Magnus' and a sharp critique of Christianity, demonstrates how fact and fiction, politics and magic were intimately connected in Parsons' mind. This is crucial if we are to understand how Parsons developed the idea of Babalon, and how the varied and sometimes paradoxical layers of meaning he added to the goddess enabled a greater variety of interpretations of her after his death.

Parsons' discussion of the black pilgrimage and the events around it seemingly indicate that he saw his relationship with Babalon as closer and more personal than that of his mentor, Crowley. Crowley never mentions Babalon appearing to him in dreams, or actively contacting him to instruct him on his spiritual journey. A deity addressing a human initiate directly to provide concrete ritual instructions and guidance was hardly unprecedented in Thelemic tradition, but Babalon never filled this role in Crowley's life.[49] Thus, Parsons' writings on the black pilgrimage emphasise the more active and vocal interpretation of Babalon as a subject in her own right. Parsons' version of the goddess intervenes directly in his life on several occasions and tells him in person what to do, even reminding him to return to his initiatory work when he has strayed. This almost mentoring role combined with the violent and sexual, sometimes sadomasochistic, imagery in which the relationship between Babalon and Parsons is couched is highly reminiscent of Crowley's concept of the Holy Guardian Angel. Babalon's function as a spiritual instructor and guide in Parsons' life also emphasises the image of the goddess as more anthropomorphic and active, and as having many more dimensions than her metaphysical function as the gateway to the City of Pyramids.

THE STAR AND THE SWORD: BABALON AS A FEMINIST REVOLUTIONARY

The essay 'Freedom is a Two-Edged Sword' is one of Parsons' most well-known works. In this sexpartite essay, Parsons expresses his disillusionment with contemporary American society, and presents his own politi-

49 For an example of such magician–deity interaction in Crowley's writings, see e.g. Aleister Crowley, 'The Paris Working', in Aleister Crowley, *The Vision & the Voice with Commentary and Other Papers*, Samuel Weiser, 1998, pp. 343–409.

cal and religious philosophy. He protests against his own treatment at the hands of the increasingly paranoid and anti-communist American government, and critiques religious and sexual repression. Ultimately, he posits the force of Babalon as the remedy that will save humankind.[50] Although Babalon is clearly attributed revolutionary and messianic functions in *The Book of Babalon*, 'Freedom' is the first known text in which Parsons explicitly relates her to secular politics. The elaboration of Babalon as a champion of social egalitarianism and, as we shall see, women's emancipation, in this text is one of Parsons' most interesting and innovative contributions to the discourse around the goddess.

Part of 'Freedom is a Two-Edged Sword' paraphrases Crowley's *Liber Oz*, which the latter wrote as a response to totalitarianism and a declaration of basic human rights.[51] In this tract, Crowley declares each individual's right to 'live by his own law' and to work, play, rest, die, drink, dwell, move, speak, write, create art, build, dress and enter into relationships in accordance with his or her will, as well as 'kill those who would thwart these rights'.[52] Although he shares Crowley's emphasis on individualism, critique of organised religion, and exaltation of free love, Parsons also attacks sexism, racism, and oppression of workers, and argues that people should be granted decent living conditions and basic resources for health, security, and wellbeing.[53] As such, his work does not exhibit the same tendencies to Nietzschean social Darwinism. Although Parsons has been described as a libertarian, there are clear socialist influences on his work, and his political philosophy is clearly much further to the left than Crowley's.[54]

Parsons devotes a significant part of 'Freedom' to critiquing sexism. He ascribes the oppression of women to Christianity's condemnation of the sexual urge, and writes that women are the ones who will finally strike back against this repression and relieve all of humanity.[55] Thus, he sees women's emancipation as fundamental to the liberation of sexuality as well as human society at large. In his view on women, Parsons diverges strongly from Crowley, who advocates women's emancipation in some texts but appears to have viewed it more as a consequence of the implementation of Thelema

50 Parsons, 'Freedom'.

51 Cf. Hymenaeus Beta, 'Foreword', in John W. Parsons, *Three Essays on Freedom*, Teitan Press, 2008, xiii.

52 Crowley, Liber Oz.

53 Parsons, 'Freedom', pp. 15–16; 20.

54 Cf. Beta, 'Foreword', ix.

55 Parsons, 'Freedom'.

than its driving force.[56] Thus, Parsons placed a far stronger emphasis on women than his mentor. In the final section of the essay, 'The Woman Girt With A Sword', Parsons explicitly links Babalon to this envisioned feminist liberation.[57] This construction of Babalon as a feminist icon is completely absent from Crowley's writings. This part of the essay also features themes of a surviving lineage of pre-Christian pagan witchcraft as a paragon of equality and liberation, epitomised in the address: 'Witch woman, out of the ashes of the stake, rise again!'.[58]

In Parsons' writings, Babalon is connected to a highly active form of femininity. Women's agency is central to his utopian vision, which involves the reshaping of society through (possibly violent) political revolution. Towards the end of the essay, it becomes clear that Parsons equates the revolutionary female force with Babalon. Unlike Crowley, who defined the Scarlet Woman by her relationship with the Beast, Babalon and the female revolutionary that are central to Parsons' philosophy are not defined by their relationship to men or the male principle. Instead, Parsons sees the liberation of women as the key to the emancipation of humanity as a whole. He also sees the popularization of female same-sex relationships and polygamy as an expression of the Babalon force increasing in the world, writing that: '...the increase of feminine polygamy and lesbianism, all indicate the development of a new type of woman'.[59] Parsons also stresses repeatedly in 'Freedom' that the new woman, epitomized by the notion of Babalon, will require men to rise to her standards, forsaking foolishness and pettiness, or she will not have men at all. The essay is concluded with a rallying cry, directed possibly at Babalon's human daughter, or possibly at womankind in its entirety. As it very clearly illustrates Parsons' conceptualisation of Babalon as a goddess of war and worldly feminist revolution, it is worth quoting at length:

> *Somewhere in the world today there is a woman for whom the sword is forged. Somewhere there is one who has heard the trumpets of the new age, and who will respond. She will respond, this new woman, to the high clamor of those*

56 See e.g. Aleister Crowley, *The Law is For All*, New Falcon Publications, 1991, pp. 303–313.

57 Parsons, 'Freedom', pp. 39–44.

58 Ibid., 42.

59 John W. Parsons, 'The Star of Babalon', in John W. Parsons, *Freedom is a Two-Edged Sword and Other Essays,* New Falcon Publications, 2001.

> *star trumpets; she will come as a perilous flame and a devious song, a voice in the judgment halls, a banner before armies. She will come girt with the sword of freedom, and before her kings and priests will tremble and cities and empires will fall, and she will be called BABALON, the scarlet woman. For she will be lustful and proud; she will be subtle and deadly, she will be forthright and invincible as a naked blade. And women will respond to her war cry, and throw off their shackles and chains, and men will respond to her challenge, forsaking the foolish ways and the little ways, and she who will shine as the ruddy evening star in the bloody sunset of Gotterdamerung, will shine again as a morning star when the night has passed, and a new dawn breaks over the garden of Pan.*
>
> *To you, oh unknown woman, the sword pledged. Keep the faith!*[60]

In a way, the sentiments expressed in Parsons' essay are a logical continuation of the vision of Babalon presented in *The Book of Babalon*, where the goddess—as demonstrated above—is conceptualised not as an initiatory function or mystical gateway, but as an agent of change come to rid the world of religious bigotry and guilt. However, the connection to women's emancipation and the downfall of male chauvinism is made far more explicit in 'Freedom'. Parsons' involvement in leftist circles thus likely influenced his view of Babalon, and this connection certainly merits further study in future research.

'An Ancient Garden and a Secret Call': Babalon and the Witch

In 1951, when Parsons' life had once again stabilised somewhat, he busied himself formulating a new religion that he dubbed 'the Witchcraft'. As illustrated above, his interest in witchcraft and the witch figure had begun earlier; Williamsons' *Darker Than You Think* and its cult of shapeshifting witches was an important influence on Parsons' ideas, and he clearly also drew on Margaret Murray's writings on witchcraft. He also compiled a collection of poems titled 'Songs for the Witch-Woman', written mostly between 1946 and his death in 1952. The poems draw strongly on Romantic and Gothic themes, featuring figures such as the Lamia, vampires, and

60 Parsons, 'Freedom', pp. 43–44.

werewolves, alongside motifs like the witches' Sabbath, Stonehenge, Merlin, and Pan. After he met and fell in love with Cameron, she appears increasingly to have become associated with such witchy motifs in Parsons' mind. In some sense, Parsons' view of Babalon in the final years of his life seems also to have been coloured by these themes. Indeed, the collection is dedicated to 'Candida [Cameron's magical name], in whom She is incarnate'; seemingly a reference to Babalon.

Parsons' essays on the Witchcraft clearly demonstrate Thelemic influences as well as his own ideas about Babalon. Although his writings on the topic are comparatively sparse, he presents the Witchcraft as a duotheistic religion focused on the veneration of a divine couple represented by Babalon and Lucifer.[61] His conceptualisation of the Witchcraft has many similarities with the Wiccan traditions that would appear in England over the next few years; Parsons describes it as a world-affirming pagan religion centred on a divine male-female pair and focused on the worship of sex, nature, fertility, and freedom, as old as humanity and surviving in secret despite centuries of Christian persecution. As noted above, he alludes to these themes in *The Book of Antichrist* and 'Freedom is a Two-Edged Sword', although he had not previously attempted to flesh them out into a religion in its own right. Although Parsons appears to have been inspired by more or less the same corpus of works in comparative mythology and anthropology that Gerald Gardner drew on, there is no evidence that the two had any contact. Thus, it seems more reasonable to say that they were both drawing on a broader discursive trend and wave of interest in witches, ancient paganism, and fertility cults. The notion of an ancient witch cult, opposed to traditional religious institutions and championing ideals of liberation and equality, was not an invention of either Gardner or Parsons, but was very much in vogue at the beginning of the twentieth century, influencing notable occultists such as Austin Osman Spare and Rosaleen Norton.[62] However, Parsons was most likely the first to integrate a Thelemic deity into this discourse.

Many late nineteenth century thinkers and authors associated the

61 John W. Parsons, 'Manifesto of the Witchcraft', in John W. Parsons, *Freedom is a Two-Edged Sword and Other Essays*, New Falcon Publications, 2001, 69–71; John W. Parsons, 'The Witchcraft', in John W. Parsons, *Freedom is a Two-Edged Sword and Other Essays*, New Falcon Publications, 2001, 71–74.

62 Fredrik Gregorius, 'Luciferian Witchcraft: At the Crossroads between Paganism and Satanism', in Per Faxneld and Jesper Aagaard Petersen, eds., *The Devil's Party: Satanism in Modernity*, Oxford University Press, 2012.

witch with social resistance and women's liberation. Although the witch motif was often used by conservative authors to illustrate the supposed dangers of feminism, the narrative of the witch-hunts was also sometimes used as a pretext for demonising the Church.[63] A prominent example is Jules Michelet's (1798–1874) *La Sorcière*, a nominally historical work that is, however, based on questionable research and inferences. Michelet's witch is a Satanist, but the author sees Satan as a paragon of goodness connected to nature, the arts, laughter, medicine and necromancy. Similar to Parsons, Michelet posits witches as champions of equality, reason, and freedom, and conversely God as the protector of the already privileged, indifferent towards the needs of the people. A similarly influential book for the conception of witchcraft as a positive and emancipatory force is Charles Godfrey Leland's (1824–1903) *Aradia: or the Gospel of the Witches*, which (in contrast to works such as Michelet's) posits witchcraft as a living religion. The book details Leland's alleged findings studying folk traditions in Italy, and tells of an ancient fertility witch cult passed down from generation to generation since pre-Christian times. Although Leland's witches are not explicit Satanists like those in Michelet's book, the witches appear to revere Lucifer alongside the Pagan goddess Diana. Thus, there are very strong similarities between the religion portrayed in *Aradia* and Parsons' own Witchcraft, and the likelihood of his familiarity with the work is strengthened by the fact that one of the 'Witch-Woman' poems is titled 'Aradia'.[64]

Obviously, the connection between an egalitarian, subversive paganism surviving in secret through the centuries, associated with women's emancipation and resistance to Christianity would have appealed greatly to Parsons. Given also the central role Babalon played in his life, it is unsurprising that Parsons made the connection between the witch cult discourse and the scarlet goddess. However, Parsons also seems to have drawn on other literary sources in the formulation of his own religion. It is here relevant to return to *Darker Than You Think*, which had been published in extended novel version in 1948. Although the clandestine, ancient witch cult of Williamson's story is considerably more morally questionable than those of Michelet and Leland, the striking similarities between some of the

63 Per Faxneld, *Satanic Feminism: Lucifer as the Liberator of Woman in Nineteenth-Century Culture*, Molin & Sorgenfrei, 2013.

64 John W. Parsons and Marjorie Cameron, *Songs for the Witch-Woman*, Fulgur Esoterica, 2014, p. 53.

story's main themes and Parsons' own vision make it reasonable to assume that the story coloured the latter's conceptualisation of the Witchcraft in some way.

Parsons melding of Babalon with the witchcraft themes is, in many ways, a logical continuation of his previous work, which he would likely have developed further, had he lived long enough. As illustrated above, witchcraft was a long-held fascination for Parsons, and ideas about witches as egalitarian subversives, resisting economic and religious oppression and practicing their craft in secret, were very much in vogue at the time. Clearly, these notions influenced Parsons strongly in many aspects of his prosaic and lyrical work, and seemingly provided a romantic language in which his socio-political vision could be couched. By drawing on this discourse, Parsons gave Babalon a past of sorts, as a goddess of witches, kept alive in secret through the centuries and finally arisen.

CONCLUSION

Parsons' interpretations of Babalon are less well-documented than a scholar attempting a reconstruction might hope. In contrast to Crowley, Parsons had to work for a living throughout most of his life, and had significantly less time to expound on his ideas. In a horrific instance of life echoing art—or in this case, ritual transcripts—Jack died on June 17, 1952, due to injuries sustained in an explosion, eerily reminiscent of his transformation into 'living flame', prophesied in *The Book of Babalon*. Finally, a great deal of Parsons' writings are lost, possibly forever; some because Cameron in the years following her husband's death developed the unfortunate habit of ritually burning his old possessions. Nonetheless, it is abundantly clear from the extant sources that Parsons was not simply a follower of Crowley, but an original magical thinker who added many interesting layers to the Babalon discourse.

Firstly, Parsons dislocated Babalon from her original position beyond the Abyss, and transformed her into an active and arguably quite anthropomorphic deity, with hopes, dreams, and a voice of her own. Whereas in her original initiatory context Babalon is more or less a static figure, awaiting the willing self-sacrifice of the adept on the pathway to enlightenment, Parsons' goddess descends into the world to speak and dictate her holy text, and instruct him in how to produce her human manifestation. She has a history as the patroness of an ancient witch cult, stretching back to pre-Christian times and kept alive in secret by visionaries and subversives across the globe. She is not a means to an end, but a speaking subject with ends of her own; rather than asking Parsons to offer up his individuality so she can birth him into the City of Pyramids, Babalon demands his blood and mortal life in order to provide for her human incarnation.

Parsons' more active interpretation of Babalon is particularly interesting in light of the fact that Crowley tended to identify the divine feminine with passivity or receptivity, viewing the male life force as the active catalyst for magical transformation.[65] In *Liber Aleph*, Crowley writes that a woman's role in magic is to 'abide joyous and obedient beneath the Man that her Instinct shall divine', becoming a 'Temple' for his work.[66] It is worth mentioning here that many contemporary Thelemites view this as a controversial passage, and it should hardly be taken as a reflection of women's roles or magical practice in the Thelemic community today.[67] Still, the contrast between Crowley's and Parsons' writings is apparent. In Parsons' vision, Babalon emerges a dominating and commanding deity, and Parsons as an ultimately dispensable tool. Here, Babalon has a future stretching beyond the adept's initiation, as a messianic war goddess leading humankind out of slavery. In this sense she bears resemblances to the god of the Old Testament leading the Israelites out of Egypt, a connection emphasised by the use of Biblical, apocalyptic language in *The Book of Babalon*.

Secondly, Parsons introduces darker, arguably satanic components into the Babalon discourse. In the narrative of the black pilgrimage, Babalon is viewed as the catalyst for a metaphysical vision quest in which Parsons confronts and embraces his dark side, and accepts the office of the Antichrist. Through Parsons' identification with this Biblical antagonist, Babalon is explicitly related to the downfall of Christian hegemony. This devilish theme is continued in Parsons' writings on the Witchcraft, in which Babalon emerges as part of a divine gender polarity with Lucifer. In this respect, Parsons builds on a genre of pseudo-historical literature and works in comparative mythology and anthropology, in which a devil-

65 Cf. Hugh Urban, *Magia Sexualis. Sex, Magic, and Liberation in Modern Western Esotericism*, University of California Press, 2006, 133–134.

66 Aleister Crowley, *Liber Aleph Vel CXI; The Book of Wisdom or Folly, in the Form of an Epistle of 666, the Great Wild Beast, to his Son 777, Being the Equinox Volume III No. VI*, S. Weiser, 1991, 171.

67 See e.g. Manon Hedenborg-White, 'To Him the Winged Secret Flame: The Social Construction of Gender in Contemporary Ordo Templi Orientis, *The Pomegranate: The International Journal of Pagan Studies* 15:1–2 (2013).

ish male deity, a strong goddess figure, and notions of social subversion and resistance played a strong role. Once again, this shows how Parsons' vision of Babalon was more than a mere reproduction of Crowley's, and the polarity with Lucifer emphasises the disconnection from the Crowleyan Thelemic pantheon.

Thirdly and finally, Parsons situated Babalon at the centre of his political vision, and his hopes for a just, enlightened, and gender equal society. He explicitly identifies Babalon with the force of female emancipation, and argues that women rather than men will be the ones to reshape society and accomplish utopia. Although Parsons vacillated over the course of his life regarding exactly how the Babalon force would incarnate, he in one passage identifies it with the intensifying struggle for women's rights, and connects it to female polyamory and same-sex relationships. In this way, Babalon acquires a socio-political significance that she had not previously held. The notion of Babalon as a champion of a feminist revolution, or as a force of countercultural liberation, is mostly absent from Crowley's writings, but has been explored and developed by later esoteric writers.

By the end of his life, Parsons believed he had succeeded in causing the goddess Babalon to incarnate on earth. Judging the validity of his claim lies beyond the realms of academic authority, and thus I will leave it to the reader to assess whether or not he was right. Nonetheless, Babalon is certainly incarnate in the minds of those who work with her, as is not least attested by the recent flurry of literary and artistic explorations of the goddess, including the works of Peter Grey and Alkistis Dimech, founders of the esoteric publishing house Scarlet Imprint; British artist and magician Amodali Zain; esoteric artist and writer Mishlen Linden and Black Moon Publishing, and many others. Although both the Beast and the Antichrist have departed this world, the final word is yet to be said.

Seven Chalices of the Lady

Grant Potts

I

IN CONTEMPORARY THELEMIC culture and its associated spiritual practices, the most evocative of goddesses is Our Lady, Babalon. In Crowley's prophetic texts, the goddess Babalon is most fully revealed in *Liber Cheth* and *The Vision and the Voice*. As much as the popularity and power of Babalon erupts from these prophetic visions, her power and resilience also resides in her antiquity, carried through the Christian mysteries in the Apocalypse of John. The Apocalypse provides a paranoid vision of the current Aeon, as it is viewed through the lens of the prior Age; nevertheless, the figures provide insight into the nature of the goddess.

Two female figures dominate the vision of that text, the 'woman clothed with the sun, and the moon under her feet, and upon her head a crown of twelve stars', and the woman 'arrayed in purple and scarlet colour, and decked with gold and precious stones and pearls, having a golden cup in her hand full of abominations and filthiness of her fornication' sitting atop the Great Beast and drunk with the blood of the saints.[1] In the Christian tradition, the woman clothed in the Sun is alternatively Mary or the church itself, while the scarlet woman is the ancient city of Baby-

1 Revelation 12:1; 17:4.

lon, oft condemned in the Hebrew Scriptures due to the extended exile of the priestly caste of the Israelite religion. For the Christian church, Babylon was thus an emblem of the world apart from the church, the city of darkness against the Church's city of light, as the Church renounced sex, luxury, and reproduction to seek the pristine, purified light of the divine in celibate austerity.

In his *Notes for an Astral Atlas*, though, Crowley berates those who would distinguish the Woman Clothed with the Sun—who he at other times identifies with the virginal Isis of the Priestess card—from the Scarlet Woman, or Babylon the Great, astride the Great Beast.[2] There is no fundamental distinction between Isis and Babalon, rather it is merely that she has received the light of the Sun, exciting within herself and the Beast with the lust necessary to give rise to the magickal child.

While the study of the texts and symbolism associated with Our Lady can lead the aspirant to the Great Work to the doorway of understanding the mysteries of Babalon, the opening of that doorway requires practice. *Liber Cheth* is described in the official instructions of the A∴A∴ as providing 'a perfect account of the task of the Exempt Adept, considered under the symbols of a particular plane, not the intellectual'.[3] Although rich in images of Our Lady, *Liber Cheth* describes practice as a work of renunciation appropriate to the New Aeon, a renunciation in which the magician is told to 'mingle his life with the universal life' not to hold it back in the austerities advocated by the monastics of the old Aeon.[4]

The richest images of Babalon occur in the account of the Cry of the 12th Aethyr of *The Vision and the Voice*, where she is described as thus:

> *Beautiful art thou, O Babylon and desirable, for thou hast given thyself to everything that liveth, and thy weakness hath subdued their strength. For in that union thou didst* understand. *Therefore art thou called Understanding, O Babylon, Lady of the Night!*[5]

2 Aleister Crowley, *Magick: Liber ABA, Book Four, Part I–IV*, Weiser, 1997, p. 503. For the association of Isis and Mary, see for example, Aleister Crowley, *The Book of Thoth*, Weiser, 1944, p. 69.

3 Crowley, *Magick*, p. 468.

4 Crowley, *Magick*, p. 661.

5 Aleister Crowley with Victor B. Neuberg and Mary Desti, *The Vision & The Voice with Commentary and Other Papers*, Weiser, 1998, p. 150.

The renunciation of Babalon is enacted in the adulteries of the mistress of the Great Beast, not the fornications that tempt Israel from their covenant with the Lord. It is rather a willful embrace of the world, a giving of oneself to all, to evoke the lust of the Father and ultimately to give birth to the Crown. On the intellectual sphere, this is the process of understanding through true interpretation, where the intellect must submit itself voluntarily to the truth of the subject, even as it gives itself over to it, so that the portion of consciousness so concerned is transformed fully into true understanding. On the corporeal sphere, this is the submission of the body to the regime of exercise to achieve the fruit of a healthy body, or to the lust of sexual desire in order to participate in the creation of a child. This is a renunciation *unto*, not a renunciation *from*. In a note in Chapter VII of *Magick in Theory and Practice*, Crowley cautions us also that 'There is no moral implication here. But to choose A implies to refuse not-A; at least, that is so, below the Abyss'.[6]

Unto what is it then that the aspirant renounces? It is, again from the 12th Aethyr, 'the cup whose blood is mingled therein, for the wine of the cup is the blood of the saints' or as expressed in *Liber Cheth*, 'the golden cup of her fornications.'[7] How is the aspirant to attain to that chalice, to 'mingle his life with the universal life'? In Chapter VII of Part 2 of *Liber ABA*, Crowley gives us further insight into the nature of this cup, as he associates the cup as a magickal weapon with the lotus flower. This lotus is more specifically the lotus in the hand of Isis, which he parallels with the cup in the hand of Babalon. He further identifies the cup with the seven lotuses of the chakras, all of which he states are 'figured by the Magick cup.'[8] Recall, that Babalon and Isis are dual figures, it is simply that in Babalon the light of the sun has been received, exciting the lust of the Work.

II

The following rite is a result of years of study and work with Our Lady, Babalon, in many forms and guises. It was originally composed and performed for the Midwinter Magickal Revival at Bubastis Oasis O.T.O. in Dallas, Texas on February 16th, 2013 EV, and has had a number of revi-

6 Crowley, *Magick*, p. 167.

7 Crowley, Neuberg, and Desti, *The Vision & The Voice*, p 149; Crowley, *Magick*, p. 661.

8 Crowley, *Magick*, p. 76.

sions and performances since, either privately or at the Babalon Chapel at Scarlet Woman Lodge O.T.O. in Austin, Texas. The rite takes substantial inspiration from a Red Tara practice I received from Chagdud Gonpa, in the Nyingma tradition of Tibetan Buddhism, and the Diamond Sapphire Gem of Radiant Light and associated Ordo Sunyata Vajra practices. Both of these sets of practices have been part of my personal practice for well over a decade.[9] There is also substantive influence (in the formula used in the consecration of the body of light) from a spirit feast I wrote for a Walpurgisnacht rite celebrated at Sekhet Maat Lodge in Portland, Oregon in 2007 EV, which was itself adapted from Jason Miller's formula for making regular offerings to spirits.[10] There is also clear influence from my own practice as a Congregant, Child, Deacon, and Priest of Ecclesia Gnostica Catholica and, of course, from over fifteen years of participation as an initiate in Ordo Templi Orientis.

The rite is primarily formulated as a group rite, with a ritual leader who reads through the script, and participants reciting or chanting as called for in the rite. Typically the rite includes an altar to Babalon where participants may leave offerings, amulets, or sigils, and the ritual leader and the participants are seated in a meditative posture of their choosing. The rite is easily adapted for individual practice. The rite has two primary foci, tightly integrated: the activation of the chakras and the central channel and the attunement of the body of light to the Thelemic current, and in particular to the mysteries of Babalon. With these foci, the seven chalices, the seven chakras, of the attendees receive the light of the Gnosis bringing them to greater Understanding of the mysteries contained therein.

9 Many of the practices associated with Ordo Sunyata Vajra, including the Diamond Sapphire, are now available in print. See Gregory Peters, *The Magickal Union of East and West: The Spiritual Path to New Aeon Tantra*, Llewellyn, 2014.

10 For the text of the Spirit Feast, see Frater Theapraxis, 'Walpurgis Night Spirit Feast, April 30th, 2007,' *Lion and Serpent: The Official Journal of Sekhet-Maat Lodge, O.T.O.* 12.2 (October 2007), p. 14–18. A version of Jason Miller's formula for offerings to spirits can be found in his *Protection and Reversal Magick: A Witch's Defense Manual*, New Page, pp. 56-59.

III
OPENING PRAYER

All vibrate: AUGMN AUGMN AUGMN

Deep echoes of the cities of Carthage, bearing forth through colonial aspirations, upon Semitic tides, through the ancient Understanding that is the domain of Our Lady, your vision resolves into an image of a desert across which two men walk, a prophet and his companion, parched with a thirst for attainment.

All recite: **Prophet of the New Aeon, known throughout the ages as Tò Μεγα Θηρίον, you are surrounded by the saints and magi of all ages. As I practice, standing in the current of your realization, may the light of the gnosis be transmitted to me and through me so that I and all others may accomplish the Great Work.**

All vibrate: ABRAHADABRA

CONSECRATION OF THE BODY OF LIGHT THROUGH THE ELEMENTS

Alone in the desert, your vision becomes that of yourself in your body, alone, in silence, and under the canopy of the night sky. As you settle into the truth of your aspirations, you generate your bodies of light and purify them through elemental powers.

Relax and settle into your body. Feel the gentle press of the air upon your skin. If you have not done so, close your eyes, and visualize that body, your legs, your hands, your skin and hair, and then allow your awareness to turn that more subtle body of light that is also your body, and visualize yourself enveloped in that pure light.

See a glowing pentacle, opening a channel to the earthly realms, becoming aware of the ground below you and the materiality of your being.

> Earth of earth, first earth within me. Dwelling place of form and presence. Bless my body so that I may be filled with light, life, love, and liberty.

All recite: **May my body be consecrated by the power of earth.**

See a second pentacle, opening a channel to the fiery elements, becoming aware of the vitality and energy of your being.

> Fire of fire, first fire within me. Dwelling place of transmutation. Enter into the heart of my body, and there transmute the impurities within into the sweet nectar of light, life, love, and liberty.

All recite: **May my body be consecrated by the power of fire.**

See a third pentacle, opening a channel to the airy elements, becoming aware of the freedom and lightness of your being.

> Air of air, first air within me. Dwelling place of movement. Sweep across my body and remove any residue or dust or ash such that all that remains is the purity of my true self.

All recite: **May my body be consecrated by the power of air.**

See a fourth pentacle, opening a channel to the watery elements, becoming aware of the mutability of your being.

> Water of water, first water within me. Dwelling place of opening. Wash over my body so that all that remains is my truest substance, guided by the law which unites us all in the sacred house of liberty.

All recite: **May my body be consecrated by the power of water.**

Now visualize a unicursal hexagram, opening up a channel to the Law of Thelema.

> Law of the law, first law within me. Dwelling place of liberty, light, life, and love. Uplift my body so that I may attain to the

Stone of the Wise, the Summum Bonum, True Wisdom and Perfect Happiness.[11]

All recite: May my body be consecrated by the power of the Law.

VISUALIZATION OF OUR LADY

All vibrate: AUGMN

In the space in front of you, the Mother of Abominations, Babalon the Great, appears and to her you pray:

All recite: Now, as I may have deviated from that true purpose that is my Will
I seek to join the Magi in gaining ultimate joy and bliss,
Both for myself and all beings.
Nu is my refuge, as Hadit is my light,
As I offer my whole being
To the Mother of Abominations,
So that my blood may be mingled with that blood of the saints,
And not one drop be withheld.
From the depths of my heart, I pray,
Evoking from Babalon's forehead, throat, and heart
A brilliant surge of rainbow light.
As the light rays touch me and all other beings,
The poisonous obstructions to my true will and to perfect awareness
—Sickness, afflictions and all other obstacles—
Evaporate like dew in the morning sun.
Health, wealth, strength, joy, and peace increase beyond measure.[12]

11 The last line recalls the Priest's closing lines to the Gnostic Mass. See Crowley, *Magick*, p. 597.

12 This prayer is inspired substantively on a Red Tara prayer received from the Chagdud Gonpa. The last line also recalls the Priest's opening lines in section VIII of the Gnostic Mass. See Crowley, *Magick*, p. 596.

All chant: A ka dua
Tuf ur biu
Bi a'a chefu
Dudu nur af an nuteru

All recite: Babalon the Great, Mother of Abominations, mingle my blood with that of the saints. Remove all obstacles and quickly grant my excellent aspirations.

All vibrate: AUGMN BABALON (×7)

MANDALA OFFERING

All vibrate: AUGMN

This world, and all others, across the span of aeons, from the four directions, and the heavens and the earth, all lands and waters, fires and air, all realms of spirit beings, infernal, astral, and blessed, in all their splendor and glory are emanated as vast and extensive clouds of perfectly pure offerings.

All recite: I offer these to you, Babylon, Mother of Abominations.

PRAYER OF ASPIRATION

All recite: By the power of having prayed thus
In a state of true love
And with dedication toward my true will,
May I master my heart and my mind.
May conditions be perfect for my practice,
May my aspirations ripen into dedication and realization,
May I attain the magical memory and master the astral plane,
May my wishes be granted, and my intentions refined.

Grant me all protections and shields necessary to remove any interferences and poisons from my path.

May the malice of others, spiritual distractions,
The harmful effects of death, disease, and disorder,
Be diminished and eliminated
So that the true wisdom of understanding may arise within
me,
And I may attain to the crown, to the Victorious City.

May I mingle my life with the universal life
May I never withhold one drop
From the golden cup of her fornication.

THE SEVEN CHALICES OF THE LADY

There is a light before thine eyes, o prophet, a light undesirable, most desired.[13]

(pause)

Attachment to ordinary appearances and clinging to your material body wane, as you allow your vision to dissolve into a field of pure light. Within that light appears the burning brand of the beast, the sun and moon conjoined. Instantly that brand transforms into an enraptured vision of Babalon the Great, the Mother of Abominations.

She is astride the great beast, facing you directly. Her eyes lock into yours.

She smiles in delight and rapture, drunk on the blood of the saints, as her hair forms a mass of flame about her head.

Her right hand is held in a gesture of welcome and offering, and her left hand grasps the chalice of ecstasy, which holds the blood of the saints.

She is bare and rejoicing, her shameless nakedness marked only by rich rubies and other jewels of aspiration.

She sits upright, in royal ease upon the seven-headed scarlet beast covered in names both blasphemous and holy.

About her is a garden of roses, and above her stands the blazing sun and the full moon.

Along the spine of her body seven chalices form at each of the chakra points, glowing with radiant rainbow light, and as you recite each sacred

13 *Book of the Law* 2:61. See Crowley, *The Holy Books of Thelema*, Weiser, 1983, p. 119.

syllable, in turn, every chalice pours out light from her body to yours.

From the lowest chalice, at the base of her spine, pours a beam of ruby light to your base, your muladhara chakra. And as you chant the sacred syllable LAM, her light nourishes of your bodily lust, dedicating it to the great work.

All vibrate **LAM**

> *Yea, though the flower wave bright in the sunshine, the root is deep in the darkness of earth.*[14]

From the chalice at her sacrum, moving up into her sex, pours a beam of vermillion or orange light to your sacrum, your svadisthana chakra. And as you chant the sacred syllable VAM, her light nourishes your joy, dedicating it to the great work.

All vibrate: **VAM**

> *Crush out the blood of me, as a grape upon the tongue of a white Doric girl that languishes with her lover in the moonlight.*[15]

From the chalice at her solar plexus, moving up into her belly, pours a beam of yellow light into your solar plexus, your manipura chakra. And as you chant the sacred syllable RAM, her light nourishes your bodily power, dedicating it to the great work.

All vibrate: **RAM**

> *O crystal heart! I the Serpent clasp Thee; I drive home mine head into the central core of Thee, O God my beloved.*[16]

From the chalice at her heart, moving up into her chest, pours a beam of green light into your heart, your anahata chakra. And as you chant the sacred syllable YAM, her light nourishes your love and sense of balance, dedicating it to the great work.

14 *Liber Cordis Cincti Serpente*, 4:43. See Crowley, *Holy Books*, p. 74.
15 Ibid., 2:54. See Crowley, *Holy Books*, p. 63.
16 Ibid., 4:1. See Crowley, *Holy Books*, p. 70.

All vibrate: YAM

I am the heart, and Thou the serpent. Wind Thy coils closer about me, so that no light nor bliss may penetrate.[17]

From the chalice at her throat, moving up into her neck, pours a beam of blue light into your throat, your vishuddha chakra. And as you chant the sacred syllable HAM, her light nourishes your voice, dedicating it to the great work.

All vibrate: HAM

All day I sing of Thy delight; all night I delight in Thy song.[18]

From the chalice at her third eye, moving up into her brow, pours a beam of indigo light into your third eye, your ajna chakra. And as you chant the sacred syllable AUM, her light nourishes your vision, dedicating it to the great work.

All vibrate: AUM

Happy are they that praise thee; for they see thee with Mine eyes.[19]

From the chalice at her glorious crown, moving up above her head, pours a beam of violet light into your crown, your shahasrara chakra. And as you chant internally the sacred syllable of silence, her light nourishes your consciousness, dedicating it to the great work.

All sit in: silence

They are gathered together into a glowing heart, as Ra that gathereth his clouds about Him at eventide into a molten sea of Joy; and the snake that is the crown of Ra bindeth them about with the golden girdle of the death-kisses.[20]

17 Ibid,, 2:53. See Crowley, *Holy Books*, p. 63.
18 *Liber Cordis Cincti Serpente*, 3:34. See Crowley, *Holy Books*, p. 67.
19 Ibid, 1:22. See Crowley, *Holy Books*, p. 55.
20 Ibid, 5:64. See Crowley, *Holy Books*, p. 83.

(pause)

> *Beautiful art thou, O Babylon, and desirable, for thou hast given thyself to everything that liveth, and thy weakness hath subdued their strength. For in that union thou didst understand. Therefore art thou called Understanding, O Babylon, Lady of the Night!*[21]

Return now to the full vision of our Lady. All seven chalices resolve into a single chalice, itself pouring forth a rainbow light, purifying your body of light of all imperfections and obstructions toward your achievement of the Great Work, the Summum Bonum, true wisdom and perfect happiness.

As you chant her mantra, allow that rainbow light to spread freely into your own body of light, and feel the splendor as the universal light transmitted through the blood of the saints enraptures the light of your own being. Once you have finished chanting her mantra, allow her form to dissolve into a natural sphere of emptiness in silent meditation:

All chant: EVOHE BABALON (×108)

(Pause for 7 minutes of silent meditation following the mantra recitation)

> *Glory unto the Scarlet Woman, Babalon the Mother of Abominations, that rideth upon the Beast, for she hath spilt their blood in every corner of the earth and lo! she hath mingled it in the cup of her whoredom.*
>
> *With the breath of her kisses hath she fermented it, and it hath become the wine of the Sacrament, the wine of the Sabbath; and in the Holy Assembly hath she poured it out for her worshippers, and they had become drunken thereon, so that face to face they beheld my Father. Thus are they made worthy to become partakers of the Mystery of this holy vessel, for the blood is the life. So sitteth she from age to age, and the righteous are never weary of her kisses, and by her murders and fornications she seduceth the world. Therein is manifested the glory of my Father, who is truth.*[22]

21 Crowley, Neuberg, and Desti, *The Vision & The Voice*, p. 150

22 Crowley, Neuberg, and Desti, *The Vision & The Voice*, p. 149.

DEDICATION OF MERIT

All recite: May all sentient beings come to realize their aspirations within the purview of light, life, love, and liberty and under the auspices of the Law of Thelema. May I quickly attain to realization of my True Will and the spiritual attainment that results from such realization. May all attain the Stone of the Wise, the Summum Bonum, True Wisdom and Perfect Happiness.

CLOSING

This is that which is written, 'O my God, in one last rapture let me attain to the union with the many'. For she is Love, and her love is one, and she hath divided the one love into infinite loves, and each love is one, and equal to The One, and therefore is she passed 'from the assembly and the law and the enlightenment unto the anarchy of solitude and darkness. For ever thus must she veil the brilliance of Her Self'.[23]

All vibrate: AUGMN AUGMN AUGMN

23 Ibid., p. 150.

"I am Babalon"

ALOSTRAEL'S STRUGGLE WITH IDENTITY IN THELEMA AS THE EX-SCARLET WOMAN

Richard Kaczynski

"SCARLET WOMAN" WAS a title that Aleister Crowley conferred upon a string of lovers who in his estimation embodied the essence of Babalon. This was no mere term of affection, but a title of office indicating that his consort filled a particular function in the Great Work relative to his role as the Prophet of Thelema, the Great Beast To Mega Therion.[1] Nevertheless, most of Crowley's magical consorts and initiatrices came into his life with no background in occultism, and after the relationship ended most vanished completely from this New Religious Movement.[2] The most notable exception was the Scarlet Woman Alostrael, Leah Hirsig (1883–1975). An interest in the occult led to her meeting Crowley in New York City. She subsequently resigned from her job as a school teacher to move to Cefalù, Italy, and co-founded with Crowley the Abbey of Thelema. Hirsig

1 "There is a considerable proportion of the contents [of the *Book of the Law*] which appears to refer to 'The Beast' and 'The Scarlet Woman' personally; but these titles may be assumed to refer to any one who happens to hold either of those offices during the whole period of the Aeon—approximately 2000 years." Aleister Crowley, "Morals of Liber AL" in *Magick without Tears*, (St. Paul: Llewellyn, 1973), 302.

2 What they may have continued to practice privately, however, is largely unknown.

devoted herself not only as the Babalon to his Great Beast, but also to the movement of Thelema itself. In her letters and diaries, she adopted its vocabulary, advocated its cause, and took to practicing magick—including keeping a Magical Record—in the style she learned from Crowley. Thus in late 1924, when she found herself replaced as Scarlet Woman by Astrid Dorothy Olsen (b. 1892), Hirsig faced a crisis not only of the heart but also of spirit, struggling to find another identity within the New Religious Movement to which she had been a prominent leader. In her dark night of the soul, she found that identity in the person of Babalon. This paper will explore Leah Hirsig's conceptualization of and identification with Babalon, how that fit with Crowley's own ideas, and how her adoption of this new identity played out during this difficult period of her participation in the Thelemic movement.

BABALON

The nomenclature surrounding Babalon derives from the Biblical book of *Revelation*, where the Great Harlot appears as the antithesis of the Woman Clothed with the Sun, much as her counterpart the Great Beast is a shadow version of the Woman's bridegroom, the Lamb. In his *Confessions*, Crowley recounts how as a child he "was fascinated by the mysteriously prophetic passages [of the Bible], especially those in *Revelation* [...] The Elders and the harps seemed tame. He preferred the Dragon, the False Prophet, the Beast and the Scarlet Woman, as being more exciting."[3]

Self-identifying as the Beast thanks to his mother, Crowley came to interpret *Revelation* as a description not of the End Times, but of the changing of the guard, the coming of a new dispensation as his Plymouth Brethren kinsfolk would have called it. Similarly as a Golden Dawn ceremonial magician, Crowley recognized the number 666 as that of the sun. Thus the Great Beast was not satanic, but solar-phallic: a symbol of the generative life-force. And Babylon—later refigured as Babalon—assumed the feminine and maternal half of that equation.

As described in chapter seventeen of *Revelation*, the Great Harlot's main features include being drunk either upon the wine of her fornication/idolatry (17:2) or upon the blood of the saints (17:6). She rides upon

3 Aleister Crowley, *The Confessions of Aleister Crowley*, ed. John Symonds and Kenneth Grant (London: Jonathan Cape, 1969), 44.

the Great Beast (17:3), is clothed in purple and scarlet, and bears a golden cup of abominations and of the filthiness of her fornication (17:4). Upon her head is written "Mystery, Babylon the Great, the Mother of Harlots and Abominations of the Earth" (17:5). These features carry over to her recontextualization in Thelema.

Thelemic hermeneutics thus owes a great deal to the apocalyptic literature with which Crowley was fascinated as a child. The first word of *Revelation*, from which the text takes its title, is the Koine Greek αποκαλυψις, which means an "unveiling" or "revelation" of divine mysteries. Note that the opening words of *The Book of the Law* similarly refer to "The unveiling of the company of heaven" (I:2), and that Crowley in his initial commentary on the text explains the passage to mean that "This book is a new revelation."[4] The Thelemic pantheon however departs from the Apocalypse of St. John by giving the aforementioned male and female figures both idealized and manifest forms. Thus—as we shall explore in greater detail below—we have the "father of life"[5] Chaos and his bride Babalon. Their "earthly emissaries"[6] or hypostases are represented by the Great Beast and Scarlet Woman. The Great Beast, Το Μεγα Θηριον, enumerates in Greek isosephia to 666, while the Scarlet Woman, Η Κοκκινη Γυνη, is right beside him at 667. Numerically, she is the "one" who rides on "the beast."

Revelation presents the Great Harlot from an androcentric view of feminine sin and debauch. Women have traditionally been punished far more severely for adultery and fornication than their male lovers. This is because women have historically been viewed as property, to be sold into marriage with a dowry to sweeten the deal. According to English law, having sex with another man's wife was "the highest invasion of property."[7] By contrast, the Great Harlot does not conform, she is not property, and she does not come virginal to the marriage bed...if she comes there at all. With the "filthiness of her fornications" mingled in her cup, she threatens male supremacy, power, patriarchy, and inheritance by mixing the bloodlines through infidelity and cuckoldry. She threatens the very fabric of society.

4 Aleister Crowley, "Liber Legis: The Comment," *The Equinox* 1913, I(7): 387.

5 From the Creed in the Gnostic Mass, see [Aleister Crowley], "Ecclesiæ Gnosticæ Catholicæ Canon Missæ," *The International* 12(3, 1918): 70–4; rpt. *The Equinox* 1919 III(1): 247–70 and Master Therion [Aleister Crowley], *Magick in Theory and Practice* (Paris: Lecram, 1929–1930), 345–61.

6 From "Liber V vel Reguli" in Crowley, *Magick in Theory and Practice*, 336.

7 J. Holt in *Regina v. Mawgridge*, 1707, Kel. J. 119, 137, quoted in *English Reports* 84, 1107, 1115.

The Thelemic pantheon recasts Babalon and her manifestation as the Scarlet Woman as the "New Woman."[8] Her appearance in the Thelemic Holy Books anticipated the societal changes that came with women's suffrage in the early twentieth century, the entry of women into the workforce during the second World War, and the introduction of the birth control pill in the 1960s. This trajectory is still unfolding today e.g., in the movement for equal pay for equal work. Her unfettered sexuality symbolizes her liberation, her equality to any man, and her freedom to explore all her possibilities, sexual or otherwise.

It is tempting to take Crowley's appropriation of Babalon as an atavism of the Greek *hierodoulous* or Hebrew *qedesha*. Both of these terms are commonly translated as "sacred prostitute," referring to a priestess or temple devotee who engages in sacred sex in service to her chosen deity. Modern scholarship, however, questions whether such practices ever existed outside of the over-sexualized minds of the nineteenth century writers with whom the notion gained traction.[9] Whether historically accurate or not, the concept nevertheless informs the context in which Crowley's thinking about Babalon emerged.

The name Babalon does not appear in Thelema's foundational text, *The Book of the Law*. In her earliest appearances,[10] from 1909 to 1913, she is a force of nature, a concept anthropomorphized as a powerful and divine being. Crowley first encounters her in *The Vision and the Voice* (1909).[11] As Crowley put it in his *Confessions*,

8 British-American writer Henry James (1843–1916) is credited with coining the term "New Woman," which in the late Nineteenth and early Twentieth centuries was used to describe the emergence of independent, educated, and career-minded women in Europe and the United States. Prominent women members of the Golden Dawn fit this ideal. See Josephine Johnson, *Florence Farr: Bernard Shaw's "New Woman"* (Totowa, NJ: Rowman and Littlefield, 1975) and Mary K. Greer, *Women of the Golden Dawn: Rebels and Priestesses* (Rochester, VT: Park Street Press, 1995).

9 See, e.g., Stephanie Lynn Budin, *The Myth of Sacred Prostitution in Antiquity* (New York: Cambridge University Press, 2008).

10 The name Babalon appears in a listing of tarot cards in one of Crowely's unpublished vellum notebooks dated 1904 (Old Series Binder 27, Yorke Collection). However, Crowley often appended later entries to his notebooks, sometimes years after the fact. Since the entry in question is undated, it is uncertain whether it predates or is contemporary with his published references to Babalon. With thanks to William Breeze for pointing out this reference.

11 [Aleister Crowley and Victor Neuburg] "Liber XXX Aerum vel Saeculi sub figura CCCCXVIII: (Being of the Angels of the 30 Aethyrs): The Vision and the Voice," *The*

The twelfth Aethyr describes the City of the Pyramids, whose queen is called BABALON, the Scarlet Woman, in whose hand is a cup filled with the blood of the saints. Her ecstasy is nourished by the desires which the Masters of the Temple have poured from their hearts for her sake. In this symbolism are many mysteries concealed. One is that if a single drop of blood be withheld from her cup it putrefies the being below the Abyss and vitiates the whole course of the adept's career.[12]

The Holy Book *Liber Cheth*, received in 1911, refers to her in its very first verse as "our Lady the Scarlet Woman, Babalon the Mother of Abominations, the bride of Chaos, that rideth upon our Lord the Beast."[13] Thus, from her first appearance in a Thelemic Holy Book, Babalon is conflated with the Scarlet Woman. However, it is the concept of Babalon as the bride of Chaos which Crowley reiterates in his contemporary writings and rituals. The polarity of Babalon and Chaos appears in the original "Star Ruby" ritual in *The Book of Lies* (1912).[14] Likewise the first two Collects of his "Gnostic Mass," written in 1913, refer to the Father as "Chaos, the Sole Viecregent of the Sun upon the Earth" and to the Mother as Babalon.[15]

Around 1913, however, Crowley's thinking veered away from the Chaos-Babalon polarity in favor of that of Therion-Babalon. These two share a correlation with the greater abstractions of Nuit and Hadit, who represent the infinite and the finite, the circle and the point. Thus in "Two Fragments of Ritual," we find that "The officers are two in number, and seek Nuit and Hadit through Babalon and the Beast."[16] In his commentary on *The Book of the Law*, Crowley identifies Babalon as a "Secret Name" of Nuit.[17] And he

---

Equinox 1911, 1(5), special supplement.

12 Crowley, *Confessions*, 622.

13 [Aleister Crowley], "Liber Cheth." *The Equinox* 1911, 1(6): 23–27.

14 Frater Perdurabo [Aleister Crowley], *The Book of Lies: Which is also Falsely Called Breaks. The Wanderings or Falsifications of the One Thought of Frater Perdurabo, which Thought is in Itself Untrue* (London: Wieland & Co., 1913 [1912]).

15 The Creed in Crowley, "Ecclesiæ Gnosticæ Catholicæ Canon Missæ."

16 P. 82 in Fra. K.Φ. [Aleister Crowley], "Two Fragments of Ritual," *The Equinox* 1913, 1(10): 81-90.

17 Aleister Crowley, *Magical and Philosophical Commentaries on the Book of the Law*, ed. John Symonds and Kenneth Grant (Montreal: 93 Publishing, 1974), 109. See also Crowley's *Confessions*, where he mentions "the reference in CCXX to Our Lady Babalon: '... the omnipresence of my body'" (599). Likewise, in his diary for 25 Feb 1924 he writes, "I shall further invoke Babalon by her name of Nuit, Lady of Starlight."

revises the "Star Ruby" ritual to replace the polarities of Chaos-Babalon and Eros-Psyche with Babalon-Therion and Nuit-Hadit.[18]

More significantly, at this time the concept of "Babalon and the Beast conjoined" becomes a sacred image of the numinous which creates and energizes the Aeon of Horus. In his epistle "De Natura ΣFINY" in *Liber Aleph*, Crowley writes, "Firstly, this Sphinx is a Symbol of the Coition of Our Lady BABALON with me THE BEAST in its Wholeness."[19] In his diary, Crowley attributes the Hebrew letter *Teth* to "Energy, Leo, the Solar Force; it is BABALON and the Beast conjoined."[20] This letter he would later attribute to the Tarot trump "Lust," which in the Thoth Tarot depicts Babalon riding the Great Beast. Finally, in *Magick in Theory and Practice*, Crowley writes expansively about how this conjunction is part of the general formula of θελημα:

> *The formula of* Thelema *may be summarized thus: θ Babalon and the Beast conjoined—ε unto Nuith (CCXX, I, 51)*[21]*—λ The Work accomplished in Justice—η The Holy Graal—μ The Water therein—α The Babe in the Egg (Harpocrates on the Lotus.)*[22]

Thus, the notion of Babalon and the Beast conjoined—or of "Our Lady Babalon and the Beast whereon she rideth"[23]—become central in the symbolism and coded language of Crowley's cosmogony.

Whatever abstract or celestial properties he attributed to the figures of Babalon and the Beast, Crowley also applied these terms to living and breathing people. In *Magick in Theory and Practice*, he writes of the magical formula ShT, "*The Angel* [Trump XX in the Tarot, i.e., *Judgement* or *The Aeon*] represents the Stélé 666, showing the Gods of the Aeon, while *Strength* [or *Lust*] is a picture of Babalon and The Beast, the earthly emissar-

18 Crowley, *Magick in Theory and Practice*, 327.

19 Master Therion 666 [Aleister Crowley], *Liber Aleph vel CXI: The Book of Wisdom or Folly in the Form of an Epistle of 666 The Great Wild Beast to his Son 777* (West Point, CA: Thelema Publishing Co., 1961), 152.

20 Crowley, *Magical Record*, 144.

21 This verse includes the line, "Also, take your fill and will of love as ye will, when, where and with whom ye will! But always unto me."

22 Crowley, *Magick in Theory and Practice*, 43.

23 See, e.g., Crowley, *Magick in Theory and Practice*, chapter 11: "Of Our Lady Babalon and of the Beast whereon She Rideth."

ies of those Gods."[24] Crowley, of course, identified himself as one of these earthly emissaries: the Great Beast, Το Μεγα Θηριον. This he did both generally speaking with the former title, and with the latter specifically as his magical motto as a Magus 9°=2▫ in the A∴A∴. But he was equally willing to anthropomorphize Babalon. In "Starlight" (from *The Book of Lies*), Crowley applies this name to Leila Waddell (1880–1932)—whom, incidentally, he never identified as a "Scarlet Woman": "AND at THE END is SHE that was LAYLAH, and BABALON, and NUIT."[25] He also referred to Hirsig as Babalon. For instance, in *Liber Nike*, he writes, "The plan is to go to Hardelot Place on Friday and spend 2 weeks with my Babalon."[26] Likewise, on March 25, 1922, his diary refers to an *I Ching* hexagram representing "The Personal Fortune of Babalon Leah Alostrael."[27] Hirsig likewise identified with the name. She noted in May 1921 that, during the operation where Crowley assumed the grade of Ipsissimus, Hirsig was proclaimed Babalon.[28] And, in June 8, 1924, her diary recorded a sex magick working whose goal was for her "To become the Babalon I need to be."[29]

ENTER LEAH HIRSIG

Leah Hirsig was a Swiss national, one of ten children to Magdalena Lüginbühl (1845–1923) and Gottlieb Hirsig (1844–1933) born on April 9, 1883, at Trachselwald, Berne. When Leah was two years old, her mother brought the children to New York to escape Gottleib's alcoholism. Growing into adulthood, the family members scattered to Switzerland, Florida, and Argentina. Leah, however, remained in New York and at age twenty-one became an elementary school music teacher.

Marian Dockerill (1878–1972), having received an introduction to Crowley through an ex-lover, brought her sister Leah to one of Crowley's Greenwich Village parties so that they could meet the notorious Beast.

24 Crowley, *Magick in Theory and Practice*, 336.

25 Crowley, *Book of Lies*, 108.

26 Aleister Crowley, *Liber Nike*, old series, binder A4, Yorke Collection.

27 Crowley, *Liber Nike*.

28 Leah Hirsig, *Three Chapters of My Life*, typescript, Aleister Crowley Papers, George Arents Research Library, Syracuse University, 28 Sep 1924, 9:00 PM.

29 Leah Hirsig, "The Magical Record of The Scarlet Woman Alostrael 31-666-31, Leah Hirsig, from January 15, 1924, to December 27, 1924 EV," binder DD1, Yorke Collection, Warburg Institute, University of London.

Both sisters seem to have had a sexually liberal streak, as Marian would later claim to have belonged to several love cults,[30] while Leah quickly succumbed to her mutual magnetism with Crowley. He was at this time making a name for himself as a painter, and on their second meeting Crowley disrobed Leah in order to paint her. When asked how she would like to be depicted, she replied, "Paint me as a dead soul." They became lovers and, by late spring 1919, she would be pregnant with Crowley's child.

Despite their intense attraction, another woman contended in Crowley's heart and mind for the mantle of Scarlet Woman. Bertha Almira Bruce (b. 1888) ran a boarding house in Detroit and helped to finance the publication of his blue *Equinox*,[31] which had just been released. For a time, Crowley counted Bruce as his fifth Scarlet Woman. Even after returning to Europe in December 1919, his diary from this period recounts a sex magick working "To have Babalon (i.e., Bertha Bruce Prykryl of Detroit) with me."[32] By mid-1920, he began expressing doubt that had been creeping in: On May 31 he wrote, "I always doubted Bertha Almeira Bruce, who is a sexual and magical partner, otherwise contemptible."[33] On June 2, in

30 Her "Confessions of a 'High Priestess' in America's Notorious 'Love Cults: By the Queen of New York's Society 'Bee Harem' and Sister of Aleister Crowley's 'Scarlet Soul' Girl, Who Reveals the Inner Secrets of Weird Rites Practiced by Cranks, Clairvoyants and Their Dupes the World Over, Including Fresh Facts on Dowieism, the Omnipotent Oom's Colony of Bluebloods, Charles Garland's 'April Farm,' and Her Astounding Ordeal Amid the Black Mass Mystics of Europe" was serialized in eight weekly installments of the St. Petersburg Times beginning on March 14, 1926, and running until May 2. A re-edited version was subsequently published in pulp format as Marian Dockerill, *My Life in a Love Cult: A Warning to All Young Girls, My True Life Story* (Dunellen, NJ: Better Publishing Co., 1928). Despite the title "High Priestess of Oom" appearing below her name on the cover, I have found no reference to her in the archives of Pierre Arnold Bernard to corroborate her claimed rank or even membership in his Tantrik Order or subsequent yoga schools. Furthermore, her name appears only once, in passing, in Bernard's biography, where she was present at a meeting between Pierre Arnold Bernard and Blanche DeVries. See Robert Love, *The Great Oom: The Improbable Birth of Yoga in America* (New York: Viking, 2010), 89. Bernard's papers are preserved in two archives: His main archive is housed with the Historical Society of the Nyacks, New York; additional material is available in the archives of his nephew's wife, Viola Wertheim Bernard, in the Augustus C. Long Health Sciences Library, Columbia University, New York.

31 [Aleister Crowley], *The Equinox, Volume III Number 1* (Detroit: Universal Publishing Co., 1919).

32 Aleister Crowley, *The Magical Record of the Beast 666: The Diaries of Aleister Crowley, 1914-1920*, ed. John Symonds and Kenneth Grant (London: Duckworth, 1972), 87.

33 Crowley, *Magical Record*, 139.

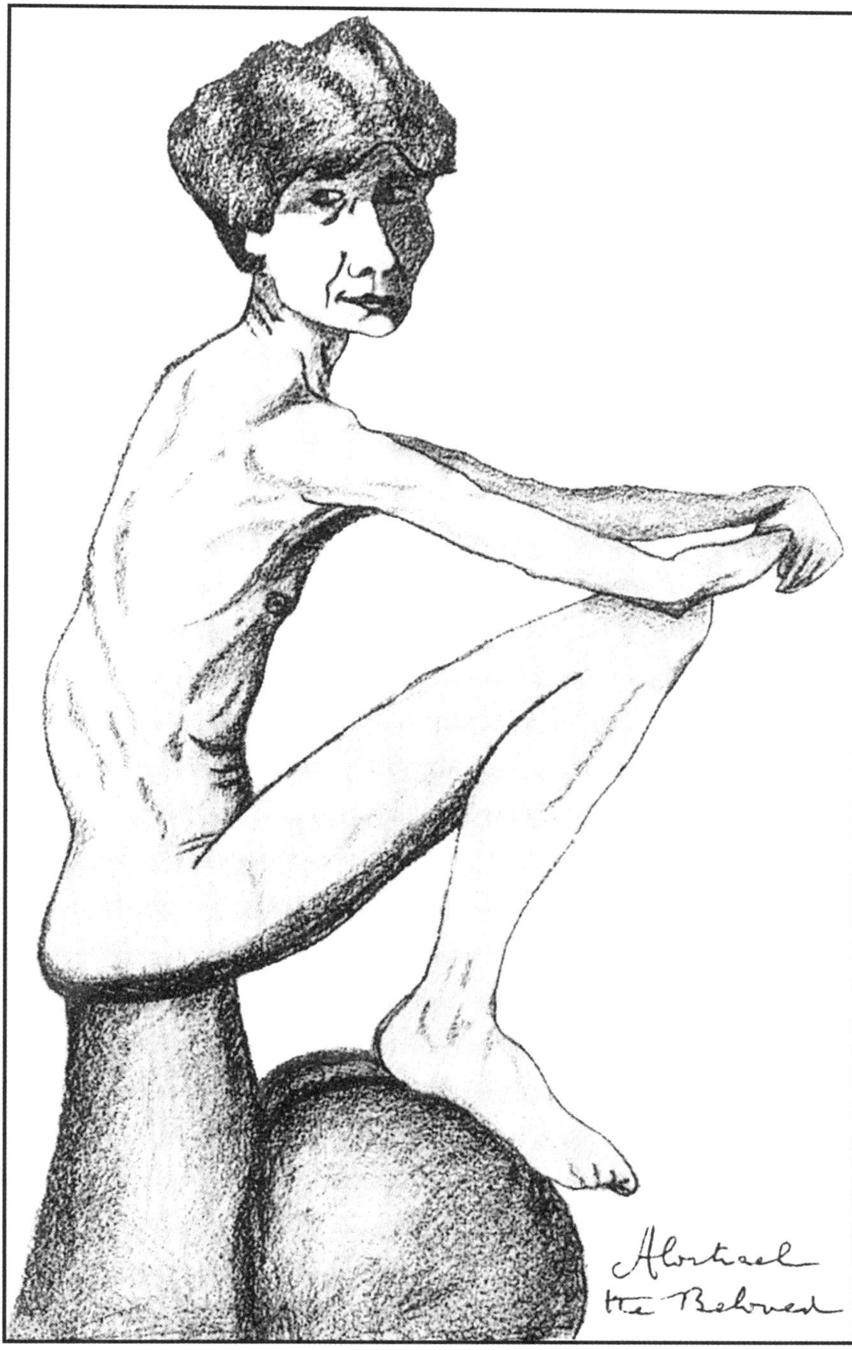

Crowley's sketch of Leah Hirsig for his poem *Leah Sublime* [image reproduced by permission of Ordo Templi Orientis]

reviewing the five Scarlet Women up to that point, he wrote, "Fifth, Almeira, whose vocation I cannot doubt, seems to have failed altogether, unless she gave me that very non-attachment I so needed. But I cannot make out whether she is still in office."[34] Not until July 1, 1920, did Crowley refer to Hirsig as his "Scarlet Whore."[35] Finally, his July 20 entry refers to her as "Scarlet Woman," and records a sex magick operation for "Alostrael to know how to use her power."[36]

Leah's grande passion with the self-proclaimed Great Beast was epic. She resigned her job teaching piano and music at Public School No. 40 in the Bronx; she could not have continued as a pregnant and unmarried teacher. Applying for a passport, she reported her intention to leave New York on board the Adriatic on October 25, 1919, stopping in France on her way to Switzerland to visit her sick sister and aged father.[37] But this was also for her confinement in preparation for childbirth. Crowley met up with her in Paris on January 10, 1920, and on February 26 their daughter, Anne Lea, was born. The *I Ching* directed them next to Cefalù, where they rented a villa with the goal of founding the Rabelais-honoring Abbey of Thelema, a social experiment in Thelema to overthrow the repressions of normal society and usher in the Aeon of Horus.

Crowley showered Hirsig with titles: Alostrael 31-666-31, 8°=3▫. Praemonstrix A∴A∴. Virgin Guardian of the Sangraal. The Ape of Thoth. Contessa Léa Harcourt. The Scarlet Woman.

And Babalon.

He was the prophet of a new age for mankind, and she was his female counterpart. She embraced the role without reservation. She kept a magical record. She practiced the techniques of magick. And the results of her experiments in astral projection are preserved in the manuscript *Alostrael's Visions.*[38] She served as Crowley's secretary in the Great Work, writing endless letters to students, supporters, and prospective benefactors. She even

34 Crowley, *Magical Record*, 145. In this same entry, he ponders whether Hollywood actress Jane Wolfe is "a, or rather the, Scarlet Woman?"

35 Crowley, *Magical Record*, 200.

36 Crowley, *Magical Record*, 229. Thanks to William Breeze for pointing out these passages.

37 Passport number 128336, issue date 14 Oct 1919, Passport Applications, January 2, 1906—March 31, 1925 (M1490), National Archives, Washington, DC.

38 Leah Hirsig, *Alostrael's Visions: Copied from the Diaries of The Beast 666 and Alostrael 31-666-31, beginning Oct. 29, 1923 e.v. Nefta, Tunisié. I–X, Cefalù, Paris.* Binder DD1, Old Series, Yorke Collection Warburg Institute, University of London.

took down Crowley's dictation of *The Diary of a Drug Fiend*[39] in a 27-day marathon. And when Crowley traveled—on business or magical retirements—she ruled the roost of students and lovers staying at the Abbey.

Hirsig's role also required that she discard conventional attitudes toward sexuality, which she did readily. En route to Europe for her confinement, she enlisted fellow passenger Ninette Shumway (1894–1990) as a nanny for her two children: the then-unborn Anne Lea, the other being three-year-old Hans Hammond (1917–1985). Shumway—affectionately known as both Shummy and Beauty—had become Crowley's lover during Leah's confinement, and before long also became pregnant.

Neither did Hirsig's sexual flexibility find its limit in this ménage à trois. When Cecil Frederick Russell (1897–1987) arrived on November 21, 1920, fresh from tending to Crowley's bookselling interests in Detroit, he was enlisted as a participant in the Cephaloedium Working, whose purposes included helping Crowley to write a commentary on *The Book of the Law*.[40] As part of the working, they disrobed and huffed ether with the goal of Russell having sex with Crowley, who would then have sex with Leah. While Leah apparently did her best during foreplay to coax Russell's participation, he ultimately found the prospect to be insufficiently arousing.

In various other ways she indulged exploration of what Mudd called the "mystery of filth" i.e. Crowley's efforts to exorcise social programming by breaking all manner of taboos and, Aghori-like, embracing the repugnant.[41] This phase is exemplified by Crowley's notorious poem, *Leah Sublime*, which he wrote on June 28. It contains the well-known stanza:

Stab your demonical
Smile to my brain!
Soak me in cognac
Cunt and cocaine;
Sprawl on me! Sit
On my mouth, Leah, shit![42]

39 Aleister Crowley, *The Diary of a Drug Fiend* (London: William Collins, 1922).
40 Aleister Crowley, Cephaloedium Working, 12 Dec 1920–20 Jan 1921, Binder A1, Old Series, Yorke Collection (serialized in *Mezla*, issues 5-6, summer and autumn, 1975, as an extract from the unpublished second volume of *The Magical Record of the Beast 666*).
41 For more, see Richard Kaczynski, "Taboo and Transformation in the Works of Aleister Crowley" in Christopher S. Hyatt (ed.), *Rebels & Devils: The Psychology of Liberation*, 2nd. rev. ed. (Tempe, AZ: New Falcon Publications, 2000), 171–9.
42 Aleister Crowley, *Leah Sublime* (Montreal: 93 Publishing, 1976; rpt. *Scratch 'n' Sniff*

As this poem foretold, he would unblinkingly explore the recesses of his sexuality, with Leah along for the ride. Adopting the feminine version of his name, "Alys," he toyed with gender fluidity as the mood struck him. He experimented with power exchange dynamics, casting Leah as a dominatrix who whipped and demeaned him to the point where he crawled on the floor and licked her dirty feet;[43] eventually, as *Leah Sublime* suggested, he would even shamefully eat some of her excrement on command ("My mouth burned; my throat choked; my belly retched" he recorded the unpleasant ordeal in his diary).[44] And, after Crowley read Herodotus' account of an Egyptian priestess copulating with a goat, he convinced Hirsig to consent to a recreation of this rite. Contrary to the sensational account which Mary Butts later provided to the yellow press, Butts's own diary clearly records that she was not present for the failed ceremony. Furthermore, Symonds quotes Crowley's diary which says that the goat—like C. F. Russell in the Cephaloedium Working—did not respond and that Crowley had to "atone" for the goat by stepping in with Leah.[45]

The Thelemites at Cefalù also experienced their share of tragedy. Jealousy strained the relationship between Leah and Ninette. Leah miscarried Crowley's son. Student Raoul Loveday died from drinking contaminated water. And the yellow press blamed it all on Crowley.

Even when the tensions were between Crowley and Hirsig, it was always them against the rest of the world. That was until the summer of 1924, when Crowley met Dorothy Olsen and everything changed. Suddenly, Alostrael was the outgoing Scarlet Woman, and Olsen was now the "Scarlet Concubine of his desire."[46]

After all these years, it was a bitter pill for Hirsig. While she was ultimately resigned to relinquishing the title of Scarlet Woman—what other

---

Leah Sublime, s.l., n.d.).

43 Crowley, *Magical Record*, 231.

44 Aleister Crowley, diary, 26 July 1920, published in Crowley, *Magical Record*, 235.

45 Butts' account for the tabloids ("Complete Exposure of 'Drug Fiend' Author," *Sunday Express*, 26 Nov 1922, 1,7) is contradicted by her diary, which reveals that she was absent from the proceedings: "Leah—apparently—if the Beast's word is worth anything, had sexual union with the goat before he was killed" (7 Aug 1921, Mary Butts Papers, Gen MSS 487, Box 2, folder 58, Beinecke Rare Book and Manuscript Library, Yale University, New Haven, CT). Crowley's diary documents this failure, and the line "I atoned for the young He-goat at considerable length." is quoted in John Symonds, "Introduction," in Aleister Crowley, *White Stains* (London: Duckworth, 1986), ix.

46 *The Book of the Law*, III:14.

choice did she have?—she focused herself on one of the other titles that Crowley had bestowed upon her: Babalon.

BABALON RISING

The seeds of Crowley's parting with Hirsig had been sown before Olsen's appearance. The Abbey was faltering after Crowley's expulsion from Italy, and Crowley and Hirsig subsequently found themselves in France while Shumway and the others carried on the best they could. Expelled from their French hotel, Crowley and Hirsig were forced to move into another place in Chelles. During all this, Crowley's health was faltering and they began losing patience with each other. In mid-September came the news that Leah's sister Alma Hirsig Bliss had arrived at the Abbey, ingratiated herself to Shumway, and kidnapped Hansi, bringing him back to the United States in an unwelcome rescue. Everything seemed to be in a downward spiral, and Crowley sought something to help him change course. That something appeared on September 16 in the person of Chicago-born Astrid Dorothy Olsen, in Chelles on holiday. She became instantly devoted to the Beast and his cause. Within days, a revitalized Crowley proclaimed her his new Scarlet Woman and announced that they were going on a magical retirement to Tunis.

The *Diary of Babalon* thus begins with Hirsig writing to Crowley the unhappy words

> *93*
>
> *I hereby renounce the title The Scarlet Woman and pass it on to the 'Scarlet Concubine of his desire,' the daughter of Babalon.*
>
> *93 93/93*
>
> *Babalon*[47]

Despite her willingness to cede the title, Hirsig felt very strongly "that there should be a link between the passing on of the title of Scarlet Wom-

47 Letter of Leah Hirsig to Aleister Crowley, 21 Sep 1924, quoted in Hirsig, *Three Chapters*, 4.

an to the next."[48] This was predicated on Hirsig's interpretation of events in September 1919, when the customary equinox password was this time dual: Ahitha-Alostrael. It was proclaimed by both Hirsig and the former Scarlet Woman Roddie Minor (1884–1979), and consisted of their magical names as Crowley's incoming and outgoing sex magick partners. As mentioned above, Crowley at this time (1919) considered Bertha Bruce to be the current Scarlet Woman; it would be several months before Crowley placed "Bruce" in the doubtful category and regarded Hirsig as the current holder of this office. Nevertheless, in Leah's mind she was effectively the Scarlet Woman who followed Minor, and she believed that the transition happened with the dual password in 1919. It represented a smooth transfer of power, ensuring continuity of the 93 Current. And Hirsig wanted her magical daughter to have that same experience.

Crowley's diary indicates that, as the sun entered the sign of Libra, he received the word of the equinox, Om, from Olsen. There is no mention of Leah, but—judging from her own record—she seemed to be satisfied with the outcome. Leah bid farewell to Dorothy and the Beast as they set out for their magical retirement, and she noted in her magical record, "The Five years of silence are over. Now for action."[49]

Leah Hirsig found herself in as dark a night of the soul as any mystic before her. Despite being rejected by Crowley, as a dedicated magician she adhered not only to the language of Thelema but also to Crowley's diary style, continuing with her magical record, sex magic, astral visions, and analyses of symbolism. She was convinced of the importance of chronicling her ordeal, emotional and spiritual, and her identification with Babalon for future generations.

The resulting account, *Three Chapters of My Life*—also called *The Diary of Babalon*—was compiled from diaries, letters and scraps of paper that she kept for the period from September 21 to December 10, 1924. In its opening pages she enters the description, "This diary is the beginning of a Magical Career of one who now knows herself as Babalon."[50] It is more than a document of the heartbreak, loss, and desperation of rejection. It illustrates her attempt to work through her pain, and to reinvent her identity in a new religious movement to which she remained steadfastly committed. In addition, this exercise sent Hirsig on an exploration of the

48 Hirsig, *Three Chapters*, 28 Sep 1924, 9:00 PM.

49 Hirsig, *Three Chapters*, 22 Sep 1924, 8:00 PM.

50 "Foreword" in Hirsig, *Three Chapters*, dated 22 Sept 1924.

mysteries of magick, and of Thelema in particular, from the female perspective rather than that of the male, of the Beast, or of the King in the Yod-Heh-Vav-Heh formula.

Thus, she began signing her letters and telegrams as Babalon. She also developed her own sigil, the "Seal of Babalon." As she described an early version, "The seal of Babalon consists of the imprint of her left forefinger with the numbers 3-4-3."[51] These numbers were arranged around the thumbprint in an equilateral triangle, but with the four on the right side of the base dropped below its proper position. She used this to seal important documents and other objects, including Norman Mudd's penis. Before long, even he was referring to her as Babalon.[52]

THE WILL TO DIE

The kidnapping of Hansi, coupled with the end of her relationship with Crowley, proved to be too much bad news at once. Leah Hirsig suffered a complete physical collapse. Under these circumstances, she yielded to an overwhelming desire to simply give up. The first chapter of *Three Chapters in My Life* is thus devoted to exploring, accepting, and even indulging her "Will do die."

She contemplated death, anticipated it, and even welcomed it. After physically collapsing from nervous exhaustion, she was convinced that the end was near (despite a doctor assuring her otherwise). She telegraphed the news to her friend, Aimée Gouraud (1871–1941). She wrote letters—generally unsent—for Crowley, Mudd, and Olsen. She began to put her affairs in order. In her will, she named Norman Mudd as her executor, leaving her few worldly possessions to him with minor exceptions: To Dorothy Olsen she left whichever of Hirsig's magical belongings that she desired. To Jane Wolfe she left her blue cape. Ninette Shumway received custody of Hans Hammond (once he was finally retrieved). Ninette's daughter, Lulu, received a little red purse. Norman Mudd received a grey wallet. And, she requested that her black and gold dress, hat, shoes, and stockings to be preserved as the raiment of Babalon.

She also left brief messages to the other English-speaking National Grand Masters under Crowley: "Let Frater Achad beware! Let Frater Pro-

51 Hirsig, *Three Chapters*, 6 Oct 1924.

52 Hirsig, *Three Chapters*, 1 Oct 1924, 7:00 PM.

gradior 'go on, go on.' Let Frater Windram—Semper Paratus—'exceed, exceed.'"[53]

Finally, she called for the prosecution of those responsible for her death, namely Lord Beaverbrook (who had attacked Crowley and the entire community at Cefalù in his yellow press), Alma Bliss (who had kidnapped Hirsig's son), and H. Roy (proprietor of the apartment from which she and Crowley had been expelled, their belongings held in lieu of payment). To facilitate this prosecution, she took a copy of the pamphlet *An Open Letter to Lord Beaverbrook*[54] and inscribed it:

> *To Lord Beaverbrook, the murderer of one of the "three women."*[55]
> *Leah Hirsig*
> *(legally)*
> *But really Babalon.*
>
> *Sept. 24, 1924 e.v.*

All these final preparations, instructions, and documents she signed with the name Babalon.

She was through wrestling with her ambivalent feelings, and resigned herself to whatever fate the Gods had in store for her. In her diary, she wrote:

> *I should have liked, as a human creature, to have died in the arms of The Beast, 666, who, as will be noted in my very first diary (commencing Mar. 21, 1919) was and is my lover, my mate, my father, my child and everything else that Woman needs in man. But I have never interfered with his Work, which was my Work: The Great Work, except in ignorance. But ignorance, where the True Will is established, does good, not harm. All the 'mistakes'*

53 Hirsig, *Three Chapters*, Spasm 1: 24 Sep 1924, page 4. The two quotes are from *The Book of the Law*, iii.46 and ii.71 respectively. The injunction to beware is not as obviously a quote, but could be construed to refer to either ii.24, ii.59, iii.2, or iii.43.

54 Norman Mudd, *An Open Letter to Lord Beaverbrook* (Paris: [s.n.], 1924).

55 This referred to a passage in a *Sunday Express* story about Crowley from November 26, 1922, which read, "Three women he keeps there permanently for his orgies. All of them he brought from America two or three years ago. One is a French-American Governess, one an ex-schoolmistress, and one a cinema actress from Los Angeles." These were Shumway, Hirsig and Wolfe, respectively.

> *made since the receipt of* The Book of the Law, *Apr. 7, 8, 9 [sic], 1904, have worked out in this way. 'There is death for the dogs' and 'There is success.'*[56]

Her meditations on her "Will do die" also led her to prepare the following declaration:

> *Babalon speaks:*
> 1. *Thelemites die without aid except that of the Gods.*
> 2. *Thelemites will be permitted to die or live as they will.*
> 3. *Thelemites will not quote from* The Book of the Law, *for their Brethren will understand.*
> 4. *Thelemites will have* The Book of the Law *and its Comment to guide them.*
> 5. *Thelemites are born and not made.*[57]

Finally, Hirsig's meditations on life and death led her to chart out various initiations, magical workings, and other significant life events, and compare them to what fruit they bore nine months later. For instance, Crowley's magical retirement in Montauk in July 1919 was followed nine months later by the founding of the Abbey of Thelema at Cefalù in April, 1920. Nine months after writing *The Diary of a Drug Fiend* in May 1922, Raoul Loveday died. And so on.

Thus Hirsig not only recognized herself as Babalon, but particularly identified with her as Magna Mater. She wrote to Crowley,

> *To Mega Therion,*
> *93*
> *The prophecy has been fulfilled.*
> *CCXX-43-45.*[58]

56 Hirsig, *Three Chapters*, 28 Sep 1924, noon. The receipt of *The Book of the Law* was actually on April 8, 9 and 10. The two quotes in her last line are from this book, ii.45 and iii.69 respectively.

57 Hirsig, *Three Chapters*, 28 Sep 1924, noon.

58 This refers to verses in the third chapter of *The Book of the Law*, which reads: "iii.43: Let the Scarlet Woman beware! If pity and compassion and tenderness visit her heart; if she leave my work to toy with old sweetnesses; then shall my vengeance be known. I will slay me her child: I will alienate her heart: I will cast her out from men: as a shrinking and despised harlot shall she crawl through dusk wet streets, and die cold and an-hungered. Iii:44: But let her raise herself in pride! Let her follow me in my way! Let her work the

I am Babalon, the Great Mother, the Mother of the Children of the New Aeon, the Aeon of Horus! I die in giving birth to my children. But I shall live again!

93 93/93
Babalon
The Scarlet Woman
Alostrael 31-666-31[59]

She also wrote her "beloved daughter Dorothy," signing as "Thy mother, Babalon." In essence, she concluded that she was dying while laboring in childbirth to her magical children. Moreover, she believed that her death would also vindicate Crowley of all the slanders made against him.

Riding this wave of despair, Hirsig finally emerged from this Apophis phase of her work and regained her Will to live. By September 30, the clouds began parting. Aimée gave her food. Mudd came to visit. Nina Hamnett sent money. "Babalon is risen," she declared in her diary, "and the children of the New Aeon live and will thrive!"[60]

YOD-HÉ-VAU-HÉ

In contemplating and assessing the fruits of her magical labors, Hirsig's thoughts naturally turned to the formula of Yod-Hé-Vau-Hé, the Tetragrammaton. Throughout his Cefalù period, Crowley had worked on the manuscript of *Magick in Theory and Practice*,[61] and in chapter three of that book he explains this formula:

---

work of wickedness! Let her kill her heart! Let her be loud and adulterous! Let her be covered with jewels, and rich garments, and let her be shameless before all men! Iii:45: Then will I lift her to pinnacles of power: then will I breed from her a child mightier than all the kings of the earth. I will fill her with joy: with my force shall she see & strike at the worship of Nu: she shall achieve Hadit."

59 Letter from Leah Hirsig to Aleister Crowley, 25 Sep 1924, transcribed in Hirsig, *Three Chapters*.

60 Hirsig, *Three Chapters*, 25 Sep 1924, 5:10 PM.

61 See "Editor's Introduction" in Aleister Crowley, Mary Desti, and Leila Waddell, *Magick: Liber ABA, Book Four, Parts I–IV*, ed. Hymenaeus Beta, 2nd rev. ed. (York Beach, ME: S. Weiser, 1997).

> *The formation of the* Yod *is the formulation of the first creative force, of that father who is called "self-begotten", and unto whom it is said: "Thou hast formulated thy Father, and made fertile thy Mother". The adding of the* Hé *to the* Yod *is the marriage of that Father to the great co-equal Mother, who is a reflection of Nuit as He is of Hadit. Their union brings forth the son* Vau *who is the heir. Finally the daughter* Hé *is produced. She is both the twin sister and the daughter of* Vau.

His mission is to redeem her by making her his bride; the result of this is to set her upon the throne of her mother, and it is only she whose youthful embrace can reawaken the eld of the All-Father. In this complex family relationship is symbolised the whole course of the Universe.[62]

Elaborating on this formula in *The Book of Thoth*,[63] Crowley argues that it underlies the structure of all fairy tales, including Beauty and the Beast, Cinderella, and Aladdin. While Crowley cautioned that these stories were but vulgar expressions of a very sublime expression of the Great Work—the divine union of opposites—Hirsig pursued a more literal interpretation of "the daughter returning the energy to the father."[64] If Olsen was indeed the magical child of Crowley and Hirsig, then Crowley had clearly placed this daughter on the throne of the mother by declaring her the new Scarlet Woman. This was not a radical interpretation, as Crowley himself had written in his diary that September, "ה Sor. Astrid appeared to complete יהוה and change the death-magnetism to a new Life."[65]

In Hirsig's mind, Olsen was but one of the children she had borne with Crowley. Indeed, they had conceived physical, intellectual, and magical children. In this case, their baby Poupée was the physical child, and the book *The Diary of a Drug Fiend* was their intellectual offspring. As for magical children, Olsen was but one of them. Hirsig claimed Frater Aud, Raoul Loveday, as another. In her analysis, she found it striking that none of these conceptions came to term: Poupée died in her infancy, after which Hirsig miscarried their son. *The Diary of a Drug Fiend* was attacked by the yellow press, and Collins let the edition go quietly out of print; it did not bring

62 Crowley, *Magick in Theory and Practice*, 22–23.
63 Master Therion [Aleister Crowley], *The Book of Thoth: A Short Essay on the Tarot of the Egyptians* (London: OTO, 1944), 54–56.
64 Crowley, *Book of Thoth*, 54.
65 Aleister Crowley, diary, 16 September 1924.

droves of seekers to the Abbey as hoped. Finally, Loveday died in 1923 of acute enteric fever.

These physical, intellectual, and magical children were part of a larger pattern of triplicities that Hirsig charted out and contemplated at this period. She noted there were three deaths of Babalon, just as her *Three Chapters* divided the first chapter into three "Spasms." She also applied this "Rule of Three" to what she identified as the three Scarlet Women: The roles of wife, mother, and whore were fulfilled by Rose Kelly, Leah Hirsig, and Astrid Dorothy Olsen.[66] Interestingly, this analysis required Hirsig to overlook the intervening Scarlet Women between Kelly and herself: Mary Desti, Jeanne Robert Foster, Roddie Minor, Marie Röhling, and Bertha Bruce. If Hirsig was distinguishing between major and minor occupants of this office, it is also telling that she placed Olsen in the "major" category. It was as if to say that if Leah had been supplanted by her own magical daughter, then that daughter must be important.

Hirsig also claimed another magical child: Norman Mudd. And it was upon him that her thinking about the Yod-Hé-Vau-Hé formula revolved. If Crowley was the king *Yod*, Hirsig the queen *Hé*, and Olsen the daughter *Hé* (final), then Mudd was the son *Vau*. If Crowley was going to enthrone Olsen by making her his new sex magick partner, then Hirsig re-interpreted Yod-Hé-Vau-Hé in terms of the parents training and initiating their magical children into maturity. Logically she, as the female "parent," should instruct Mudd in the same way that Crowley was with Olsen. Identifying Mudd with Parsifal the "pure fool" and with the similarly naïve Dummling of folklore,[67] she took him on as her sex magick trainee.

This was more than a tit-for-tat response to Crowley. As Djurdjevic points out, "to properly understand Crowley and Hirsig in this context, we need to approach the sexual as the mystical."[68] In Hirsig's mind, completing the Yod-Hé-Vau-Hé formula was essential. Up to that point, Crowley had sired no sons: all his physical children had been daughters, and his one son with Hirsig never came to term. But she predicted, "Now that Parsifal knows how to use his lance,"[69] Olsen would be able to bear Crowley an heir.

66 Hirsig, *Three Chapters*, 2 Oct 1924.

67 For Dumling, see e.g., "The Fool of the Family" in Ascott Robert Hope, *Stories of Long Ago* (John Walker & Co: London, 1881), 154–60.

68 See Gordan Djurdjevic, "Our Lady Babalon and Her Cup of Fornications: Approaches to a Thelemic Goddess," *Clavis* 2013, 2: 69–81.

69 Hirsig, *Three Chapters*, 28 Sep 1924, 9:00 PM.

And so *Three Chapters* describes a ritual that Hirsig conducted with Mudd's participation. They feasted on tea, butter, bread, milk, ham, black grapes, and figs. Then she explained to him

> *this was a marriage feast now that the Prince had found the slipper of Cinderella and could carry her off to his castle; that Dummling had brought the feather home to his father and had therefore earned the hand of the Princess. Also, that Parsifal, having found the lance would now be able to use it.*[70]

Mudd was not quite getting the picture, so Hirsig "gave my son, Parsifal, instructions and advice about his Lance." They consummated the lesson with not one but two acts of sex magick for reverence unto Ra-Hoor-Khuit.

This interpretation of the Yod-Hé-Vau-Hé formula liberated Hirsig from being on the short end of the revolving door known as "Scarlet Woman." If the Beast could proclaim the arrival of a new sex magick partner, then so could Babalon. At this point, her diaries (like Crowley's) recounting each instance of a sex magick working and the goal thereof—frequently strength for Babalon, to fill Parsifal with Babalon's force, or to establish the Kingdom. On the first full moon after the autumnal equinox, she received her own word for the upcoming six month period:

FE⊙⊃T

The manuscript of *Three Chapters of My Life* contains a page, on A∴A∴ letterhead, dated October 17 where she lists her Word, I Ching hexagram, and other oracles in a column to the right of those issued by Crowley at the autumnal equinox, as if to indicate that her results with Mudd provided a parallel to the results that Crowley obtained with Olsen.

ANGER

In addition to the themes of death and parenthood running through *Three Chapters of My Life*, another unsurprising theme is Babalon coming to terms with her anger. Early on in the manuscript, Hirsig quips, "I look like a Fury. I *am* a fury, *The* Fury, but I am not in a fury."[71] Eventually, however,

70 Hirsig, *Three Chapters*, 4 Oct 1924.
71 Hirsig, *Three Chapters*, 22 Sep 1924.

she grew resentful of constantly living hand-to-mouth while Crowley honeymooned at the Majestic Hotel in Tunis with his new Scarlet Woman. On October 28, she wrote a letter to Crowley which she ultimately decided not to send:

> *To Sir Aleister Crowley*
> *Edward Alexander Crowley Esq.*
> *To Mega Therion and all the rest,*
> *Saluti*
>
> *The* Sir *means as little to me as "Lord" Beaverbrook—Aleister is a mere wish phantasm (all wrong except as a nom de plume) and even Emily Bishop may have been unfaithful!*
>
> *The question remains "Who are you?" For practical purposes you are Ed. Alex. C. legally, and Aleister Crowley as a writer. What you'd better do is find out who you are really, just as we'd better all find out including your dear daughter V.L.*
>
> *At present you seem to be a very stupid young bridegroom bent on providing your bride with rich garments etc. but not having made proper preparations beforehand. It is extremely unwise for a young man to marry in haste—he usually doesn't even have the leisure in which to repent—the* siren *doesn't give him a chance. You are no more a Magus than you are a cunt. You seem to disregard all Holy books etc. in your sexual stupidity. They may be partly wrong but not entirely. You seem also to forget that Babalon makes the bridge for the Abyss—or something to that effect (your vellum copy of 30 Aethyrs is tied up for lack of 333 francs)—and that you never crossed it really any more than Achad did. If you can find a filthier female to represent Babalon (myself, thank you) at the moment, do so.*
>
> *Your extremely pathetic letter, saying you are on your way to Tozeur with 100 francs if you are lucky etc. arrived today. This scribble is due partly to that bit of pathos tho' not entirely. In fact, as I pause to eat a peasant soup made in my little nest (I have one now, have you?) I find that I too have any number of things to say to you but am not nearly angry or interested enough to say them. I don't suppose I ever will be and they will keep till you recover.*[72]

Despite venting in this letter, she concluded that she really wasn't angry enough to say everything that she had to say, or to send it. (Given that the

72 Hirsig, *Three Chapters*, Appendix to Chapter 2, 28 Oct 1924.

letter is preserved in the typescript of *Three Chapters* that Hirsig had prepared for Crowley, and that it survives in the Crowley Papers at Syracuse University, one presumes that he eventually did see it.)

The dark clouds were parting. By November 12, she noted that the purpose of her current burst of journaling had "exhausted and purified itself... after 11 days of rain from the Cup of Babalon."[73] Finally, on November 29, she collected together all the scraps of paper, loose sheets, unsent letters, and diary pages of the past two months and began typing

> *my* Babalon Diary, *a single copy for 666. Typed the "Death" period Sept. 23–Sept. 30 also Sept. 24 (1st death stunt) documents. I had qualms many times as to whether I wasn't wasting time but I'm not. I want to get out a complete record of that period. And if one can be so—I don't know what to call it—when one is dying, why not to the nth power when one is alive—or supposed to be.*[74]

On December 3, having finished typing the most emotionally challenging material, she noted more philosophically:

> *Somehow my despair has passed by. In typing the Sept. 23–29 stunt, I see how supremely happy I was then because I was so very busy doing what seemed at the time a tremendous task, sparing nothing to get it done—and after each of the three critical periods had passed I slept a peaceful happy sleep. That is as it should be when Thelema gets going. It's worth while living with that in view—perhaps some centuries hence.*[75]

Typing up her diary was a magical act, an exorcism, a meditation, "a revelation indeed."[76] Just after midnight, early in the morning of December 10, she closed out her diary—signing it Babalon—eager and hopeful to see what the universe would bring in future chapters of her life. Her next diary—beginning December 29, 1924—was titled "Diary of ? Known on Earth as Leah Hirsig."[77]

73 Hirsig, *Three Chapters*, Appendix 2 to Chapter 3, 11 Nov 1924.
74 Hirsig, *Three Chapters*, 29 Nov 1924, 11:00 PM.
75 Hirsig, *Three Chapters*, 3 Dec 1924, 12:15 AM.
76 Hirsig, *Three Chapters*, 8 Dec 1924.
77 Diary of Leah Hirsig, 29 December 1924–5 February 1925, Old Series, Binder DD3, Yorke Collection.

CONCLUSION

On reflection, Hirsig would consider these chapters of her life to be madness. Nevertheless, she continued to serve the Order and Thelema in general, whether it was rushing to Olsen's side to help when she was pregnant[78] or joining Crowley at the conference in Weida in 1925. At the end of that year, she bore a son, Alexander, to fellow Thelemite William George Barron. Thereafter, however, she became a nearly invisible character in Crowley's life: Her name no longer graced his diaries, and their only communications were limited to rare letters from her concerning *The Book of the Law*, wherein she frequently challenged Crowley's role as prophet because he failed to follow the book's instructions. Ultimately, Crowley wearied of Hirsig's letters and declared her a "centre of pestilence" per the Short Comment (i.e., for discussing *The Book of the Law*), instructing all members of Ordo Templi Orientis to shun her and to destroy unread any communications from her. In response, she wrote to Crowley on December 26, 1929, renouncing both him and her title. Another letter followed in 1930, in Mudd's hand, renouncing all her magical oaths and obligations to Crowley. Returning to the United States, she resumed her former career as teacher. Although naturalized as a United States citizen since 1916, Leah Hirsig eventually moved back to Switzerland and died at Meiringen in 1975.

78 Contrary to Hirsig's prediction of a son, Olsen miscarried early into this pregnancy.

Dreaming of Babalon and the Bride of the Land

Caroline Wise

AUGUST 12TH 2004. It is high summer. The moon is dark, veiled from the world. It is exhilarating, flying over the landscape. It is a *sensuous* experience. There is a feeling of complete freedom, my loose hair wild in the wind. The air is alive. Crackling. Magnetized. Sense is heightened. The sky is a deep peacock blue, moody yet vibrant, lush and dark, back-lit. I look down and see hills like soft green cushions; rounded, plump, pregnant bellies. Breasts soft yet taut. The grass is emerald, but the hues change in the shadows of the hills as I travel. This moment, and the landscape, are poised in balance at that tipping point between ripe fruit and putrescence, beauty and decadence, lushness and rot.

I am startled when these sculpted hills beneath me reveal the place as the environs of Glastonbury. There are few houses or buildings of any kind, just the land with some tracks, and the hills and the woods and the rivers and the springs. I recognize the landmarks. I am ambivalent about Glastonbury. I love the surrounding country, the Glastonbury Zodiac, that vast circle of celestial beasts mapped out in the Somerset hills and streams, for its magic and beauty and mystery. I dislike much of the town. I groan. Glastonbury! Even in dream, I'm aware of the cliché, but fascinated by this bird's-eye view, and wonder what is to be shown.

There is a tantalising rumour that John Dee knew of the landscape zodiac. These celestial figures were laid down by the legendary Phoenicians, claims Katherine Maltwood, the artist who re-discovered them. *Phoenician* shares a root with phoenix, and with *phoînix,* crimson, and *phoinós,* blood red. Aquarius, the sign of the new aeon, is represented by a phoenix in the Glastonbury Zodiac, and incorporates the Abbey, whose blood stained the Tor when its Abbot and priests were martyred; the Tor itself, and St Edmund the Martyr's Hill is on one wing of the fire-bird. There is a lot of blood in this landscape. Chalice Hill, and the white and red springs also dwell within the phoenix.

I shudder as I fly over the up-turned chalice of the Tor. The stem of the Chalice is St Michael's Tower, the remains of a church destroyed in an earthquake. Its aura is menacing and I want to pass it quickly. The blood of the martyrs runs into the Chalice well at the base. The dull red waters of death mingle with the ferrous-red waters of life that come from deep within the earth. At the winter solstice the dance of the dying and resurrecting solar god is played out when the sun appears to roll down this tor. Arthur, that cuckolded king, is said to be sleeping inside, waiting for his reawakening, a sleeping beauty. I am flying on, no need to dwell on this. Now below is Wearyall Hill, the place where, in legend, Joseph of Arimathea came after the crucifixion, and stabbed his thorny staff into the earth, on the sign of Pisces. He's staked his claim, staked the goddess down for the Piscean age. What good is she, when the guardian of the grail is always 'wounded in the thigh', a euphemism for impotency? Joseph came, or his legend did, to bring the game 'Salvation or Burning' to this land. Glastonbury sees the first foundation in England of the new faith that will have the sex instinct cast in shame, birth waters stained with sin. This faith will pin down women and label them either virgin or whore and burn them for good measure.

Flying further on I see that the landscape is subtly moving now, undulating almost imperceptibly, taking the form of a vast woman; a landscape giant, a grass goddess, studded here and there with the blood red poppies of Lammas, symbolic of remembrance of the dead sacrificed to the war engines. Those young men are reborn in the scarlet flowers, literally on the old battlefields in France, and symbolically here.

The goddess is physically manifesting. Of course the goddess of the earth is physical, I think as I see her below. She appears languid, wanton and innocent, luscious and at ease, self-absorbed, and dreaming. She is open to the bliss of the sunshine, thighs shifting, arms stretching as if stirring in sleep. Her grassy head lays on them; her chest is rising and falling. Her lust for the sun is purely instinctual; she will open herself and take her fill on her own terms. She is the goddess unveiled. It is mesmerizing.

The air is buzzing as I swoop lower to see. Now the moving land becomes many women, writhing contentedly around a great earth goddess, a green Electric Ladyland. I realise that the area I am looking down upon now are the places associated with Saint Bride. St Bride hides the pre-Christian goddess Brigid in her mantle. I am hovering over the place known as the Beckery and the suggestively named Bride's Mound, associated with the virgin St Brigid. Bride's Mound has a sacred spring, dry now. A stone marks its place. There was a Saxon chapel dedicated to Mary Magdalene at the Beckery once. The Harlot saint and the Bride shared the well. It's ironic that this well no longer flows when this county gets devastated by floods. The famous Glastonbury blue grail was found in this well of Brigid in the early 20th Century. It was used by three sisters to serve Mass. Heretical and historical, on a quiet mystical level this opened the way for the return of the functioning priestess to these lands.

The solar goddess Brigit is the Lady of Flame. She is a fiery arrow, no passive moon goddess reflecting the sun god's glory. The light of the sun goddess has been dimmed these days.

In her myth Bride is born in a halo of sunlight. Priestesses kept her flame alight across the sea in Ireland, as priestesses had done for the flame goddess Vesta in Rome. Bride-Brigit is goddess of the sun and the earth and the waters. Farm animals, the cows and the sheep, are of her domain. Lambs are born around the time of her Irish festival, Imbolc. She is a fertility goddess. Some say the word means ewe's milk, others say it means first milking. The solar swan and the earthy goose are her birds. In the West of Scotland, the Gaels would declare 'Bride has come' when a serpent came out of a hole in the earth at spring.

I'm seeing the goddess in the landscape with her priestesses, as I look down. The Green Lady, the Verdant Woman. The fields around Bride's Mound were once called The Brides; perhaps the grass priestesses writhing around the goddess of the dream vision represent these.

"Ah, this is all about Bride, but there's something else too" I say, and feel myself being urged to travel on, to turn. Her holy wells are places of mystery, openings to the womb of the earth. The green land is her bed. Bride/Brigid is the fire in the smith's forge, a place of creation. She is midwife, the saline seas her birth waters. Stolen into the Christian faith as the mid-wife of Jesus, and of saints, she continues.

As I look on this tableau of green women, green goddesses, thinking of Bride, a number appears in my vision, between me and the earth, big figures, red with a gold aura sparking urgently, reminding me of the graphics of a slot machine, lighting up when you have won a prize. 156 it flashes. 156. 156!!! I want to continue my night flight, but I am jolted by this screaming number. As I am pulled into wakefulness a voice vibrated inside me as the number continued to flash, 'find me in this land', it said.

156, the number of Babalon, was unexpected among the Somerset Hills. What was Babalon, cipher for wild untamed and un-restrained female sexuality doing at the place of the Virgin Bride?

DOWN TO EARTH

The dream was so dramatic and detailed, it over-shadowed me for days. I decided to answer the Babalon call and quest in the physical landscape to understand better. I kept putting it off, deciding it was either impenetrable or too simple, being just a play on the idea of the Virgin Bride and Holy Whore, two sides of the same coin, sharing a bed. *I am deflowered, yet a virgin; I sanctify and am not sanctified.*

The main symbol of Babalon is the Chalice, a symbol with much significance in the Glastonbury mythos. In Christianity, the Chalice of the communion is a most sacred object. Its hidden symbolism is of the womb of Mary. Less hidden, it is the cup that contained the sacred blood from Christ's death. It is probably based on earlier traditions. Its sacredness is reflected in the anointing of the cup with *chrism,* a substance containing olive oil and balsam that has been consecrated by a bishop. In Glastonbury's environs, the symbol of the chalice is strong and it shapeshifts through the ages. This area is a drowned world in ancestral memory. It lies below sea level, and it was deluged in the 7th millennium BCE. Each hill became an Island. This was Dion Fortune's Atlantean vision of Avalon, where a sacrifice must be made to the goddess of the waters by a sea priestess.

These days the valleys regularly fill with mist, a chalice of the *in*-substantial. This re-claimed land is a primal chalice. At Glastonbury's Chalice well, situated between the tor and the rounded mound of Chalice Hill, red Chalybeate waters pour from a lion's mouth. Just above this is the white spring, with its calchite waters. In a superb flourish of *perichoresis*, the earth goddess releases the white and red springs side by side, leaking out from the up-turned cup, letting us know there is quickening inside, no matter what abominations have taken place above. As the Tor lies within the phoenix sign of Aquarius in the Glastonbury Zodiac, a new age is promised, the phoenix rising and knocking over the cup of the old and spilling the contents out into the world. The magical revival has dawned, and now instead of executions, we see witches and druids drum and dance the songs of life and love above. I am sure there have been many conceptions there. The red and white springs rise and mingle under the chalice of the Tor, symbolic of the Elixir Rubeus, the effluvium of Babalon, the Scarlet Woman, the menstruum of the lunar current, as described by Kenneth Grant. Chalice Hill swells gently, newly pregnant, nurturing, wondering, at rest.

Here is Babalon the Earth Mother in her most fertile sense, the one we meet in the Gnostic Mass.

> *And I believe in one Earth, the Mother of us all, and in one Womb wherein all men are begotten, and wherein they shall rest, Mystery of Mystery, in Her name BABALON.*

And later—

> *Mother of fertility on whose breast lieth water, whose cheek is caressed by air, and in whose heart is the sun's fire, womb of all life, recurring grace of seasons, answer favorably the prayer of labour, and to pastors and husbandmen be thou propitious.*

By the late 12th Century, the poet Robert de Boron merged the legend of the Grail with the Christian myth of Joseph of Arimathea, who uses the chalice of the last supper to catch the remaining drops of Christ's blood as he hung on the cross. Joseph becomes the guardian of the Holy Grail in the Christianized Arthurian legends, and he sends the grail cup to Britain. As the legend evolves it becomes Joseph himself who visits Glastonbury with the sacred chalice.

Katherine Maltwood saw the fish shape of Wearyall Hill in the sign of Pisces, the vessel of the Christian age. Here, she said, Joseph landed by boat, as the hill was still an island, and the sacred blood poured upon the altar of the fish from the grail chalice he brought. Some say the grail chalice was the womb of Mary Magdalene herself, carrying the living child of Christ from the Holy Land. Mary arrived here with Joseph, says the legend. She was despised by the church as a harlot, a fallen woman, and her name was linked to many of the abominations of the Roman Catholic Church in their treatment of women and girls. Modern re-telling now cast her as the anointed one, initiatrix of the secrets of sacred sexuality, and Priestess of Isis to her sacrificed priest of Osiris, the risen god. Her Chalice is the alabaster jar of spikenard, the oil in The Song of Songs. It is said to have the scent of female sexual arousal. Mary Magdalene's presence in Glastonbury is in Magdalene Street, brazen and unashamed in front of the ruined abbey of the martyred abbot.

As the sacred chalice moves into the Arthurian legends, the Knights of the Round Table must quest for this Grail, and they must engage in the play of courtly love and its tantric undertones. A faked burial of King Arthur and Guinevere is placed at Glastonbury Abbey and the pilgrims come and the coffers fill. Guinevere is herself painted as the archetypal Scarlet Woman.

In 2005 I visited Glastonbury around Lammastide to see a friend. I wanted to unravel the dream. Was Babalon manifest in this landscape? We visited Kingweston, a place with Templar associations. It is in the Leo figure in the Glastonbury Zodiac, fitting for the name, a kingly lion in the West. Some twenty years before, the author Andrew Collins had worked the Glastonbury Zodiac as an initiatory journey, and his intuition and research led him to believe that that entrance to the Zodiac in this respect was from the figure of Leo. You start from Leo and 'ride the lion' around the circle of stars reflected in their earthly monuments. I felt that the figure of the lion might shine some light on the Babalon dream. The Leo sun was high in the sky, a year on from my dream, and taking shelter from the heady heat we entered the church. All around us was a frieze of The Fall. My friend, a priestess of the Goddess Brigid, dipped her finger in the holy water stoop and placed it on my forehead, spontaneously, and said 'I anoint you as a priestess of the Magdalene'. She was as surprised as I was, and said she was compelled to do it.

Riding the lion onwards, he takes us to the sign of Virgo, the virgin. If he is the king, there are signs that she is a queen. Swans, the royal birds, swim in the flooded fields and roads.

The Virgo effigy stands slightly aloof from Leo. She has the effect of being independent of the other signs of the zodiac. She bears the name Mother Cary, as the River Cary delineates much of her shape. To some she is the Caileach, the hag of winter. Maybe she becomes so after summer, but she has her fertile time, with baby, with corn. The landscape effigy of Mother Cary appears to hold out a sheaf of corn, offering the harvest to all. She is like a corn dolly in the land. The Lion king comes to her. She is fecund. She becomes pregnant and she gives birth to the golden harvest. She is virgin in the sense of an independent woman. Although she is not a secret, Cary does not make access easy. We drive round and round, following the signs, literal and symbolic, but keep getting lost. She is shorn of corn

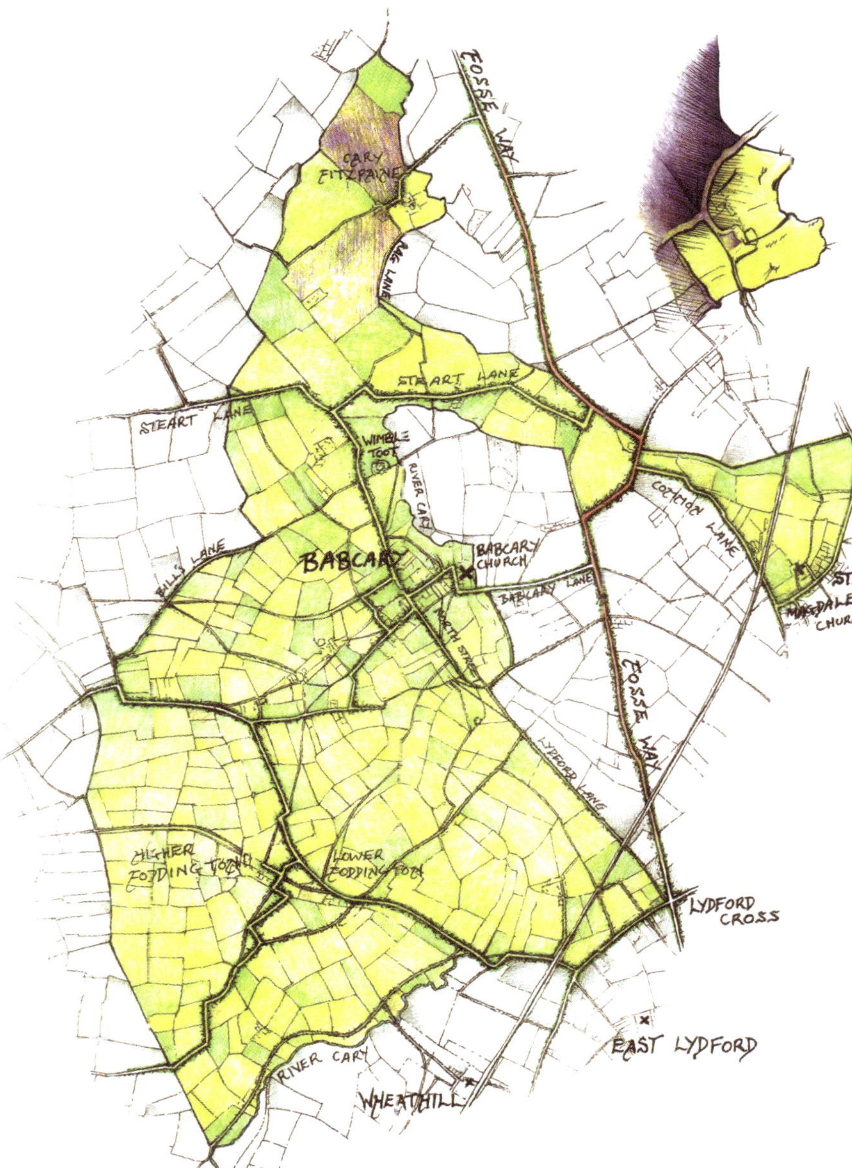

Image courtesy Yuri Leitch.

now the harvest is in, but she is beautiful unveiled. Eventually we prove ourselves worthy and she reveals the way to her sacred places. In Babcary lies her pregnant belly—*babe carry*—the virgin must protect the unborn child. The nipple of her effigy is at a Bronze Age barrow called Wimble Toot. The track to this place is blocked off but there is a path for seekers to find. John Wadsworth who researches the Glastonbury Zodiac, says

> *For she sits apart from the other signs, somewhat detached, 'beyond the pale' (pale being an old word for fence); a woman whose unashamed sexuality is anathema to the patriarchal religious structures that she inevitably subverts. She is the fallen woman of Christianity, and we find the only church in the Zodiac dedicated to Mary Magdalene on Virgo's wheatsheaf at Keinton Mandeville. We may envisage her also as Magdalene's Arthurian counterpart Guinevere, furthest from Avalon yet nearest to Camelot, fiercely guarding the integrity of the feminine principle in our round table landscape.*

WALKING ON THE WATERS

> *Upon earth she is ever-fecund; heaven she is ever Virgin.*

Standing on Wearyall Hill, in Pisces, where the chalice arrived in legend, I cast about for the next place to visit. There are fantastic views from the top over the Somerset Levels to the west. To the east lie Chalice Hill and the dominating Tor. To the northwest are Brean Down and Brent Knoll, the terrain on which Dion Fortune's initiatory novel The Sea Priestess is based. Much of the area around the Glastonbury environs is neither land nor water, it is the magical in-between. Ancient Yew tracks have been found, the sweet tracks across the marshes and the wetlands of Meare. One walks on boards as the waterfowl nest and coo around. Like the Temperance card and the Star card of the Tarot, one foot can be in water and the other on land. The women on both cards pour from their chalices, one naked, one chaste. Both guide. Babalon and Bride?

Sitting by the sea and contemplating the dream meaning, much of the ideas below were formed. This place of the Sea Priestess was not an easy place to be. The Sea Priestess, Vivienne le Fay Morgan, is an initiator of men to the goddess, an awakener of their sexuality, albeit with British under-statement and restraint. Dion doesn't want the net curtains twitching. The name Morgan le Fey is borrowed from the Lady of the Lake in the

Arthurian legends, the lady who chooses who will be king. She is in charge of bestowing and restoring his sword. This seemed promising. Brent Knoll is called Bell Knoll in the book and is where the magic starts. The protagonist describes the headland Bel Head as a place of the sun god (Baal Head) where there had once been bel-fires. It was

> *Shaped like a couchant lion, the place with his tail to the sea and the farm lay between its paws, getting what shelter it might from the westerly gales. The slope that led to the lion's chest had at some time been terraced... Miss Morgan remarked at once on the lion-form, and pointing to the terraces between its paws said 'that was where they grew their vines.' It had been used as a temple.*

It was with some trepidation that I entered the realm of the Sea Priestess in my Babalon search. Fortune's goddess demands sacrifice.

Dion Fortune has the reader and protagonist drawn towards a great goddess by the mysterious priestess, a representative of the physical landscape and the sea and the ancient Atlantean legends of the place. The Priestess says

> *Those who adore Isis of Nature adore her as Hathor with the horns upon her brow, but those who adore the celestial Isis know her as Levanah, the Moon. She is the great deep whence life arose, she is the ancient and forgotten things wherein our roots are cast. Upon earth she is ever-fecund; in heaven she is ever Virgin. She is the mistress of the tides that flow and ebb and ebb and flow and never cease. These things are the keys of her mystery, known only to the initiated.*

Is the goddess this priestess serves leading closer to the Babalon in my dream? Here she is Magna Mata, Matter, the Great Mother, who takes on the masks of Isis, the sexual initiator of Osiris, and Hathor, of love and dance. Rhea is the fierce mother, honoured with raucous chants and dances and crashing symbols. Binah is the bitter sea, the womb, and understanding and contemplation. Ge is the personification of the earth. She awakens the latent sexuality, if Dion would only let go of her reins. Dion's reins do not represent *the passion which unites them*, her's are those of caution, over anxious that liberated woman may show full expression of the sexual impulse, but like the Scarlet Woman, she does want to stir something in the man, his 'sun upon earth.'

We read how men were given in sacrifice to the lust of the sea, tied to rocks in a cave below the lion rock, every part of them devoured by the crashing waves of the sea goddess. Euphemism abounds to protect the uninitiated. Ultimately the sea priestess sacrifices herself to save these drowned lands from the waters, caught up in a cycle of incarnation that she is trapped in as initiator. This is not a goddess for our time. This is not a liberating goddess. Even those who serve her well can be sacrificed. This is a goddess of the Old Aeon. The priestess may take the lead, but the goddess here is very much of Fortune's times (era), for she says

> *Isis of Nature awaiteh the coming of her Lord the Sun. She calls him, she draws him from the place of the dead, the kingdom of Amenti, where all things are forgotten, and he comes to her in his boat of millions of years, and the earth grows green with the springing grain. For the desire of Osiris answereth into the call of Isis. And so it will be in the hearts of men, for thus the gods have formed them. Who soeth denieth this is abhorred by the gods.*

In *Freedom is a Two Edged Sword*, Jack Parsons says

> *Among the ancient Hebrews the name of god was...IHVH. This is perhaps the most magnificent formula ever devised for symbolizing at once the whole process of nature and the highest secrets of magic. Yod symbolizes God, as the primal father, the solar-phallic creative will, or fire. He symbolizes god as the mother, the feminine generative principle, the passive will, or water. Vau symbolizes God as the sun, the male child of the father and mother, the will to go, air. He final symbolizes god as the daughter, Babalon, She who is to come, earth, the virgin who unites with the father, stimulates him to reactivity, and begins the generative process all over again. The cycle is closed, the process is eternal, and contains within itself the seeds of all possibility.*

Like the Sea Priestess and her endless incarnations, Parson's idea is that the feminine principle is passive, there to serve the solar-phallic creative will, and 'the cycle is closed'. What's liberating about being stuck in a cycle? Is their sexually unrestrained Scarlet Woman only to serve their desires? The doctrine of the wheel of Karma may be an endless cycle, but each turn of the wheel brings change. Parsons sexual mysteries chime well with that of the Roman Catholic Church. Is the sex therapist Priestess of Dion Fortune and the Babalon imagined by Crowley helpful to modern women and men? Few magicians today have experience of the stifling world before the late 1960s, let alone know the Book of Revelation and the oppressive religion of Crowley's mother. The sexual repression of the past, of the church, reflected in society became a fulcrum for the re-emergence of Babalon. In the west there is a shifting of gender and sexuality occurring, a great freedom, hard won and still being fought for and claimed. How does Babalon as envisaged by Parsons serve them? Why should they serve her?

BABALON BOUND

BABALON, as the Great Mother, represents MATTER, a word which is derived from the Latin word for Mother. She is the physical mother of each of us, the one who provided us with material flesh to clothe our naked spirits; She is the Archetypal Mother, the Great Yoni, the Womb of all that lives through the flowing of Blood; She is the Great Sea, the Divine Blood itself which cloaks the World and which courses through our veins; and She is Mother Earth, the Womb of All Life that we know.

The revival of the earth goddess is well underway. She is revered and dishonored at the same time, as is the case with women. Babalon as Matter, the *Magna Mata*, the ever-fertilising land, lays fracked, poked and drilled for black fluid now more precious than the gold she was robbed of as Ishtar. Her waters have a half life only vampires can dream of, and her hair, the trees of eternity, roughly shorn, the punishment for the harlot of the old aeon. Ripped out for roads and palm oil. The earth goddess is stripped bare in the market square. Women in the developing world have never had it so bad, as the neo-pagans here dance round the maypole.

> *The concept contained within Babalon is that of the mystical ideal, the quest to become one with all.*

Like starry Ishtar, Babalon, has had her jewels and her bracelets ripped from her. Ishtar has had her robes torn as she is forced to descend through the seven gates to be tortured by her sister self. Virgin or Whore, Maiden or Mother. Woman, Hate Thyself. Babalon may deny no one, and this may be eternal, but how much more should she take? The wells, symbols of the sacred feminine, are dry, but the river banks have burst. The goddess is revered more than ever, yet seems stuck in her dungeon. Unrestrained female sexuality is quickly ring-fenced. Even those who proclaim her do this. The Arthurian Knights must quest for the grail, follow the rose petals, go through ordeals, serve the Grail, and understand it. When they have found her, they put the goddess in a virtual chastity belt.

Moving through the ages, there are orders formed and lodges, fetishising this principle into something for the secret and the few, attainable only by studying arcane ways. The goddess is on the pedestal again, the chalice upturned to make the pillar. We commodify her. We mystify the natural. We must climb an initiatory and hierarchical ladder to know what is natural. Wild female sexuality is given the title Babalon, but she is there title or not. Her earthly priestesses are given a title, Scarlet women, and thus categorized, the title that can be given and taken; she is rudely appointed!

> *Seven eunuchs guard Her with drawn swords; No Man may come nigh unto Her.*

Babalon represents the liberated woman and the full expression of the sexual impulse. So why *take* the liberty? Let's break her chains and oaths and restore her bracelets and rings, and let her walk out into the world. She does not need a phalanx of body-guards, be they eunuchs, Templars or impotent kings. She doesn't need to be a guarded secret. She can be free of the strip-searching, the strip-mining, the leering. *Let to her all power be given.* Babalon is for all who want her. Let her be un-staked from the Piscean Age, let *'the Lion know not where she walks'*, unless she wants him to.

DREAM MATA

What was she showing me in this landscape? The Earth is symbolic of the female generative force, the sun of Brigid the female solar power, fertilising, ripening, her champion Cary in Virgo, ever conceiving and pregnant through the wheel of the year. The sexual earth, all giving, our alpha and omega.

Traversing the Zodiac full circle, if not by a circular route, and visiting all the places seen from above in the dream-flight, it was in the remote quiet beauty of Virgo where I found her best in the land and answered her request. This representation of the Goddess is self-possessed and contented, the untrampled goddess, turning through the seasons of maiden, mother, and crone, and rebirth, offering her wheatsheaf-chalice freely. I return each summer, and take her roses. The Earth is our mother, the earth gives us all. She gives and gives and denies no one. We must give all back. She will take us all as piles of dust eventually. The earth *is* fortitude. The Earth is our mother, we must take care of her.

Babalon Rising:

JACK PARSONS' WITCHCRAFT PROPHECY

Erik Davis

IN THE FORTY YEARS or so following the death of John Whiteside Parsons in 1952, his name—Jack Parsons from here on out—circulated principally among magic folk, critics of Scientology, and historians of modern rocketry. In the new century, however, the tale of the SoCal rocket scientist-cum-sex magician has proven a hot commodity, told and retold in a series of articles, biographies, graphic novels, movie scripts, and reality TV shows that have transformed Parsons into one of the most storied figures in the history of American occulture. The superficial reasons are easy to see: with its charismatic blend of sex, sorcery, technology and death, Parsons' story haunts a dark crossroads of the Southern California mindscape, scrawling a prophetic glyph in the wet pavement of postwar America. Indeed, his tale is so outrageous that if it did not exist, it would need—as they say—to be invented. But if it *were* invented—that is, if his life were presented as the fiction it in so many ways resembles—it would be hard to believe, even as a fiction. The narrative would seem overly contrived, at once too pulp and too poetic, too rich with allegorical synchronicity to stage the necessary suspension of disbelief.

In this essay, I want to explore an unremarked aspect of Jack Parsons' life and thought, what I will call his *magickal feminism*. In his 1946 text *Free-*

dom is a Two-Edged Sword, Parsons issued a call for women to take up the spiritual, sexual, and political sword—a cry for female autonomy that also eerily anticipated the militant witchcraft that would find historical expression in California over twenty years later. Before we sketch these links, however, we need a quick review of his extraordinary life.

Parsons was born in Pasadena in 1914 and raised in privilege by his mother and grandparents, although the family later fell on hard times. A pampered and bookish child, Jack attempted to conjure up the devil at age thirteen and balked in terror at his apparent success. He also became interested in chemistry and rocketry, then largely the province of boys who, like Parsons, consumed pulp science-fiction magazines like *Amazing Stories*. Today, when we say that something "isn't rocket science," we forget that in the early 1930s, few prominent scientists took space rocketry seriously at all. This didn't stop Parsons, who built model rockets with his pal Ed Forman, and later hooked up with a Caltech student named Frank Molina, who in turn helped bring their experiments with rocket propulsion under the guidance of the legendary Caltech professor Theodore von Kármán. Setting up in the Arroyo Seco, just above the Devil's Gate dam, the team began experimenting with stationary rockets, and eventually moved their tests to the Caltech campus itself—at least until a few wayward explosions forced the group, now labeled the "suicide squad", to return to the Arroyo. After the group scored some successes useful for the war effort, Parsons made, in the summer of 1942, his most significant technical breakthrough: the creation of a solid fuel dubbed GALCIT-53, whose subsequent development would lead directly to the Minutemen and Polaris missiles of the postwar era. In the forties, Parsons and Forman started the Aerojet Corporation, while also co-founding the Jet Propulsion Laboratory with Molina and others.

Parsons had managed to transform a reckless hobby into a profitable and cutting-edge technology, but the brazen and confident fellow was equally devoted to his magickal career during these years. Parsons was already familiar with the rudiments of magical practice when he came across a copy of Crowley's *Konx om Pax* on the shelves of a Pasadena used car dealer in 1938. Inspired, Parsons then visited the Agape Lodge No. 2 in Hollywood, which at that moment was the only functioning lodge of the Ordo Templi Orientis. Jack and his wife Helen were initiated in 1941 under Wilfred Smith, and by 1943 the charismatic Parsons, who initially impressed Crowley as the perfect person to usher Thelema into a new era, became head of the lodge. At the same time, Crowley and others in the lodge were concerned about Parsons' dark-side dabbling in "black magic", "voodoo", and "witchcraft", all of which were seen as excessively dark or crude magical currents at the time (these reactions—from Crowley no less!—remind us as well of how much the boundaries of "proper" occult practice would change during the coming decades). Parsons' wildness also dictated the social character of the so-called "Parsonage": the redwood Pasadena mansion at 1003 South Orange Grove Ave. that he and Helen transformed into a bohemian rooming house that also served as the new home of the lodge.

Parsons continued to read the pulps, and attended meetings of the Los Angeles Science Fiction Society. Here he befriended Robert Heinlein, Ray Bradbury, and the redhead L. Ron Hubbard, whom Parsons described to Crowley as "the most Thelemic person I have ever met." In 1946, Parsons invited Hubbard to play the role of scryer in the Babalon Working, perhaps the single most storied rite in the history of American occultism. As we will explore later in this essay, Babalon is a polyvalent archetype within Thelema, at once symbolizing the Earth Mother, the supernal initiatrix beyond the Abyss, and a practical current of sexual mysticism embodied in the office known as the Scarlet Woman. Parsons believed that the energy of Babalon was the balance and complement to the explosive violence that characterized the Aeon of Horus, and as such had a leading role to play in the historical era that was just beginning to dawn.

The first part of Parsons' ritual, designed to evoke an "Elemental," resulted, in Parsons' mind at least, with the relatively synchronistic appearance at his home of the striking redhead Marjorie Cameron, his next and last great love and sex magic partner. Later, in February 1946, alone beneath the two power lines whose crossing framed his favorite power spot in the Mojave, Parsons evoked Babalon, who appeared before him and commanded him to write down *Liber 49*—a bold and, it must be said, resoundingly unsuccessful attempt to add a fourth chapter to Crowley's *Book of the Law*. As Michael Staley argued in *Starfire*, "In terms of content, level of inspiration, and style, *Liber 49* is nothing like *The Book of the Law*; and on this basis alone, the claim can be looked at askance."[1] More recently, Peter Grey has described Parsons' text as "a poor production with some howlingly bad lines only redeemed by a few shots of brilliant blood red clarity."[2]

1 Michael Staley, "Beloved of Babalon," in Michael Staley, ed., *Ecpyrosis: The Best of Starfire Vol 1*, (London: Starfire Publishing Ltd, 2010), 92.

2 Peter Grey, *The Red Goddess* (London: Scarlet Imprint, Summer Solstice 2008), 163.

The oddities of Parsons' *Book of Babalon*, an incomplete manuscript that contains *Liber 49* and other texts, have contributed to the somewhat uneasy relationship many Thelemites have with Parsons' magical legacy. Though Crowley was grooming Parsons to succeed him, Master Therion thought the Babalon Working was ridiculous. He also grew disenchanted with Parsons' erratic emotionality and—rather ironically—his erotic obsessions. William Breeze, currently the Frater Superior of the O.T.O., also does not withhold criticisms of Parsons, accurately noting that "Jack had tried to do with magick what he successfully pulled off with chemistry and rocket science: reading beyond his level of experience, skipping preliminaries, bootstrapping himself, rewriting the rules to suit himself."[3] For Breeze, Parsons was ultimately a "failed" magician—a failure that also proved disastrous for the institution of Thelema in the immediate postwar period. The loyal Smith had been knocked aside to make way for Parsons, but, by the end of 1946, Parsons turned his back on the O.T.O., selling the Parsonage and resigning as head of the lodge.

Over the next six years, Parsons' career, love life, and state of mind grew increasingly erratic even as he plunged into a solo magickal path. He wrote a few powerful texts, took the oath of Magister Templi before his old mentor Smith, and began to develop a new and more "modern" magical religion freed of the "claptrap" of the O.T.O., a path that he called "the Witchcraft." Because of his associations with political radicals and his hedonistic lifestyle, Parsons was eventually barred from the military-industrial complex he helped to build, and earned his keep pumping gas and making explosive effects for Hollywood. In June 1952, a day before moving to Mexico with Cameron, he was horrifically maimed from an apparently accidental explosion in his home laboratory. He died a few hours later. Upon hearing the news, his mother killed herself, and Cameron plunged into an agonizing grief that in some sense never left her.

Back in the pivotal year of 1946, Parsons had written "Freedom is a Two-Edged Sword", a remarkable proto-libertarian essay whose political, religious, and erotic concerns were inspired in part by Crowley's recently issued "Liber OZ" and in part by Parsons' growing spleen at America. In the final section, "The Woman Girt with a Sword", Parsons presents a vision of a militantly empowered feminist witchcraft that was radical for its time and remarkably prescient. Castigating the religion of Jehovah as a

3 William Breeze, "Foreword," in John W. Parsons and Marjorie Cameron, *Songs for the Witch Woman* (London: Fulgur, 2014), 11.

"tyrannical and superstitious patriarchy" that treats females as "an inferior animal," Parsons bemoans the contemporary fate of woman. "How long have you served in chains, a slave to the lust of pigs and the guilt of pigs?" He ascribes this servitude to women's love of males, whom he characterizes as "bewildered frightened children, playing games against the dark." Pessimistic about men's politics and men's science, Parsons looks back fondly on the era before patriarchy, a romantic nostalgia that would not enter popular consciousness until the 1970s: "It is not a matriarchy as we imagine it—a rule of clubwomen, or frustrated chickens. It is an equality. The woman is the priestess; in her reposes the mystery. She is the mother, brooding yet tender; the lover, at once passionate and aloof; the wife, revered and cherished. She is the witch woman."

To be sure, Parsons' anti-patriarchal song of praise would probably not pass full muster with many feminists today, his vision being at once heterosexist, essentialist, and, in a pulp fantasy sort of way, slightly cheesy. In Parsons' spiritual mythology, man is the hero, with woman the hierophant who compels man to make himself magically worthy of her fecund mysteries, which are still tied to male potential. "The future is with you. For you are the mother of the new race, the redeemer and lover of the new men, the men who shall be free." That said, Parson's evocation remains remarkable for its militancy: "Come back, woman, come back to us again!...Witch woman, out of the ashes of the stake, rise again!...Be cunning, oh woman; be wise, be subtle, be merciless."

A similar pivoting marks Parsons' vision of liberated female eros. Critiquing the "frigid woman," he cries "Go to the mountains and the oceans and the forest, go naked in the summertime, that you may regain the old joy, and love gladly and freely under the stars." This might seem like a stereotypical male Dionysian fantasy, but Parsons' next lines more surprisingly anticipate the body image critiques and celebratory consciousness raising that would come to characterize the many feminist currents of the future. "But the body is not beautiful? Here is a secret. The body is molded by the mind. Embrace fear, repression, hate; then look upon the body—or rather do not look upon it. But go free; love joyously, without restraint; run naked a little. Then watch the cheeks flush; see the breasts swell—the supple contours, the flowing rhythm."[4] He ends the essay with a martial evocation of Babalon, "girt with the sword of freedom," a figure

4 These quotations are from John Whiteside Parsons, *Freedom is a Two-Edged Sword: Essays* (Las Vegas: Falcon Press, 1989), 39–44.

whose incarnation into political reality he also linked in a contemporaneous essay to women's "demand for increased freedom, the rejection of both the tyrannical husband and the child lover, [and] the increase of feminine polygamy and lesbianism."[5]

Archetypal assemblages arise and echo through history in nonlinear patterns of resonance. Parson's vision of a gynocentric, erotically libertarian, and explicitly martial and anti-patriarchal proto-witchcraft began developing almost ten years before Gerald Gardner's publication of the considerably tamer *Witchcraft Today* in 1954, and over twenty years before the appearance of the New York City feminist group WITCH, an acronym that stood, at least in some accounts, for "Women's International Terrorist Conspiracy from Hell." Formed in Halloween 1968, WITCH was inspired by the wacky Movement activism of the Yippies, and was less focused on the specifically feminist issues that would soon come to the fore in radical women circles. In Cynthia Eller's words, "These first feminist witches did not gather to worship nature, but to crush the patriarchy, and to do so in witty, flamboyant, and theatrical ways."[6] In their 1968 manifesto, WITCH claimed that "witches and gypsies were the original guerillas and resistance fighters against oppression—particularly the oppression of women... Witches have always been women who dared to be: groovy, courageous, aggressive, intelligent, nonconformist, explorative, curious, independent, sexually liberated, revolutionary."[7] Writing a decade later, the feminist theorist Mary Daly would strike a similar tone in her "gyn/ecological" work of "re-calling/re-membering/re-claiming our Witches' power to cast spells, to charm, to overcome prestige with prestidigitation, to cast glamours, to employ occult grammar, to enthrall, to bewitch."[8] This reclamation included the power not only to seduce and enjoy, but to focus and direct militant aggression. In *Pure Lust*, Daly writes that "The Metamorphosing Sage rides her Rage. It is her broom, her Fire-breathing, winged mare...Rage is not a 'stage.' It is not something to be gotten over. It is transformative, focusing Force."[9]

5 *Freedom is a Two-Edged Sword*, 91.

6 Cynthia Eller, *Living in the Lap of the Goddess: the Feminist Spirituality Movement in America* (New York: Crossroad, 1993), 53.

7 Ibid.

8 Mary Daly, *Gyn/Ecology: the Metaethics of Radical Feminism* (Boston: Beacon, 1978), 318.

9 Mary Daly, *Pure Lust: Elemental Feminist Philosophy* (Boston: Beacon, 1984), 375.

From the perspective of magical praxis, however, it is fair to say that the militant witch was more pose than potion within radical feminism. "By the late 1970s," Ronald Hutton notes, "witchcraft had become a symbol without a practice in most feminism."[10] However, while the second-wave feminism of the seventies focused on a host of concrete political goals, the practice of "consciousness raising" also transformed the inner life of many feminists. This, coupled with the opening to lesbianism and changing sexual roles, broadened the focus for many feminists towards the energetic features and potentials of the liberated female body. This "essentialism" developed into a loosely focused feminist spirituality that inevitably began to feed and comingle with popular witchcraft. In 1978, the Pagan historian Margot Adler noted that some Wiccan practitioners viewed the term *witch* "as a word to be reclaimed, much as militant lesbians have reclaimed the word *dyke*."[11] In other words, rather than rewrite the figure of the witch into a gentle New Age healer, many Wiccans drew productive energy from the very negativity that charged and animated the archetype.

The unambiguous origin of radical feminist witchcraft lies in Southern California, where Zsuzsanna Budapest, a hereditary witch from Hungary who moved to Los Angeles in 1970, founded the women-only Susan B. Anthony Coven no. 1 in 1971. Radically detuning the masculine/feminine polarity that structured Gardnerian Wiccan, Budapest saw spiritual work as continuous with the discourse and militant practice of radical feminism and particularly lesbian separatism. Her manifesto states that "We believe that just as it is time to fight for the right to control our bodies, it is also time to fight for our sweet womon [sic] souls." This spiritual militancy employed a good deal of pragmatic kitchen witchery that resembled American rootwork more than the more anodyne ritualism of some Pagan witchcraft. The coven's "Anti-rape squad" publicly shamed male rapists, and ushered victimized women through the legal process by teaming them up with butch dykes who would keep aggressive cops at bay. Once the rapist was apprehended, a black candle in the shape of a penis would be ritually burned. "A witch who cannot hex cannot heal," Budapest wrote. "Cupcakism, turning the other cheek, is not for witches."[12] Though Budapest's most famous student, Starhawk, offered a kinder, gentler, and more inclu-

10 Ronald Hutton, *The Triumph of the Moon* (New York: Oxford, 1999), 344.

11 Margot Adler, *Drawing Down the Moon,* (New York: Viking Press, 1979), 42.

12 Z. Budapest, *The Holy Book of Women's Mysteries* (Berkeley, CA: Wingbow Press, 1989), 2, 48.

sive model of witchcraft activism, she too would sometimes articulate an aggressive militancy that stands out against the more tepid New Age and ecumenical visions of spiritual feminism. "So-called negative emotion—anger—is valued ...as a sign that something is wrong and that action needs to be taken," she wrote in the 1979 collection *Womanspirit Rising*. "Witches prefer to handle anger by taking action and making changes rather than by detaching ourselves from our feelings in order to reach some nebulous, 'higher' state."[13]

None of the feminist witches from the seventies are likely to have read Parsons, and none of them, it should be stressed, needed his peculiar prophecy. That said, I don't believe it is an accident that militant witchcraft arises most vociferously in Los Angeles, whose powerful magical currents draw from decades of local Thelemic practice, and the corresponding presence of the Babalon current so brazenly established by Parsons. Here I am using the term "currents" not only in the sense familiar to esoteric scholars, in which a "current" is a historically identifiable but constantly developing mode of discourse and practice. I am also interested in a more haunted and energetic sense of current as a kind of psycho-geographical charge. So while there are certainly direct connections between Parsons and the Los Angeles magical culture of the sixties and seventies, principally through the influence of the amazing Marjorie Cameron, we don't need to speculate about such points of contact to understand the intertwining of times within a particular nexus of space. In light of what comes later, we can also follow the flow backwards—upstream so to speak—and ask questions of emergence that resonate with figures of later manifestation. Here in particular I would like to return to Parsons and consider the question: From what gleamings did Parsons derive his vision of the self-empowered feminist witch? Though we can never nail down the dense psycho-dynamics of such a singular soul as it journeys through the labyrinths of archetype, I think we can locate three seedbeds for Parsons' prophetic vision: pulp literature, the Thelemic lore of Babalon, and Parson's own unusual sexual ethics.

13 Starhawk, "Witchcraft and Women's Culture", in Carol Christ and Judith Plaskow, eds, *Womanspirit Rising* (San Francisco: Harper & Rowe, 1979), 264.

Parsons was a life-long lover of fantastic literature, weird tales, and science fiction, material that undoubtedly fed his magick, his science, and his erotic imagination. Though he does not to my knowledge mention the book, as a youth Parsons almost certainly read Rider Haggard's 1886 novel *She*, the mega-selling *Star Wars* of Victorian fantasy adventures. The novel's eponymous and sometimes vengeful heroine, Ayesha or She-Who-Must-Be-Obeyed, is a white queen of an African tribe who espouses a savage and Nietzschean social Darwinism. For Ayesha, all human motives are reduced to sex, wealth, and power. "Our life is one long crime", she says. "We destroy that we may live."[14] Haggard's book can be seen in some ways as an interrogation of Victorian sexual values, though an only partially subversive one—for every kink there is a correspondingly smooth accommodation. For example, the tribal people first encountered by the British explorers invert the normal rules of courtship by displaying aggressive female come-ons. As Haggard critic Norman Etherington noted, the author "appears to endorse simultaneously the feminist proposition that women should be given more choice in romance and the conventional man's desire for women who will fulfill his sexual fantasies without prompting."[15] Ayesha, an independent and murderously cruel leader, features a similar ambivalence, for after falling in love with the explorer Leo, she grows submissive, and pledges to love, honor, and obey him. That said, the character Ayesha carved a radical, even revolutionary archetype into fantastic literature, a woman at once violent, exotic, and desirably in command. Freud was fascinated by the character, and Jung believed she embodied the anima, the unattainable ideal female whose pursuit through the labyrinth of projection had destroyed many a male. Etherington also presents a psychoanalytic argument, concluding that Ayesha ultimately represents "the desired but unattainable mother."

Parsons certainly had a close and curious relationship with his mother, but we will leave such speculations aside in light of a far more important literary influence on his adult fantasies: Jack Williamson's excellent 1940 short story (and later novel) *Darker Than You Think*, one of Parsons' favorite fictions. An imaginative reflection of the sexually repressed Williamson's own Freudian analysis at the Meninger Institute, the horror story concerns the journalist Will Barbee's embroilment with the confident and charis-

14 H. Rider Haggard, Norman Etherington, ed., *The Annotated She* (Bloomington, Indianapolis: Indiana University Press, 1991), 136.

15 *The Annotated She*, xxx.

matic red-head April Bell. Bell's "lithe free grace", it turns out, depends on her actually being a werewolf bitch, a shape-shifter who seduces Bardee into her ancient witch cult through the Lovecraftian route of dream. In one dream, Bardee is changed into a saber-tooth "were-tiger" while Bell remains in her human form: "nude and white and beautiful, her red hair streaming in the wind", she *mounts him*. Though radiating the cruel ambivalence of a film noir femme fatale, April is at the same time magnetic and liberated, and the psychoanalytic process represented by Barbee's seduction by this aggressive and sexually amoral woman is a threatening but ultimately positive vanquishing of repression. The last line of the novel describes Barbee, back in wolf form, as he "picked up her exciting scent, and followed her into the shadows."[16] In the words of the psycho-biographer Alan Elms, the ultimate fate of "Will" in the story represents a "triumph of id over superego".[17] Though the randy and psychoanalytically informed Parsons needed no such erotic encouragement, the figure of the threatening, darkly erotic, and supernatural anima figure certainly informs his aggressive woman girt with a sword.

If pulp fiction represents a "low magic" of the psycho-sexual imagination, we can turn to Thelema, and especially the blood-red radiance emanating from Babalon, to find more numinous—though still highly erotic—exemplars of magickal female power. The nature and function of Babalon in Crowley's magickal imagination and system of practice is a matter most recondite, and I trust other contributors of this volume to lead us through this arcana. Here I simply want to offer the uncontroversial assertation that Parsons' transformation of the Babalon current both carries on and significantly reframes Crowley's powerful re-imagination of the Biblical figure. That said, I also think it is important to respect the distinction that Carl Abrahamsson makes between Babalon as archetype and Babalon as a magical formula, two features that I shall briefly address in turn.[18]

Though Crowley's vision of Babalon directly emerges from the scarlet images and purple prose embedded in *The Book of the Law*, we should begin with the apocalypse that closes the New Testament. The Babylon who appears in *Revelation* is, of course, the personification of a place: the

16 Jack Williamson, *Darker Than You Think* (New York: Garland, 1975), 162, 282.

17 Alan C. Elms, *Uncovering Lives: the Uneasy Alliance of Biography and Psychology* (New York: Oxford University Press, 1994), 129.

18 See Carl Abrahamsson "Babalon", in Carl Abrahamsson, *Reasonances 2000–2013* (Scarlet Imprint, 2014), 59–68.

ancient city of Jewish exile that was itself almost certainly a cipher for the more present hegemony of Rome. As such, she incarnates the *city as such*, whose wanton luxury is rendered all the more corrosive through its whorish proximity to kings and rulers. Significantly, though she rides the sovereign beast, Babalon herself does not reign, but rather prostitutes herself to power. In the Enochian magic of John Dee, which forms the matrix of Thelema's scarlet Lady, "Babalon" remains a signifier of wickedness and harlotry. But in the sort of inverted affirmation we saw above, whereby derogatory terms like "dyke" and "witch" are validated and extolled, Crowley's visionary encounter with Babalon in *The Vision and the Voice* turns this sluttishness on its head.

In the 12th Aethyr, Crowley encounters a charioteer whose ruddy cup echoes the golden cup "full of abominations and filthiness" that Babylon enjoys in *Revelation*. Here the cup itself is full of blood, an intoxicating wine that Crowley somewhat counter-intuitively names "compassion." The logic, however, is compelling, even brilliant. The Mystery of wanton Babalon is precisely her selflessness: "she hath yielded up herself to everything that liveth, and hath become a partaker in its mystery. And because she hath made herself the servant of each, therefore is she become the mistress of all." Here the Biblical rejection of harlotry is reclaimed as the saint's infinite generosity, not unlike the utopian phalanxes of Charles Fourier, whose "sexual philanthropy" ensured that pleasure was distributed even to the infirm, the repulsive, and the kinky. However, despite her position atop the Beast, Babalon is far from a commanding figure; indeed, it is precisely her "weakness" that "hath subdued their strength." This is not the "woman girt with a sword" announced by Ra-Hoor-Khuit in the third book of *Liber Legis*, a figure who, it must be emphasized, is not identified with the "Scarlet Concubine" we meet a few lines later. Even as the Lady of the City of Pyramids, the Babalon we meet in *Liber 418* is not martial.

Things become spicier when we turn to the Babalon who becomes the central topos for Crowley's vision of sexual mysticism. In *Liber Cheth*, her ruddy cup becomes at once the Holy Graal and the sacred orifice into which the magician expends himself in an act of radical self-abnegation that catalyzes an erotic *nigredo*: "Then shall thy brain be dumb, and thy heart beat no more, and all thy life shall go from thee; and thou shalt be cast out upon the midden, and the birds of the air shall feast upon thy flesh, and thy bones shall whiten in the sun." Babalon's acolytes are, in a sense, called to emulate her own compassionate abjection, a submission that, to speak in less covert sexual terms, introduces a distinct element of masochism to the scenario. The *chela* here is urged to "slay thyself in the fervour of thine abandonment unto Our Lady." At the same time, it is still the supplicant's "quenchless lust" that drives the scene, and not Babalon's own desire. In *Liber Aleph,* a later text, Babalon's role as magickal "top" comes through more boldly, as she "plieth Her Scourge upon me, even upon me, To Mega Therion, to compel me to Creation and to Destruction..." Once again, though, Babalon remains a supernal Mother, albeit an incestuous and drunken one, "wallowing in Joy." There is no sword in sight.

Within Crowley's own practice of sexual magick, the Babalon current was "stepped down" into the office of the Scarlet Woman, whose characterization in the third chapter of *The Book of the Law* of course already provided a typology for Babalon. We need only recall Leah Hirsig's oath to recall the continuity of this office and shameless Babalon: "I will work the way of wickedness, I will kill my heart, I will be loud and adulterous, I will be covered with jewels and rich garments, I will be shameless before all men, I for token thereof will freely prostitute my body to the lusts of each and every Living Creature that shall desire it."[19] The Scarlet Woman incarnated the pride, luxury and sacred sluttishness of Crowley's supernal archetype, while providing the Beast with the concrete opportunity to continue transgressing the Christian taboos that in some sense he never could (or wanted to) abandon.

As with many intense and transgressive sexual relationships, Crowley's treatment of Hirsig and his other Scarlet Women present a complicated and not always pretty picture. The stress of trying to uphold your spiritual mentor's grandiose spiritual and sexual projections should not be underestimated. As Carl Abrahamsson delicately puts it, "For many of these women, I'm sure the concept [of Babalon] created great challenges."[20] Moreover, as the scholar Hugh Urban suggests in his well-informed if one-dimensional account of Crowley in his *Magia Sexualis*, "Crowley seems to have regarded women as rather limited and ultimately expendable companions in spiritual practice".[21] Similar critiques have been directed towards traditional Tibetan tantric practice, of course, and the origin of both complaints remains what can only be called the patriarchal stain. Urban turns to *Liber C vel Azoth*, a practical text of heterosexual magick linked

19 Cited in Abrahamsson, op cit., 64–65.

20 Ibid, 64.

21 Hugh Urban, *Magia Sexualis: Sex, Magic, and Liberation in Modern Western Esotericism,* (Berkeley: University of California Press, 2006), 133.

to the 9th degree work in the O.T.O. Here Crowley writes that "Man is the guardian of the Life of God; woman but a temporary expedient; a shrine indeed for the God, but not the God."[22] Every man and every woman may be a star, in other words, but those stars burn with a solar-phallic light.

At the same time, it is important to emphasize that Crowley's Babalonian vision played a direct and instrumental role in establishing the figure of the Goddess within modern—as opposed to traditional—witchcraft. In his initial version of the Charge of the Goddess, Gerald Gardner, who Crowley initiated into the O.T.O., put a good deal of Crowley's "scarlet" language from the Gnostic Mass (and *Liber Legis*) into the mouth of his Wiccan high priestess, voicing the Star Goddess:

> *I love you: I yearn for you: pale or purple, veiled or voluptuous. I who am all pleasure, and purple and drunkenness of the innermost senses, desire you. Put on the wings, arouse the coiled splendor within you. Come unto me, for I am the flame that burns in the heart of every man, and the core of every Star.*

This language was later drastically changed by Doreen Valiente, who offered a less lusty but more pastoral and regal portrait of the deity. On a more "meta" level, Valiente's "overwriting" of Crowley's visionary language also represents the complex ways that Crowley's legacy has been cloaked within popular postwar Wicca, which has always had trouble with the Beast's distinct lack of feminist sentiments. So, for example, Starhawk presents Crowley's definition of magic in Dreaming the Dark, within quotation marks, but nonetheless does not attribute the citation to him or mention him anywhere in the book.[23] Similarly, many less informed Wiccans and feminist witches have denied any connection with the Thelemic current that, through the complex of images that bind female energies in the *Book of the Law* to the figure of Babalon, directly shaped the lineaments of the modern Goddess.

To return to Parsons, we might locate his "Woman Girt with a Sword" at the halfway point between Crowley's Babalon and the independent goddess of later popular witchcraft. In Abrahamsson's words, "Parsons reformulated what Crowley had already defined," drawing the Babalon current away from Crowley's solar-phallic fixations and releasing it into a post-patriarchal or proto-feminist frame that amplified the martial element. With

22 Ibid.

23 Starhawk, *Dreaming the Dark* (Boston: Beacon Press, 1988), 169.

Parsons, the two images that are clearly distinguished in *Liber Legis*—the "woman girt with a sword" (III.11) and the "Scarlet Concubine" (III.14)—are conflated in Babalon, who is now not only wanton, but armed, dangerous, and demanding her freedom. This transition is made abundantly clear in Parsons' poem "The Birth of Babalon," usually included within the *Book of Babalon*. The poem begins with a restatement of Crowley's figure, with her wine and compassionate harlotry:

BABALON is too beautiful
for sight of mortal eyes
She has hidden her loveliness away
in lonely midnight skies,
She has clothed her beauty in robes of sin
and pledged her heart to swine
And loving and giving all she has
brewed for saints immortal wine.

In the immediately following stanzas, however, the figure shifts abruptly—"But now"—into distinctly Parsonian imagery, which links Babalon to both the sword and the flame:

But now the darkness is riven through
and the robes of sin are gone,
And naked she stands as a terrible blade
and a flame and a splendid song
Naked in radiant mortal flesh
at the Birth of BABALON.[24]

The emphasis on "birth" here also reminds us that, for Parsons, the maternal potential of Bablon does not only underscores her archetypal power but announces her capacity to incarnate in the flesh, in the human world. In contrast to Crowley's more metaphoric (and savvy) understanding of the Scarlet Woman as a mobile office of Babalonian ritual, Parsons seems to have literally believed that Babalon was going to take or had already taken physical incarnation. While this belief helps us appreciate the particular burden that Cameron carried in her life, it is also important to register, again, the paradoxical *autonomy* of this vehicle. In *Liber 49*, Parsons' chan-

24 *Ecpyrosis*, 122.

neled text, Babalon promises to provide a female "vessel" but commands Parsons to "Seek her not, call her not. Let her declare." Significantly, this vessel, "single in will," is also linked to the language and imagery of witchcraft: "And she shall wander in the witchwood under the Night of Pan, and know the mysteries of the Goat and the Serpent, and of the children that are hidden away."

This is strange and powerful stuff, both echoing and extending Crowley's more incantatory prose. But overall, as noted above, *Liber 49* is a singularly unconvincing "sacred" text, its obsessive force undercut by bursts of terrible prose and an erratic emotionality that suggests an almost adolescent naivete on Parsons' part. The 59th verse is particularly representative in its bizarre combination of prophecy and immature smut:

> *Yea it is even I BABALON and I SHALL BE FREE. Thou fool, be thou also free of sentimentality. Am I thy village queen and thou a sophomore, that thou shouldst have thy nose in my buttocks?*

Babalon demands liberation in forthright terms that cannot help but evoke the language of the civil rights and feminist movements to come. Here we are far from Crowley's wanton initiatrix, whose demands are seemingly restricted to pleasure. At the same time, Babalon scolds Parsons—the "fool", the pulp Parcifal—for precisely the features of romantic sentiment and masochistic submission that mar *Liber 49* and criss-cross his broken and extraordinary life. Moreover, Babalon makes her claim with a graphic, ridiculous image that cannot allow us to forget for a moment the clammy psycho-sexual dimension of Parsons' remarkable vision of militant deity. Indeed, in "village queen" I cannot help but hear the echo of She-Who-Must-Be-Obeyed, Etherington's "desired but unattainable mother."

No doubt the pampered child Parsons had an interesting relationship with his mother, who spoke volumes by killing herself once her son had left the world. But there is nowhere to go with such potentially cheap psychoanalyzing. More important here is Parsons' adult sexual ethics, and the ways these forced him to relate to the choices and independence of the women in his life. Parsons was a passionately sexual person with self-admitted bisexual leanings, and his adventurous nature found easy purchase in his bohemian social milieu. Many people in both the Agape Lodge and the Parsonage practiced free love, an experimentalism that perhaps was inspired by the sexual magic enshrined in the higher grades of the O.T.O., but was more likely due to the erotic realities of a mid-century Angelino demimonde linked to political radicalism, Hollywood hedonism, and the nascent stirrings of the sexual liberation movement. (It is hardly accidental that Harry Hay, who founded the ground-breaking homosexual Mattachine Society in 1950, and later co-founded the Radical Faeries, sometimes played organ for the Agape Lodge's Gnostic Mass.) Though free love had been a part of American radicalism and the esoteric fringe since the nineteenth century, more modern sexual practices like wife-swapping and "swinging" were just coming into their own in mid-century America, and there was nothing like today's discourse of "polyamory" to support the conflicts and complexities that inevitably arose. In "Freedom is a Two-Edged Sword," however, Parsons attempted to give the sort of open relationships he pursued an ethical foundation based in a proto-libertarian notion of transactional autonomy. In a couple, he wrote, "neither party, whether the relationship be in or out of wedlock, has any right or jurisdiction over the love or affection, the body or sex life of another for longer than that other desires." Sexual possession, in contrast, turns marriage and partnership "into a gruesome joke by the ever-present specters of jealousy and suspicion."[25]

However foolish he might appear at times, Parsons attempted to practice what he preached. He somewhat brazenly took up with his wife Helen's younger and vivacious half-sister Sara, aka Betty, who according to Crowley's letters was something of an "alley cat." Parsons was brutally frank with Helen about his sexual preference for Betty, and this greatly wounded his wife. Though Helen soon availed herself to Smith's bed, the two men's friendship remained strong. Similarly, Betty's own subsequent adventures with L. Ron Hubbard did not infuriate Parsons. To Crowley, he admitted that Betty had transferred her sexual attentions. "I think I have made a great gain and as Betty and I are the best of friends, there is little loss. I cared for her rather deeply but I have no desire to control her emotions, and I can, I hope, control my own. I need a magical partner. I have many experiments in mind."[26] In other words, though the affair caused Parsons significant pain, this did not prevent him from working intimate magick with the man who stirred his jealousy—at least until Hubbard, with Betty at his side, absconded with a great deal of Parsons' cash. Far more importantly for our purposes, however, is the fact that Parsons

25 "Freedom is a Two-Edged Sword," 27–31.

26 Russell Miller, *Bare-Faced Messiah: the True Story of L. Ron Hubbard* (New York: H. Holt, 1988), 118.

did not attempt to "control" Betty. He wanted her free. In cleaving to the ethical principals he outlined in his essay, he affirmed her right to wield her own independent erotic will, even if that meant putting a very painful sword to their affections.

A number of authors have pointed to Parsons' masochism in all this, but I think it is also important to emphasize that Parsons sincerely believed that women had a right to their own erotic self-determination—and that this sword-wielding bid for autonomy aligned them with the social dynamics of Babalon and the new Aeon. All of these themes were put into exceptional play once Parsons encountered the fearless, highly talented, and erratic Marjorie Cameron, who also possessed a head of burning red hair. When they first met, following the initial phase of the Babalon Working, they barely left Parsons' bedroom for two weeks. Parsons wrote Crowley that he had found "my elemental", though he also came to suspect that Cameron was carrying something of Babalon as well—presumably a very different esoteric energy, though one that was arguably no more suited to a flesh-and-blood woman. At the same time, as Parsons' biographer George Pendell astutely noted, "In Parsons' mind she was his very own creation, but this did not mean she was in his thrall."[27] When Parsons suggested they open up their relationship, she heartily agreed. During their six years of marriage, she had many lovers, left Los Angeles for long stretches of time, and caused Parsons considerable pain as well as a less familiar emotion: doubt. Some of the resulting ambivalence can be sensed in some of the Parsons poems recently published in *Songs for the Witch Woman*, which are accompanied by Cameron's extraordinary images. In one poem, a black goat cavorts with a golden girl, but it is the girl who has demon's eyes. In another verse, a seemingly innocent dancing girl is revealed to be bait for unwary men, with spiders waiting in the wings to attack.

Echoing Crowley's complex relationships with his Scarlet Women, Parsons placed a heavy magickal load onto Cameron's shoulders. Though she did not take to magick immediately, she eventually took lessons from Parsons, who playfully called her his "witch." Even when it was unclear if Cameron would return from Mexico, where she worked alongside a number of Surrealist painters, Parsons believed that she was his magickal heir, just as he presumed to be Crowley's. In early 1952, Cameron did return to Los Angeles in order to support Parsons during a particularly bleak time in his career. Her return partly inspired his final turn towards what he called

27 George Pendell, "Introduction," *Songs for the Witch Woman*, op. cit., 19.

"the Witchcraft": a modern, stripped-down magical organization that would transcend the "claptrap" of the O.T.O. Together the couple elected to move back to Mexico, a decision that can be seen, in part, as Parsons' final turn towards Babalon. Not only was he following Cameron into her world, but in the months before the move, he became fascinated with Ixcuina/Tlazolteotl, an Aztec goddess of filth and STDs who rules over sexual misdeeds as well as their purification. But even after his death, Parsons' transfigured Babalon continued to exert her power through Cameron. She incarnated the Scarlet Lady with chilling aplomb in Kenneth Anger's 1954 film *Inauguration of the Pleasure Dome*, and went on to influence an underground network of artists, actors, and bohemians who helped establish Angeleno counterculture, including Wallace Berman, George Herms, Dennis Hopper, and Curtis Harrington. Cameron, who burned much of her work and never made a career of her art, was certainly a fragile vessel; a broken Babalon who never forgot the charge that both animated and oppressed her. William Breeze reports that even late in life, Cameron still wondered if it were possible that she could really be an elemental—as striking a reminder as any of how the gods we construct construct us in return, in fragments and in flame.

On the Nature of Abomination

Daniel A. Schulke

AS DEIFIC FORCE and form, the Lady Babalon presents many hypostases to the practitioner of magick: consort of the Great Beast, cup-bearer, whore, conqueror, and Intercessor of the Great Abyss are amongst those better known. Clothed resplendent in purple and red, she is the divine fornicator and idolatress of divine bearing, and dweller of the wilderness. One of the most intriguing facets of her array of powers, and one of the least understood, is her guise as Mother of Abomination.

In its common usage, Abomination is that which is repulsive or abhorrent and precipitates loathing. Its surface manifestation is the 'monstrous', provoking offense, recoiling, self-righteous indignation, and outrage, a reaction both visceral and moral. As a magical arcanum, particularly in a Thelemic context, Abomination is considerably more complex, often subjectively defined. More importantly, it is a critical magical formula, and a vital but often ignored force in the spiritual development of the magical practitioner.

Initially emergent as an entic occult presence in the ceremonial angelic workings of Elizabethan magicians John Dee and Edward Kelley,[1] the

1 John Dee and Meric Causabon. *A True and Faithful Relation.* During these operations

spirituous presence *Babalond* was resonant with an older template long entrenched in Western mystical consciousness. This first recension of the Mother of Abominations appeared as the Whore of Babylon in the prophetic New Testament *Book of Revelations*. In a particularly rich complex of emblemata and pagan spiritual attributes, she is described as woman richly arrayed; sitting upon many waters, or upon a great beast; the Mother of Harlots; and bearing a golden cup filled with 'abominations and filthiness of her fornication'.

Viewed from the perspective of John of Patmos, prophetic author of the *Book of Revelations*, 'abomination' most likely alluded to a number of repulsive matters relevant to his Christian audience at the time, for example, apostasy, heresy, or that which ran counter to a developing Christian orthodoxy. Abomination in *Revelations* thus relates to the activities of the Beast, the Dragon and the Harlot; their children are the abominations against God. Like many religions, as Christianity developed over time, its list of abominations multiplied and diversified, often driven by conflict at its peripheries with other religions, spiritual practices, and social norms. In our own time, amongst the adepts of the Temple, this biblical definition of abomination could refer to those who are free from the shackles of Yaweh.

To Dee, whose magical operations catalogued in *A True and Faithful Relation* gave rise to the modern angelogical theurgy of the Enochian magical system,[2] the understanding of 'abomination' was likely very complex and based, in part, on the sin of iniquity. This is evidenced by the angels' chastisement of Dee during the operations for he and Edward Kelly's sins, particularly the latter's Lust of Woman.[3] This was one of many flaws shackled to the condition of mortality, and stood in opposition to the Great Work, for to Dee, the Goal of the Wise is achieved

> *by the true Philosophical method and harmony proceeding and ascending, as it were, gradatim, from things visible, to consider of things invisible: from things bodily, to conceive of things spirituall: from things transitory, and*

the initially received name of the entity was BABALOND, the spirit of harlotry.

2 The term *Enochian magic* in modern magical parlance refers to the material received in the spirit operations of Dee and Kelley, such as the Holy Tables and the language angelicall.

3 The *True and Faithful Relation*.

> *momentary, to mediate of things permanent: by things mortall (visible and invisible) to have some perseverance of immortality.*[4]

The mortal world, and its failings, were thus for Dee the realm of error and potential falsehood, as Dee wrote concerning the Spiritual Records:

> *Oute of this boke shall be restored the holy bokes, which haue perished euen from the begynning, and from the first that liued. And herein shalbe deciphred perfect truth from imperfect falshode, True religion from fals and damnable errors, With all Artes: which are propre to the vse of Man.*[5]

In addition to its more empyrean implications, the magical scope of abomination also extends to a retinue of very personal aversions and repugnances. In contemplating the personal atrocities of Dee, it is important to consider the contextual emergence of the spirit Babalon in Dee and Kelley's operations of angelic spirit congress. Her appearance as 'The Daughter of Fortitude' occurred following Dee and Kelley's agreement to share all things in common, including their wives, in obedience to the received message of the angel Uriel. This sexual transgression of marriage vows breached the bonds of body and heart, but also the understanding of marriage as a sacrament of God, and its is likely that all involved had strong aversions to the arrangement, at least initially. This said, the magical rite of the *orgia*, hearkening to the temporal liberation of bonds, is a magical formula well known from antiquity and can be an effective vehicle for the generation of power, ecstasy, and prophetic gnosis, as well as fragmentation of the ego. Importantly, it places the appearance of Babalon in Dee's work in the context of the liberating Arcanum of fornication, and the struggle to embrace that which one abominates. Interestingly, the issues of license and permeable sexual relationships would, centuries later, also attend upon another magician who conjured Babalon, John Whiteside Parsons (1914–1952).

Within the Thelemic purview of Babalon, we may attempt to discover the magical notion of Abomination in the writings of the Master Therion (Aleister Crowley), ostensibly the first and most prolific scribe of that esoteric tradition. Examination of the subject in Therion's work is tricky, for on the surface, his work occasionally engaged powers and practices that

4 John Dee. *A Letter, containing a most brief discourse apologeticall*, 1592.

5 Whitby (ed.), *John Dee's Actions with Spirits*, II, p. 378.

many consider repugnant, such as coprophagy and animal sacrifice, but these exemplars must be seen as integral to the arcana for the specified magical operations in which they occur, and dwell among the more sensationalized aspects of his work.

'Abomination of Desolation' is a phrase originating in the Bible,[6] often in apocalyptic prophecy using the specific form *the abomination that maketh desolate*. Theological scholarship does not entirely agree on its meaning, but its usage is often as a concrete noun and refers to idols, in some cases the profanity of their erection in a place formerly considered sacred. In Thelema, the phrase is also of considerable import, and it is found in Therion's received work *The Book of the Law*, the mystical text upon which the foundation of Thelema rests:

> *That stélé they shall call the Abomination of Desolation count well its name & it shall be to you as 718.*[7]

Via the kabbalistic pathways of gematria, the number 718 means 'persistence' and 'dryness.' It is also the name of the Stele of Revealing itself; a mystery whose significance Therion never elucidated upon. Further extrapolation of the phrase *Abomination of Desolation* yields 'overflowing', an apt correspondence with Our Lady Babalon. The apparent contradiction implied by 'dryness' and 'overflowing' is balanced perfectly when one remembers that Babalon resides in the Great Desert of the City of Pyramids, as well as bearing the Cup of Abomination itself. The two concepts equally resonate with the Cup through the disruptive magical arcanum of Opposition,[8] an essential component of its nature, as well as that of the Lady Babalon.

For some who live according to the magical philosophy of Thelema, the phrase *Abomination of Desolation* refers to the glory of the Flesh. This recalls the ancient Gnostic rejection of corporeality, but instead of abhoring the flesh, one glories in it. This turns the notion of idolatry on its head, not only by reckoning the Self as a signified (yet embodied) form of the divine, but also by assuming a stance of ownership of one's own corporeal-

6 Daniel 9:27, 11:31, 12:11; Maccabees 1:54; Matthew 24:15–16, Mark 13:14.

7 *Liber Al vel Legis*, Ch. 3, v. 19.

8 Consider the kindred alchemical formula *Solve et Coagula et habebis magisterium*, or, in chemistry, the oxidation-reduction equation. Similar mottoes and formulae permeate the inner mysteries of Sabbatic Witchcraft.

ity, despite the mortifications imposed by material existence. In examining the words and deeds of Crowley, in some instances his idea of abomination appears linked with the constraint or suppression of the body, its drives, and thus the powers wherewith Nature has endowed it:

> *Do not think then that by Non-Action thou doest follow the Way of the Tao, for thy Nature is Action, and by hindering the Discharge of thy Potential thou doest perpetuate and aggravate the Stress. If thou ease not Nature, she will bring thee to Dis-Ease. Free thereof every Function of thy Body and of every other Part of thee according to its true Will. This also is most necessary, that thou discover that true Will in every Case, for thou art born into Dis-Ease; where are many false and perverted Wills, monstrous Growths, Parasites, Vermin are they, adherent to thee by Vice of Heredity, or of Environment or of evil Training. And of all these Things the subtlest and most terrible, Enemies without Pity, destructive to thy will, and a Menace and Tyranny even to thy elf, are the Ideals and Standards of the Slave-gods, false Religion, false Ethics, even false Science.*[9]

Here, a kind of tyranny of stasis is invoked which not only perverts nature, but will ultimately, if left unchecked, turn against the magician's own divine nature. Crowley's grotesque language implicitly aligns this—as well as a putrid clustering of other falsehoods—with deformity, disease and rottenness, effectively marking out its footprint in the terrain of the abominated or demonic. Considering this passage alone, is it clear that for Crowley these forces occupy not only a Thelemic *terra damnata*, indicative of magical pathology, but also serve to harass and corrupt that most holy adytum of the cult, the True Will. At the core of all of these negative principles is a tendency toward incessant subversion and dilapidation of the magician, a gyre in the Current which serves as a repository for its flotsam.

This highlights Thelema, in part, as a doctrine of magical liberation. The True Will must be liberated from the False Will, even as the walker of high magick's path must be emancipated from the ideological slaveries of contaminated gods and human institutions. Yet in Crowley's magical cartography, the nature of abomination also extends to philosophical zones which traditionally have also embraced ideas of liberation, whether it be of the individual, certain groups, or humanity as a whole. In *New Comment, Liber AL vel Legis* he writes:

9 Aleister Crowley. *Liber Aleph*, Ch. 30 Αδ De Via Libertatis.

> *Our humanitarianism, which is the syphilis of the mind, acts on the basis of the lie that the king must die. The king is beyond death; it is merely a pool where he dips for refreshment. We must therefore go back to Spartan ideas of education; and the worst enemies of humanity are those who wish, under pretext of compassion, to continue its ills through the generations. The Christians to the lions! Let weak and wry productions go back into the melting-pot, as is done with flawed steel castings. Death will purge, reincarnation will make whole, these errors and abortions. Nature herself may be trusted to do this, if only we will leave her alone. But what of those who, physically fitted to live, are tainted with rottenness of soul, cancerous with the sin-complex? The Christians to the lions!*[10]

This stance, whether useful or not for the individual magician, must also co-exist with the hard reality that the very conditions which elicit humanitarianism as an active response arise from the Abominable. Humanity's depredation of itself, despite the rise of innumerable religions and their soteriologies, is an historical constant;[11] Crowley's view of the matter is clear, unwavering, and documented abundantly.[12]

'Abomination' for the Thelemic initiate may thus be thought of as a subjective concept, intensely personal and ultimately abhorrent, but as an Arcanum also functioning as a kind of constant across the field of magick---the alienated powers or aversions of the Adept or Seer. This is reflected in part in the Master Therion's admonition:

> *Go forth, o my Son, o Son of the Sun, rejoicing in thy Strength, as a Warrior, as a Bridegroom, to take thy Pleasure upon the Earth, and in every Palace of the Mind, moving ever from the crass to the subtle, from the coarse to the fine. Conquer every Repulsion in thy self, subdue every Aversion. Assimilate all Poison, for therein only is there Profit. Seek constantly therefore to know what is painful and to cleave thereunto, for by Pain cometh true Pleasure. Those who avoid Pain physical or mental remain little Men, and there is no Virtue in them. Yet be thou ware lest thou fall into the Heresy which maketh*

10 II, v. 21

11 Hence one justification for various models of magical predation and parasitism, as with some so-called 'Left Hand Path' groups in modern occultism.

12 "It is useless to oppose the baseness of humanity; if one touches pitch one runs the risk of being defiled. I am perfectly content to know that the vileness of civilization is rapidly destroying itself; that it stinks in my nostrils tells me that it is rotting and my consolation is in the words of Lord Dunsany." Aleister Crowley, *Confessions*, p. 188.

> *Pain, and Self-sacrifice as it were Bribes to corrupt God, to secure some future Pleasure in an imagined After-life. Nay, also of the other Part, fear not to destroy thy Complexes, thinking dreadfully thereby to lose the Power of creating Joy by their Distinction. Yet in each Marriage be thou bold to affirm the spiritual Ardour of the Orgasm, fixing it in some Talisman, whether it be Art, or Magick, or Theurgy.*[13]

Here abomination itself is invoked as both 'Poison' and 'Aversion.' Although Crowley's modality for confronting it magically differs slightly from expression to expression ("conquer," "subdue," "assimilate" etc.) the message is unified by an unbending 'all or nothing' approach: a true magician must embrace abomination fully and consciously, even if such a conjoining is violent and painful. Conjugation is the means by which the poison is transmuted and becomes exploitable, in accord with True Will.

This is the Sacrifice unto the Cup of Babalon,[14] wherein nothing is withheld, and finds resonance in the Great Labor through the alchemical stage of calcination. Through the agency of furnace and crucible, the blessed Salt is yielded. The fire of Our Furnace, the inferno of Magical Ordeal, must be of sufficient heat and duration, and the crucible impeccable. An incomplete calcination cannot generate the Stone: this is the 'drop withheld' from the Cup that serves to infect the operation.[15]

This total and uncompromising principle of magical union accords well with the oracle of Babalon as received in the 1946 magical operations of Jack Parsons and Marjorie Cameron:

> *Thou shalt offer all thou art and all thou hast at my altar, withholding nothing. And thou shalt be smitten full sore and thereafter thou shalt be outcast and accursed, a lonely wanderer in abominable places.*[16]

Restraint, which Crowley himself associates with disease, is an affront to the goddess, particularly regarding the sacrificial offering, and even more

13 Ch. 24. χ DE VOLUPTATE POENARUM.

14 The devotee will note that Verse 49 of *The Book of Babalon* provides a sevenfold (6+1) formula of the sacraments of Babalon's cup: tears, sweat, semen, blood, love, and faith. The seventh ingredient is secret. Although not explicitly 'sacraments of Abomination,' averse formulae of the Cup may be extrapolated.

15 The alchemical interaction between Babalon and the Initiate is a critical arena of power, which awaits serious research and exposition.

16 *Liber 49*. v. 13.

explicitly the offering of Self. Whether by withholding oneself from Babalon, or by merely approaching her altar, the postulant unto her mysteries will be accurst, thrown alone into a wilderness whose chief characteristic is its 'abominable' nature. This particular verse also glyphs Babalon's function as the gatekeeper of the Great Abyss, for one understanding of the 'abominable place' whereto the aspirant is thrown is the post-initiatic destruction of personal epistemology which Crowley signified as the Night of Pan.

The breadth of the deific form of Babalon—at least in terms of her written magical exegesis—was widened with the emergence of Jack Parsons' *Liber 49*, previously cited. Ostensibly dwelling in the heretical shadowlands of Thelemic textual recension, *Liber 49* was self-declared as the fourth chapter of *The Book of the Law*, though it is not regarded as such by the major magical orders espousing Thelemic doctrine.[17] Regardless of its ultimate entic origin or status within the 'Thelemic canon', it may be studied as a refraction of the Babalon Current through Parsons and Cameron, and offers many valuable lessons for the practitioner.[18]

In the first context, the very text of *Liber 49* itself may be counted a species of abomination, in consideration of the wider ambit of Thelemic texts and their degrees of classification. Her self-declared identity as a 'devious song'[19] could apply equally to her macrocosmic magical attributes, but also specifically to her voice as manifest through *Liber 49*. This casts Babalon in the principal rôle of disruptor of the established order, which is not always the same thing as a liberator.

The location of the Babalon Working, the Mojave Desert of the southwestern United States, is also interesting and harmonizes with certain attributes of the Lady, and of her description of 'abominable places.' Occupying a rain shadow terrain, the severe climate limits human presence, and those souls which do pass through must be prepared for ordeal. Containing Death Valley, its heat can be lethal, and dust storms are well established. The Mojave is the dwelling place of several species of poisonous reptiles, and of bats, owls, and toads—the faunal retinue of witchcraft. Arguably, the plant most emblematic of the Mojave is the punishing cholla cactus

17 Ordo Templi Orientis (O.T.O.) and Argentum Astrum (A∴A∴). Verse 73 of *Liber 49* implies Babalon as the Daughter in the Yod-He-Vau-He magical formula, and thus the 'fourth'.

18 This stance is aligned neither with the Judaizers of the Temple, nor its defilers.

19 *Liber 49*, v. 10.

(*Cylindropuntia* spp.), of which three species are represented. Though by day this desert is an unforgiving landscape, even in the winter when temperatures are moderated, by night sky clarity is unparalleled offering an ideal crucible for operations of both lunar and stellar gnosis, an essential strand of the Babalon current.

As an essential consideration of Parsons' work with the Babalon current, it must be acknowledged that Abomination finds its kindred in the soul-scapes of witchcraft, characterized by erotic nightmare, grotesquerie, and trespass against the normative. Parsons linked witchcraft with the emergence of Babalon and her mysteries, and the manner of her manifestation and subsequent events in Parsons' life may be characterized as transgressive and abomination-emanant.

More than this, the historical Abomination of Woman across many spheres of human power, especially science, magic, and religion, also colors Parsons' magical outlook:

> *The sexual perversion of Christianity becomes obvious when it is realized that* "The Holy Ghost" *(The Sophia) is feminine. The very Tetragrammaton, Yod He Vau He, means: Father-Mother-Son-Daughter and asserts the splendor of the biological order. How could life proceed from a strictly masculine creation? What miracle could possibly be superior to the miracle of copulation, conception and gestation? In the corrupt and demonic Jehovah, the priesthood blasphemed nature in order to perpetuate a tyrannical and superstitious patriarchy. Woman was insulted and affronted with the calumny of immaculate conception—then, by this mystery mongering, a premium was placed on moral and spiritual sterility. This sublimation of the sex-urge has been the basis of the power of the church and is the source of much of the psychosis rampant in the modern world.*[20]

What Parsons called 'The Witchcraft' was an imagined magical history of *Homo sapiens* seen in part as a rejoinder to the abuses of government and religion, and partly as a manifesto of magical liberalism.[21] Beautiful and stirring as the vision is, it also ignores the widespread anthropological reality of witchcraft being synonymous with *maleficia*, and the incidences in which conflicts between witch-groups have resulted in murder, lynchings,

20 Jack Parsons. *Freedom is Two-edged Sword*, Chapter 2.

21 Jack Parsons. "We Are the Witchcraft," *Freedom is A Two-Edged Sword*, New Falcon, 1989.

and other atrocities.[22] Nonetheless, the alignment of historical witchcraft narratives and iconography has been focused to a large degree on the malignant feminine, whose 'chaotic sexuality' and seductive nature in most instances opposed a more male, and churchly order.[23]

The alignment of Babalon with witchcraft is especially apropos when considering her aspect as the Mother of Abominations. Indeed, presented through a certain lens, the historical narrative of European Witchcraft may be seen as a repository of religious abomination: fornication, sodomy, cannibalism, necromancy, infanticide, grave desecration, intercourse with demons, blaspheming the sacrament, and scores of other depraved acts are accorded the witch. Far from being simple criminal charges applied to a persecuted class, these characteristics existed in ritual frameworks (real or contrived) which may have owed as much to pre-classical folk religion as it did to the deliberate inversions of Christianity.[24]

Additionally, witchcraft as a concept, practice, and symbol-set is nothing if not 'of the body', its basis arising in part from the enfleshed sorcery of atavistic resonance. Folkloric complexes such as the Wild Hunt, the philter-bearing seductress, and the haggard crone serve as examples whereby the essentialism of witchcraft assumes highly visceral forms. The linkage between witchcraft and magical projections of female sexuality is ancient, and indeed the visceral aspects of Babalon recall the sexual lechery and sensual pleasures of the female *Sahacat* witches as well as others of medieval lore.[25] Similarly, the Lady Babalon, in addition to her more specified spirituous emanations, may be considered to be Thelema embodied, not merely extant in a hypostasis of liberation but awakened in the flesh of the practitioner through *active* magical engagement. Grant aligns Babalon with 'the darkness of Matter' in distinction to the Light of the Beast.[26]

Though witchcraft as a mythos and folkloric stratum long predates Thelema, it too contains a diverse set of magical practices and philosophies in modern esotericism. One such modern recension of organized witchcraft practitioners is the magical order *Cultus Sabbati,* a body of ritual

22 One modern example being the practice of 'medicine murder' in which human body parts are cut from living victims for their power in witchcraft.

23 Zika, Charles. *The Appearance of Witchcraft.* Routledge, 2007, pp. 70–98.

24 See Ginzburg, C. *Ecstasies: Deciphering the Witches' Sabbat.* Moshe Idel argues in *Saturn's Jews* (2011) that Judaism in Europe also contributed significant lore to the construct of the witches' Sabbat.

25 Weyer, Johan. *De Prastigiis daemonum,* 1583 (trans. George Mora, MRTS, 1998).

26 Kenneth Grant. *The Magical Revival,* Starfire Publishing, 2010 (1972) p. 24.

practices patterned upon the magical and mythic strata of the medieval Witches' Sabbat. Curiously, its genesis lies in the historical intersection of English and continental cunning-folk practice including divination, charming and spellcraft, with the lodge-based neo-masonic ceremonialism of the late 1800s. Although the Witches' Sabbat emerges from several distinct magical, folkloric and religious strata, the blasphemed Christian rites (such as the Black Mass), though often overstated, are an important link with the arcana of Babalon, both as a force of disruption, and an inversion of the usual order of things. The Grand Formulae of the Witches' Sabbat lies in intercourse with the Other, that which the self abominates, for the liberation of ecstasy.[27]

In the metaphysic of Sabbatic Witchcraft, Abomination is known as the aborted child of Self, those alienated portions of the magical body resulting in disembodied and pathological entity.[28] Through the nigromantic art, this corpse is raised from the dead and restored to vitality, embodying not only the apotheosis of its former being, but all the horror and wretchedness of its former moribund state. This act, when achieved, is referred to as *self-overcoming* and mirrors certain aspects of ego-death during the initiatic process known in Thelema as crossing the Abyss, of which Babalon is the governess. The often-misunderstood magical zone known as the Abyss is not only the void traversed from Ego (presence) to Non-Ego (supernality) but is the region containing all that is Other, and hence, abominable.

That the whore should relate to certain aspects of the Abyss is not surprising, for it is an apt magical metaphor, not only as applicable to aspects of sexual morphology and function, but also for the characteristic threefold physical states of aggression, vulnerability and *ecstasis* which by nature indwell the sexual act.

Whilst it is true that the magical formulation of 'Crossing the Abyss' as it is currently understood in the Sabbatic Witchcraft bears certain influences from Thelema, an older substrate has long been present in some lineages of English Witchcraft. This is known as 'crossing over the hedge.' This enigmatic expression, grounded in the rural British magic of

27 The engagement so mentioned finds its ritual exemplars in the rites of the Star Ruby, Reguli and Samekh, respectively, in which Babalon is invoked as direction, power and deity, into both magical circle/temple and within the body of the practitioners themselves.

28 The germ of the idea is that such power, left in an essentially quarantined and condemned state, not only creates a draining effect on the magical body but also severs the magician from an important source of personal power.

the 1800s, may refer to a number of magical arcana, including flight of the witches to the nocturnal Sabbat and is intimately bound up with the concepts of sacrifice, dissolution, dissociation, and attainment of ecstasy. However, its foundational form references the passing over a boundary between the known and the unknown, and the successful return to the point of departure. Its primary referential in the physical landscape is the hedge, that mass of thorns, trees, brush, darkness, and physical interference that divides one plot from another. For the witch, passage over (or through) the hedge denotes a successful stage in the process of Initiation, where one is 'blooded in the thorn-patch', returning both less and more than one previously was. In its higher manifestations, the witchcraft rite of 'crossing over the hedge' involves the projection of one's spirit during the High Sabbat through the physical and aethyric membranes which usually obstruct attainment of the ecstatic state. To cross over is difficult enough; to return and reconstitute without negative compromise to the physical vessel is miraculous, an act requiring constant practice, as well as totality of sacrifice—a theme familiar to devotees of Babalon.

In contemplating Abomination and Babalon's relation to witchcraft, we may also consider the motif of the witches' cauldron, that vessel infused with every tincture of the damned and rotten; a concentrator of offal, poisonous creatures, demonic force, and the malformed. Comparison between the witches' cauldron and the Cup of Babalon is tempting, but imprecise: the Greek word for the Whore of Babylon's drinking vessel is *potérion* (ποτήριον) or 'drinking cup'; witches' cauldrons are, in general, vessels of making and concoction rather than of libation. A closer correspondence may be derived on the basis of the esoteric morphology of the cup and its Arcanum as the vessel of feminine mystery: the Witches' cauldron and the manifold vessels portrayed in late medieval and early modern depictions of witches are often considered resonant with the womb, vagina or anus.[29] Crowley likewise associates the Cup of Babalon with the Yoni, as the Outer Robe of Concealment, the precious stones of the Pearl and Star Sapphire, and also the magical formula VITRIOL.[30] These associations strengthen when one considers the biblical description of the whore's cup as being filled with the filth of her fornication.[31]

29 Zika, Op. cit.

30 *Liber 777*.

31 *Book of Revelation* 17:4.

Kenneth Grant connects the cup with arcanum of the Vinum Sabbati, a mystery of the nocturnal sorcery of the *lamiae.* In accord with the nature of Abomination reflecting alienated power and falsehoods, Grant notes that that the symbol of the cup and its contents—originally a mystery of the primordial goddess—have fallen over the millennia under the influence of diverse myths, magical traditions, and projected phantasms.[32] This has lent a distorting influence to it, rendering magical perception of its form mutable and capable of casting glamours, a quality associated with both witchcraft and the Cup itself. In explicating the esotery of certain sex magic operations, Kenneth Grant also aligns the Cup of Babalon with the *smashan* or cremation ground.[33] It is important to note as well that Grant considered witchcraft a degenerate form of a more perfect and ancient species of high magick, despite the considerable amount of text he devoted to it in his publications:

> *Witchcraft, as generally understood (or misunderstood) is a degradation and an abomination of this science, at one time universally used by Initiates... the use of menstrual blood and the urine of whores sprang from misinterpretation of the lunar Current and its confusion with chaotic sexual practices which, over the centuries, infiltrated some of the lesser Tantras and earned for them the detestation of Initiates.*[34]

Beyond the superficial impulses of disgust which veil the symbol, and regardless of the ascribed legitimacy of either magical philosophies, the awful contents of Babalon's Cup are of supreme magical import to both Thelema and the Sabbatic Tradition, forming the resultant protoplasm of the co-mingling of All with the Lady. For the magician, Abomination is not embraced for its outwardly-destructive potencies or sinister glamours, but for its inwardly-confrontational power, and potential to transform. Additionally such a stance, if it can be attained, fulfills the Thelemic mandate *Love is the Law, Love under Will,* a motto which can be said to be in accord with some ethe of witchcraft.[35] This is also a stance the Master Therion

32 Kenneth Grant. "Vinum Sabbati." *Carfax Monographs*, privately published, 1959-63.

33 Grant, *The Magical Revival*, p. 150.

34 Kenneth Grant. *Aleister Crowley and The Hidden God*, Starfire Publishing, 2013 (1973) pp. 94-95.

35 In September 1993, the witchcraft order Cultus Sabbati formally accepted *The Book of the Law*, as part of its lodge affiliation with the Typhonian Order of Kenneth Grant.

expressed throughout his literary and magical corpus, as well as within the moral and sexual parameters of his many relationships, male and female.

Lest the magical concept of Abomination be conflated with exteriorized fetish, it is essential to note its subjectivity and the complexity this presents for the practitioner and devotee. Defining the contents of the Foul Cup are easy if we turn to the words and understanding of others, but to behold its complete form, one must gaze into the mirror and behold the reflected monster, rather than the mask of its idealized form. Here Abomination assumes its critical Interior Manifestation—the alienated Self; the places one dares not tread. An essential quality for transmutation is containment within the alembic:- All must embrace the process, elsewise the *numen* of the operation is bled beyond into the periphery, and the vessel is broken.[36]

Likewise, the magical tension between the Thelemic pursuit of True Will and the Embrace of All necessitates a dual stance in which the practitioner is both active and passive, the former for the virtue of cardinal action, the latter for the acceptance of the unseen and Ineffable which lies behind the Veil. This is a stance the Master Therion well expressed in many writings.[37]

The total sacrifice unto the Cup of Babalon finds a kindred arcanum in the Draconian recensions of Sabbatic Witchcraft. Specifically, the rite known as *Ka: The Hieros-Gamos*. In the Draconian recensions of Sabbatic Witchcraft, the Sacrifice unto the Cup of Babalon is in resonance with the ophiolatrous *Rite of Ka: The Hieros-Gamos*. The aim of this primal ritual is to bind the entirety of the practitioner's mind, spirit, and body to the Great Serpent *Azhdeha*, spirit of magick entire, and the collective stellar emanations of the constellation of Draco. Undertaken during the last complete lunation approaching to Winter Solstice, the practitioner pours the totality of his or her essence into a specially-prepared votive urn, the so-called

36 Sincere and complete magical embrace of abomination, principally as *other,* finds ancient antecedence in the tantric Chöd sādhanas in Tibetan Buddhism and Bon. Often practiced in charnel grounds, it engages the horrific, repulsive, and improper as the means of flaying the Ego, and serving the remains up to previously summoned demons and hungry ghosts. However the understanding and efficacy of the act lies in the doing, not in the reading and observing.

37 "Know naught! All ways are lawful unto innocence. Pure folly is the key to initiation. Silence breaks into rapture, Be neither man nor woman, but both in one." *The Book of Thoth.* The verity of this magical formula is also expressed in emblematic-imagic fashion through Atu XIV, Art.

Marriage Vessel, which receives serial offerings of blood and sexual secretions resonant with the lunar progression and given wholly to the Great Serpent.[38] During the initial month-long ritual working which incepts the seven-year cycle of Draconian praxis, a taboo of sexual devotion solely to the Great Serpent is customarily observed, not for the sake of outward abstinence to the mortal world, but rather that no portion of the practitioner be withheld from the Serpent.[39] The *Ka* rite as reified represents a particularly advanced ceremonial pedigree of witchcraft, but the substance of its origins lie in the vessel-sorcery of early modern English cunning-craft, which included vessels for the habitations of familiar spirits, and the fashioning of witch-bottles for protection or cursing.

More esoterically, Babalon's Arcanum of embracing All, and withholding nothing from the cup of Sacrifice, invokes the Sabbatic concept of 'Walking the Blade of Cain', the narrow and precarious third way lying between the sinistral and dextral paths, whose razor edge cleaves the unworthy aspirant in two. In the composite traditions of Sabbatic Witchcraft, the historical figure of Cain is revered as the Initiator, or the force of Initiation. In this archaic folk narrative, Cain's transgression against God, the murder of the profane Abel, and subsequent wandering exile are seen as a sublime initiatic formula of the Craft, and are resonant with the themes of sacrifice and wandering of the 'abominable places' in *Liber 49*. Though likely arising out of late medieval syncretism of Brythonic folk sorcery, Romany lore, and popular biblical mysticism, this formula is in accord with the *fragmenta* concerning the ancient Gnostic sect of the Cainites, who in order to find salvation had to 'pass through all things'.

Cain is but one part of the initiatic complex of Traditional Witchcraft; other British traditions of witch-sorcery feeding the Sabbatic Current account the Devil himself as the Initiatic force which awakens and empowers the sleeping witch, amongst others.[40] This phenomenon of the Devil being the initiating power of the practitioner of magic is in resonance with Crowley's correspondence between the Initiator Aiwass as both his Holy Guardian Angel and Satan-Lucifer.[41] In other Sabbatic traditions, Lilith, a

38 Andrew D. Chumbley. 'Hieros Gamos: The Rite of Sacred Marriage between Man and Serpent.' *The Dragon-Book of Essex. Xoanon*, 2014 (1998), p. 75.

39 It is axiomatic that sexuality, both male and female, suffers under the constraint of prudery, much as do the transmutative powers of the alchemical laboratory without benefit of the Labour.

40 For example, Lilith, mother of Witches, or Sabatraxas, atavistic *daimon* of the Toad.

41 *Magick in Theory and Practice*, 1929, p. 193.

nocturnal demoness known for transgressive sexuality and lasciviousness, is the initiating power, through an ancient bloodline of both flesh and spirit. The traditional witch Andrew Chumbley, past magister of the Cultus Sabbati, aligned the Thelemic hypostases of Babalon, the Beast, and their bastard child Seth-pa-kharad with the witchcraft complex of Lilith, Mahazhael, and Cain, respectively.[42]

The magical wastelands of the abominable, if they truly repulse, are both personal to the magician, and alienated from the Self. Accordingly, a bifurcative state of the magical path, due to its fragmented nature, offers diverse choices for the way ahead and not all are singular. In this meshing of planes, the Initiate confronts that which is loathsome both within and without, in order that nothing prevent the crossing of the Abyss. This, ultimately, is what Abomination refers to in the Thelemic ethos: all sense impressions, all sense of Self, must be annihilated.

As a magical practitioner, I have often advised my colleagues in such situations to take the thorny path, the way of difficulty and obstacle, because, as the legends of old teach, the gods show little interest in mortals who walk the way of ease. The hard way is ever rejected because of personal aversion to what it promises. Such is the way of Abomination. The alchemists noted the value of the feculence of their Art: whether as the generalized state of Nigredo, or as a more specified *caput mortuum* of a single operation, not only was putrescence accorded the potentials of great power in the Labour, it was also acknowledged to 'contain all'. At the very least, in its state of perpetual decomposition, the heap or dung and ordure provided the baseline thermal nourishment for incubation, circulation, and ripening. Such was the golden causeway, and also a profound mystery of Our Lady.

Less important than the parameters of any given abomination is the initiatic power it contains when one embraces it consciously and wholly. The overarching principle embodied in the Cup of the Lady is thus one of initiatic power conveyed by the successful union of opposites. In its more complex mystical recensions, the writings and ritual practices of Sabbatic Witchcraft reflect what is known as the Formulae of the Opposer. Although these magical axiomata underlie many historical traditions of sorcery, including the witchcraft of the Sabbat, it has been best articulated in modern esotericism in the works of the Cultus Sabbati.[43] Briefly de-

42 Andrew D. Chumbley. "Wisdom for the New Flesh". *Starfire* Number 5, 1994.

43 Andrew D. Chumbley. *Azoëtia, A Grimoire of the Sabbatic Craft* (Xoanon, 1992) *Qu-*

scribed, the Formula circumscribe the relation between the magical practitioner and the 'Other'—whether alienated, demonic, or abominable—and are frequently characterized by a transgressive stance against Self and all law which it is subject to. In its ritual actuation, as well as an embodied principle governing the spiritual path, the formula is one of liberation, releasing previously inaccessible powers and understandings by overturning strongly-held personal conceptions of propriety, attraction, aesthesis, and personal comfort. If successful, its action may be favorably expressed in the alchemical metaphors of conjunction and sublimation; when unsuccessful it is the catastrophic combustion of the volatile Mercury.[44]

What is the essential magical power that allows the embrace of Abomination? Will, the philosophical Mercury of Thelema, and Love, its Alkahest. Yet their usage for the embrace of All is not a simple formula, for inasmuch as Love and Will may be singular, they may also exist in multiple gradients; they instruct by their embodiment, but they may also teach through the situation of their absence. Often, the essential medicine found wanting for the True Embrace is honest and thorough self criticism—a virtue essential for the development of any seeker, in any tradition of spiritual and magical power. Implicit in the approach of the devotee is a mandate for union of the corporeal Temple: Vessel and Elixir as one, both hallowed and accurst. For as it was prophesied, though the Lady's Cup contain all manner of filth, its substance is of Gold.

---

tub (Xoanon, 1995), and *The Dragon Book of Essex* (Xoanon, 2014) as well as Daniel A. Schulke, *Lux Haeresis* (Xoanon, 2011).

44 The high explosive Hg(CNO)2 (Mercury fulminate), highly unstable and susceptible to detonation by mere friction or jostling, and whose unsafe handling precipitated the laboratory explosion which killed Jack Parsons in 1952. Johann Kunckel, an early Swedish chemist trained in the alchemical tradition, is generally credited with its first isolation, derived from dissolution of mercury in *aqua fortis*, with the addition of Aqua Vitae, progressively warmed in a dunghill.

Rite of the Seven Keys of the Kingdom

(IN NOMINE BABALON)

Robert Fitzgerald

PROCEDURE

✠ Bathe and Robe
✠ Purify and Consecrate
✠ Star Ruby
✠ Kings and Seniors
✠ Keys 16 and 17, English/Enochian
✠ Star Sapphire
✠ Compassing the Star of Babalon
Chanting letters
lighting candles at points
placing the cups
✠ Pa—Un—Pa—Un—Ur—Med—Drux x 49
✠ 19th Key
✠ Liturgy (Daughter of Fortitude; excerpts Liber 418; Liber Cheth)
✠ Prayers of Devotion
✠ Casting the Sign of Our Lady (red and blue triangle)
✠ Communion/Feeding the Cups (Wine, Elixir and Blood)
✠ Reception of the Seven Keys
✠ License to In-dwell

✠

The purpose of the ritual is to achieve Communion and Congressus with Our Lady of Abominations. The Seven Keys are the Powers of Her train, each to be received as given by Her to each practitioner. Ideally at least two, but better three or four servants are best for the proper exaction of the rite. Let it begin at midnight, and let each step be lovingly and immaculately executed, without thought of time or lust of result. Each practitioner shall fill spirit, mind and body with the love for Her. Let nothing be undone nor forgotten, lest the entire Opus fail and incite Her fury. All shall be prepared to give All that they are, lest the Sacrament be profaned.

RITUS

At least one hour prior to the rite, each servant shall take a hot bath with oils of jasmine and rose. Hyssop shall be boiled and its water used to robe. Standing naked without the Temple, each servant shall anoint themselves with the water, saying:

Thou shalt purge me with hyssop, O Lord and I shall be clean:
Thou shalt wash me, and I shall be whiter than snow.

Robing, the servants shall declare:

> By the figurative mystery of these holy vestures, I will clothe me with the armour of salvation in the strength of the Most High, Ancor; Amacor; Amides; Theodonias; Anitor; that my desired end may be effected through thy strength, O Adonai, unto whom the praise and glory will for ever and ever belong! Amen.

The servants shall enter the Temple proper.

To purify, a servant shall take up the bowl of hyssop water and shall make a perfect triangle, starting in the north, moving to the east and then to the west, sprinkling the waters and saying in a clear voice:

For pure will, unassuaged of purpose,
delivered from the lust of result, is every way perfect.

Lighting a stick of sandalwood incense, the servant shall then consecrate the Temple and make a perfect triangle, starting in the south, moving to the west and then to the east, and making the Mark of the Beast in the air at each point (Ä), saying:

I am uplifted in thine heart;
and the kisses of the stars rain hard upon thy body.

Standing at the center of the Temple, a female servant shall exact the Ritual of the Ruby Star, with Force and Fire in her voice and limbs.

The servant chosen as Summoner shall then call the Kings and Seniors of the Angelic Holy Table, with Rood and Voice in the following order:

NORTH (Make the Sign of the Cross with each name, above and below)
King: Eldprna
Seniors: Anodoin ✠ Arinnaq ✠ Apdoce ✠ Alndvod ✠ Adoeoet ✠ Aetpio

EAST
King: Bataiva
Seniors: Autotar ✠ Hipotga ✠ Haozpi ✠ Htmorda ✠ Aaoxaif ✠ Abioro

SOUTH
King: Iczhhca
Seniors: Acmbicu ✠ Lhiansa ✠ Lhctga ✠ Lzinopo ✠ Aczino ✠ Aidrom

WEST
King: Raagiol
Seniors: Soaiznt ✠ Ligdisa ✠ Lgaiol ✠ Laoaxrp ✠ Saiinou ✠ Srahpm

The Angelic Retinue so duly summoned shall be asked to form the 'perfect circle' and to inform and enliven the mind, body and spirit of the servants in the task at hand, in the name of 'Babalond'.

The 16th Key shall be recited by a female servant, first in English, then in Enochian:

O thou second flame
The house of Justice which hast thy beginning in glory;
And shalt comfort the just:
Which walkest on the earth with feete 876

That understand and separate creatures:
Great art thou in the God of Stretch-forth-and-Conquer.
Move and shew yourselves
Open the mysteries of your Creation
Be friendly unto me
For I am the servant of the same your God
The true worshipper of the Highest.

Ils viuialprt salman balt ds acroodzi busd od bliorax
balit dsinsi Caosg lusdan Emod dsom od tliob
drilpa geh yls Madzilodarp Zacar od
Zamran odo cicle Qaa zorge Lap
zirdo Noco Mad hoath Iaida

The 17th Key shall then be recited by a male servant, first in English, then in Enochian:

O thou third flame whose wings are thorns to stir up vexation:
And hast 7336 lamps living and going before
Whose God is Wrath in Anger
Gird up thy loins and harken
Move and shew yourselves
Open the mysteries of your Creation
Be friendly unto me
For I am the servant of the same your God
The true worshipper of the Highest.

Ils dialprt soba vpaah chis nanba zixlay dodsih
od brint Faxs hubaro tustax ylsi sobaiad
I vonpovnph Aldon daxil od toatar
Zacar od Zamran odo cicle Qaa
zorge Lap zirdo Noco
Mad hoath Iaida

Standing at the center of the Temple, a male servant shall exact the Ritual of the Sapphire Star, in perfect equipoise and stature.

The Servants shall then lay out in unison and with perfect symmetry in red chalk, or else in prepared powders (comprised of the collected blood, menses, seed and ashes of the Elixir of those present), the Star of Babalon upon the floor at the center of the Temple. This shall be exacted whilst all chant Her name by its letters in the Angelic Alphabet forty-nine times, until the Star be perfectly traced: Pa-Un-Pa-Un-Ur-Med-Drux. White candles shall be lit and placed at the points of the Star, along with red chalices, preferably made of crystal. The servant chosen to be the Oracle of Her Voice shall take their place within the Star. All else shall remain without.

The 19th Key shall be recited by the Summoner, first in English, then in Enochian. The name 'Babalond' shall take the place of the name of the Aethyr.

O ye heavens which dwell in the Body of Our Lady Babalond
And are mighty in the parts of the Earth
And execute therein the Judgement of the highest
To you it is said, Behold the face of your God, the beginning of comfort:
Whose eyes are the brightness of the heavens:
Which provided you for the government of the Earth,
And her unspeakable variety
Furnishing you with a power and understanding
That ye might dispose all things according to the providence
And foresight of him that sitteth on the holy Throne
And rose up in the beginning saying,
The Earth let her be governed by her parts and let there be division in her,
That the glory of her may be always the ecstasy and ascension of orgasm.
Her course, let it run with the heavens:
And as a handmaid let her serve them:
One season let it confound another:
And let there be no Creature upon or within her the same:
All her members let them differ in their qualities:
And let there be no one creature equal with another
The reasonable Creatures of the Earth and Men
Let them vex and weed out one another:
And in their dwelling places, let them forget their names:
The work of man and his pomp, let them be defaced:
His building let it become a Cave for the beasts of the field:
Confound her understanding with darkness.
For why?
It rejoiceth me, the Virgin and Man.

One time let her be known, and another time a stranger:
Because she is the bed of an Harlot, and the dwelling place
of him that is fallen:
O ye heavens arise, the lower heavens beneath you,
Let them serve you:
Govern those that govern:
Cast down the downcast such as fall:
Bring forth with those that increase:
And destroy the rotten:
No place let it remain in one number:
Add and Diminish until the stars be numbered:
Arise, Move, and Appear before the Covenant of his mouth,
Which he hath shewn unto us in his Justice:
Open the Mysteries of your Creation:
And make us partakers of the undefiled knowledge.

Madriax dspraf fargt ge tilb Babalond chis Micaolz saanir
Caosgo od fisis balzizras Iaida nonca gohulim Micma adoian
Mad Jaod bliorb sabaooaona chis Luciftias peripsol ds abraassa
noncf netaaib Caosgi od tilb adphaht damploz tooat noncf
gmicalzoma Lrasd tofglo marb yarry Idoigo od torzulp
iaodaf gohol Caosga tabaord saanir od christeos yrpoil tiobl
Busdir tilb noaln paid orsba od dodrmni zylna Elzaptilb
parmgi peripsax od ta qurlst booapis Lnibm ovcho symp
od Christeos Agtoltorn mirc Q tiabl Lel Ton paombd dilzmo aspian
Od christeos ag L tortorn parach asymp Cordziz dodpal od fifalz
Lsmnad od fargt bams omaoas Conisbra od auauox tonug Orscatbl
noasmi tabges Levithmong unchi omptilb ors
Bagle Moooah olcordziz L capimao ixomaxip od cacocasb gosaa
Baglen pii tianta ababalond od faorgt telocvovim
Madriiax torzu oadriax orocha aboapri
Tabaori priaz artabas Adrpan corsta dobix Yolcam priazi arcoazior
od quasb qting Ripir paaoxt sagacor vml od prd-zar cacrg Aoiveae cormpt
Torzu Zacar of Zamran aspt sibsi butmona ds surzas tia baltan
Odo cicle Qaa od ozazma plapli Iadnamad

The Liturgy Unto Our Lady shall now be recited, each in turn, by the servants without.

DAUGHTER OF FORTITUDE

I am the Daughter of Fortitude and ravished every hour of my youth. For behold, I am Understanding, and Science dwelleth in me; and the heavens oppress me, they covet and desire me with infinite appetite: few or none that are earthly have embraced me, for I am shadowed with the Circle of the Stone and covered with the morning Clouds. My feet are swifter than the winds and my hands are sweeter than the morning dew. My garments are from the beginning and my dwelling place is in myself. The Lion knoweth not where I walk, neither do the beasts of the field understand me. I am deflowered and yet a virgin. I sanctify and am not sanctified. Happy is he that embraceth me: for in the night season I am sweet and in the day, full of pleasure. My company is a harmony of many Cymbals and my lips sweeter than health itself. I am a harlot for such as ravish me and a virgin with such as know me not. For lo, I am loved of many, and I am a lover to many; and as many as come unto me as they should do have entertainment. Purge your streets, O ye sons of men, and wash your houses clean; make yourselves holy and put on righteousness. Cast out your old strumpets and burn their clothes; abstain from the company of other women that are defiled, that are sluttish, and not so handsome and beautiful as I, and then will I come and dwell amongst you: and behold, I will bring forth children unto you, and they shall be the Sons of Comfort. I will open my garments and stand naked before you, that your love may be more enflamed toward me.

(The Liturgy continues with excerpts recited from Liber 418: the Babalon section from the 12th Aethyr, LOE; the song which begins, 'Omari tessala...' and its English translation from the 2nd Aethyr ARN; and the entirety of Liber 156, Cheth Vel Vallum Abiegni)

Now shall the assembled servants fervently pray with devotion unto Our Lady from their hearts. The Summoner shall cast forth the Red and the Blue Triangle about the Star of Babalon, and let Her be called in Speech and in Silence. Let communion with Her be achieved, both within and without Her Star, and in the Body of Her chosen oracle, depending on the purpose of the Ritus. Let the Cups be filled with the Wine of the Sabbath. Let Her speak, as She so wills. Let the Keys be received by each in their own fashion, as She so wills. Let the License to In-Dwell be given, first by the Summoner, and then by the servants. Let Her light abide.

✠ Fiat ✠ Fiat ✠ Fiat ✠

Emblematic Arcana of Babalon

Frater A.I.

LAMEN OF BABALON THE BEAUTIFUL

THE MYSTERIES OF Our Lady are manifold, and these powers may be expressed in infinitely diverse emanations. Among these are the emblems to serve as heralds of her charge, esoteric concentrators of specific aspects of her power. Each serves as a Veil for that which may only be revealed through Union with the Beloved.

SEVEN-HEADED APOCALYPTIC BEAST AND THE CITY OF THE PYRAMIDS

EMBLEMATIC LAMEN OF THE 17TH PATH TO OUR LADY BABALON BEING THE DISPOSING INTELLIGENCE OF CAIN, OR ATU VI 'THE BROTHERS'

The House of Babalon is established in Binah, straddled between the manifest and unmanifest world and this is reflected in the dualism expressed by the double spheres. The material world is a reflection and the dualism is expanded by the zodiacal sign of Gemini. The sign of the twins has been explained by the Master Therion as the story of Cain in Atu VI 'The Brothers' as related in *Liber 418 The Vision and the Voice*, The Cry of the 2nd Aethyr, which is called ARN:

> *In the first place, there is again the woman riding on the bull, which is the reflection of BABALON, that rideth on The Beast. And also there is an Assyrian legend of a woman with a fish, and also there is a legend of Eve and the Serpent, for Cain was the child of Eve and the Serpent, and not of Eve and Adam; and therefore when he had slain his brother, who was the first murderer, having sacrificed living things to his demon, had Cain the mark upon his brow, which is the mark of the Beast spoken of in the Apocalypse, and is the sign of initiation.*
>
> *The shedding of blood is necessary, for God did not hear the children of Eve until blood was shed. And that is external religion; but Cain spake not with God, nor had the mark of initiation upon his brow, so that he was shunned by all men, until he had shed blood. And this blood was the blood of his brother. This is a mystery of the sixth key of the Taro, which ought not to be called The Lovers, but The Brothers.*
>
> *In the middle of the card stands Cain; in his right hand is the Hammer of Thor with which he hath slain his brother, and it is all wet with his blood. And his left hand he holdeth open as a sign of innocence. And on his right hand is his mother Eve, around whom the serpent is entwined with his hood spread behind her head; and on his left hand is a figure somewhat like the Hindoo Kali, but much more seductive. Yet I know it to be Lilith. And above him is the Great Sigil of the Arrow, downward, but it is struck through the heart of the child. This Child is also Abel.*

Dead Abel is here shown in the heart of the lamen within a vesica, the latter referring to the Kteis of the Great Mother, thus the symbolism of birthing the son, Light from Darkness is evident. This is the path which connects Binah to Tiphareth and contains the mystery of Life, Death and Faithfulness. According to the *Sepher Yetzirah*:

The seventeenth path is called the Disposing Intelligence. It disposes the righteous to faithfulness, and clothes them with the Holy Life-Breath; and it is called the Foundation of Beauty in the place of the Supernals.

Foundation=Yesod=Moon=9
Beauty=Tiphareth=Sun=6

Together they are Cancer [a double-sign like Gemini]

This is the secret union betwixt mother and son and
a hieroglyph of the Chariot.

CHARIOT GRAIL

This Chariot glyph is composed of several elements significant to Babalon. The central star is derived from Liber Al; I, 60 '*Five Pointed Star, with a Circle in the Middle*' and is a reference to the Scarlet Woman. Together with the other stars its number is 11 *'as all their numbers who are of us.'* A star is the geometric figure of the number 5, qabalistically Geburah, being Strength on the Pillar of Severity. Thus aligned with the triangle geometrically representing Binah, the Path of the Chariot is here connoted. As the receptacle of the Blood of the Great Mother, the glyph also represents a form of the Grail, being supported also by the triangle and the watery symbolism of Cancer, the sign assigned to this Qabalistic Path.

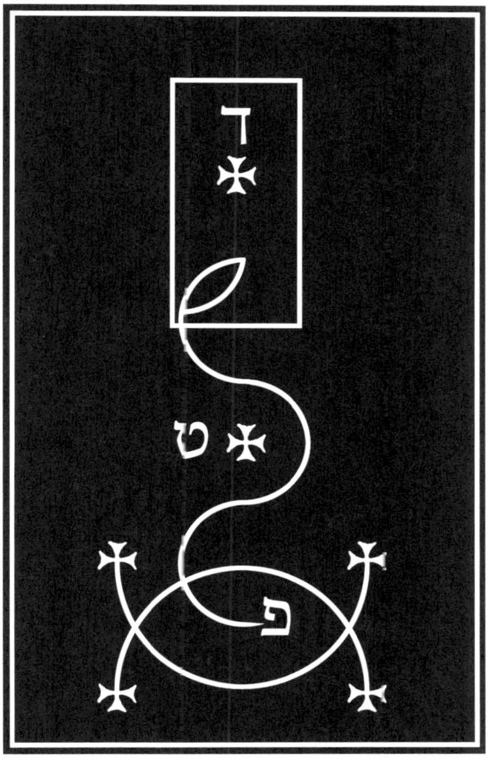

TRESTLEBOARD OF THE SIDEWINDER

Neophytes in such matters would do well to chalk or paint the trestleboard upon the temple floor to serve as a prompt until repitition brings it on as a natural action and an activated formulation of specified qabalistic currents known unto the wise as the Way of the Side-Winder. The arcana of the formulae employ the forms represented by the three horizontal paths on the tree, acting as steps in an AGAPE with the mystery of Babalon, the mouth, serpent and door. This is the trinity of mother, father, son reflected in Venus, Mars and Leo [Sol]. Further projected as an inversion upon the supernals Binah as mother and Chokmah as father, it leaves Tiphareth as the 'son'.

The Way of the Side-Winder is the preparatory ouevre preceeding the Station of the Daath-Cross where operations involving the formulation of a Babe of the Abyss transpire. This child of the bornless supernals Atu XI LUST is the secret fire of desire and the serpent of the Garden of Eden. The alchemists told a qabalistic joke by nailing [vav | tiphareth] a serpent to a cross. The symbol of the Brazen Serpent not only exemplifies the formula 'solve et coagula' but also counts the gematria of serpent [nephesh] and Messiah [messiach] as being of the same enumeration. The formula is reflected on a third triplicity of Magus, High Priestess and Babe of the Abyss. [*see* OVUM ABYSSUS INFANTULI]

The three-fold Way of the Side-Winder provides entrance to one of the Hidden Paths on the Tree, a path connecting Binah to Daath. Here one experiences the laying of the Egg from Mater Dolorosa: will, desire and belief of the babe within this egg of blackened light. Born from the bornless blackness full of potential and primal power. Once mastery over the egg-form is attained, the adept may perform the rites at the Station of the Daath-Cross of the Abyss.

A turning of phrase and uncoiling serpent shall bring the door a-swinging.
[The Three Horizons]

Horizon of the Mouth [Peh=80] *Mars*
This is the voice of the Aeon, a Blasted Tower and renderer of the Rainbow of Promise
[Speech in Silence]

Horizon of the Serpent [Teth=9] *Leo*
'O Lion and O Serpent that Destroyed the Destroyer Be Mighty among us.'
[Silence in Speech]

Horizon of the Door [Daleth=4] *Venus*
Upon the Door of Daath thou shalt knock and NEMO shall answer thee.
[Silence]

80+9+4=93=AGAPE 'divided for Love's sake for the chance of union.'
'There is the dove, and there is the serpent.'
[Empress & Lust]

The Hidden Path connecting Binah to Daath is the Akasic Egg of the blackened Throat, the ovum of the Secret Flame. New-born life hatching from a Pile of Dust. On Otz Chaim, the Path of the Egg forms a triad with the Magus and High Priestess who together bring forth the Babe of the Abyss.

OVUM ABYSSUS INFANTULI*

*Egg of the Babe of the Abyss, the Latin acrostic being; OAI. See Liber LVXI v. 38 *'I, Apep the Serpent, am the heart of IAO. Isis shall await Asar, and I in their midst.'* OAI=70+1+10=81. 81 is also; 'Gods' [ALIM]=1+30+10+40 as well as 'I' [Anoki]=1+50+20+10 and providing a secret signifigance not only to the letters, but also the method of the A∴A∴ as denoted by the reversal of the IAO formula. Instead of employing the current of the dying god, the OAI shows how a god may be conceived. 'O Lion and O' Serpent that destroyed the destroyer be mighty amoung us'. Here, Black Osiris shares his generative power via the serpent. The serpent is the germinating creative fire spewed from the mouth of the dragon. This secret fire is incubated in Silence, beneath the veil of the Priestess of the Silver Star. This current is further expressed via the elements of air and fire conjunct in the sign of Capricorn. Alchemically this would be the heat of the philosophic egg being regulated by the combination of those active elements. Thus the 'Season of the Goat' marks the period of gestation.

Egg [Hebrew: BeTzaH]=2+10+90+5=107. 107 is also Oel the ruling angel of LEO and the 5th astrological house [Hebrew: OVAL]=70+6+1+30

STATION OF THE DAATH-CROSS

[Armed with trident and sickle]
NEMO parts Thy veil like a split sickle-moon
[Sign of Silence followed by the Rending of the Veil of the Abyss]

Cross-roads crowned with whirling might
Supernal Mother Dolorosa
Starry Father of the Sea
[Enter the Frontiers of the Abyss in an Egg of Blackened Light]

Tears will purify the Egg [water, purify]
And Blood will Consecrate [blood, consecrate]
Solar incubation shell-shod [fire, enliven]
Daath-Cross of the Abyss Bless [Sign of the+]
O Morning Star and Crescent [sol et luna]
O Revealer and Concealer[nox et lvx]
Illumi-Birthed Ovum of the Pyramids [golden child born
of a black mother]
A Hidden path is Laid, it is Laid.

CUP OF FORNICATIONS

CONTRIBUTORS

AMODALI is a magical practitioner, artist, musician and writer from Lancashire in the North of England; specializing in research on the sexual mysteries of Babalon and the metaphysics and phenomenology of female occult anatomy. Her multidisciplinary body of work has manifested internationally for over 25 years through ritual perfrmances, music, art exhibitions and magical research undertaken under the auspices of 'Incarnadine Temple'. In recent years, Amodali has given talks on the magic of Babalon at events such as the 'Ecology, Cosmos and Consciousness' Lecture series in London and the Esoteric Book Conference in the United States. Her forthcoming book *The Marks of Teth* will be published by Three Hands Press in 2016.

ERIK DAVIS is an author, scholar, award-winning journalist, and podcaster based in San Francisco. His wide-ranging work focuses on the intersection of esoteric religion, media, and the imagination. He is the author, most recently, of *Nomad Codes: Adventures in Modern Esoterica* (Yeti), and also wrote *The Visionary State: A Journey through California's Spiritual Landscape* (Chronicle), the 33 1/3 volume on *Led Zeppelin IV* (Continuum), and *TechGnosis: Myth, Magic, and Mysticism in the Age of Information*, which has recently been reissued with a new afterword.

GORDAN DJURDJEVIC is a contributor to the anthology *Aleister Crowley and Western Esotericism* (Oxford University Press, 2012); co-editor, with Henrik Bogdan, of the collection of essays *Occultism in a Global Perspective* (Acumen, 2013; Routledge, 2015); and the author of *Masters of Magical Powers: The Nath Yogis in the Light of Esoteric Notions* (VDM, 2008); *India and the Occult: The Influence of South Asian Spirituality on Modern Western Occultism* (Palgrave Macmillan, 2014); and, with Shukdev Singh, *Sayings of Gorakhnath: Selected Translations from the* Gorakh Bani (Oxford University Press, forthcoming).

ROBERT FITZGERALD is a native Californian, a practicing Thelemite of over thirty years, and a devotee of Babalon. *A Rose Veiled in Black* is the first work he has co-edited for Three Hands Press.

FRATER A.I. is a practitioner who embraces Western ceremonial magic and its allied modalities including Crooked Path sorcery, planetary and sigil magic. His work has appeared in *The Psalter of Cain* (Xoanon, 2012) and *Clavis Journal.*

BARRY WILLIAM HALE is a multi-media artist from Sydney, Australia. His work is a synthesis of art and magick, image and sound. He is part of the duo known as NOKO, whose purpose is the conjuration of spirits through voice, electronics and visual graphic arts. Babalon is his muse.

MANON HEDENBORG-WHITE is a Ph.D. candidate in the History of Religions at Uppsala University, Sweden. Her dissertation project explores the history and development of the goddess Babalon, with an emphasis on issues of gender and sexuality. She has published and spoken on a number of subjects related to modern Western esotericism and gender, as well as the connection between folk religiosity and resistance in the cult of the Mexican death saint, Santa Muerte.

RICHARD KACZYNSKI is the author of *Forgotten Templars: The Untold Origins of Ordo Templi Orientis* (2012) and *Perdurabo: The Life of Aleister Crowley* (2002; rev. exp. ed. 2010), widely considered to be the definitive biography of the Great Beast. He is also a contributor to several recent academic anthologies, as well as books such as *A Concordance to the Holy Books of Thelema* and *The Golden Dawn Sourcebook*. Richard has written and lectured internationally on these and related topics since 1990. By day, he is a social psychologist, biostatistician and research scientist whose 1993 doctoral dissertation examined metaphysical beliefs and experiences among occult practitioners.

TIMO KETOLA was born in Helsinki in 1975. Since 2005 he has lived in central Italy where he works with book design and general illustration, as well as exploring traditions such as woodcarving, bronze casting and fine-art prints.

HANA LEE is a non-medium specific creative with a degree from San Francisco Art Institute. Lee's work depicts reflections of liminality, and the shapes realized and transformed within. As the sphere binds the subconscious and conscious continuum, what manifests reveals a fragment of the counterpoint.

SARAH LINDSAY is a multi-media artisan living in the Pacific Northwest who binds her anachronistic work with the hand of spindle, shuttle and needle. Her artwork explores the areas of symbolism and hexencraft, specifically the apotropaic arte. Her work has recently been exhibited at True Love Gallery in Seattle, Washington as part of 'CONSTELLATION—An Ouverture to the Zodiac' and also appeared in the astrological journal *The Ascendant*.

LINDA MACFARLANE is an artist and devotee of the Great Goddess. She has created illustrations for a number of magical texts including *Magical and Philosophical Commentaries on the Book of the Law*. In 1973 Linda, with her husband Peter Macfarlane, co-founded 93 Publishing as a method of assisting Kenneth Grant in his re-introduction of Crowley and Spare material to a new generation of readers.

MITCHELL NOLTE is a freelance illustrator and artist located in Melbourne, Australia. His art and personal interests involve magick, mysticism, Thelema, Alchemy, dreams and fantasy. The imagery serves as a vehicle for many worlds and entities, such that the human spirit can birth with love, imagination and will.

GRANT POTTS, PH.D., has been active in the magical community in the United States his entire adult life, and has been an initiate of Ordo Templi Orientis since 2000. He has served O.T.O. in a number of capacities, both on a local and national level, and currently serves as Master of Scarlet Woman Lodge in Austin, Texas, as well as a member of the Committee for the Advancement of Thelemic Families. In his professional life, he serves as chair of a Department of Philosophy, Religion, and Humanities at a major community college, where he also teaches introductory classes on Philosophy and Religion.

NICOLE DIMUCCI POTTS is a self taught henna artist and owner of Scarlet Bee Henna, and has practiced the art of henna for 17 years. She will be an instructor at this year's Henna Intensive and Retreat in California, teaching the Magical Art of Henna. Nicole has been a member of O.T.O. since 2008, and is currently serving as a Priestess for her community. Professionally, she works in education, currently for Austin Community College, and raises her very magical 4 year old daughter.

LIV RAINEY-SMITH specializes in the superannuated art of hand-pulled xylographic prints. Her imagery emerges from dreams, visions, esoteric traditions, and a longstanding love of historic art. She designs, cuts, and prints her original woodcut editions in Portland, Oregon.

DANIEL A. SCHULKE is a writer on the subjects of folk magic, witchcraft, comparative religion, and ethnobotany. His essays have appeared in the prominent esoteric journals *Starfire, The Cauldron, Clavis,* and *Abraxas.* His book *Veneficium,* concerning vectors of poison usage in magical traditions, was released in September 2012 by Three Hands Press.

ROBERT C. STEIN is a Professor Emeritus of Biology from Buffalo, New York. He became involved in the work of Thelema in 1982 and founded Pyramid Camp/Lodge in 1984. In 1985 he spent a year preparing and performing the ritual *Liber Nu* in a comet impact crater in Australia. His primary interest is the Class A Liber XXXI (manuscript), Liber XXVII and Liber CCXXXI. His *modus operandi* is to rely on original literature, especially before 1985. He does have other interests too.

CAROLINE WISE is a former owner of the Atlantis Bookshop in London. In the 1980s, when she was at Skoob Books, she initiated the republication of Kenneth Grant's work. Her interests and practice concern the goddess in all her forms, animal mythology and welfare, and working with psychism, dreams and the sacred landscape. She is the author of *Finding Elen, the Quest for Elen of the Ways* and has contributed to several books on the Goddess.

A Rose Veiled in Black was first published at Winter Solstice 2015 EV by Three Hands Press. The first printing consisted of 777 standard hardcover copies, 49 copies in quarter crimson goat, and seven slipcased copies in full crimson goat. A softcover edition, featuring a unique cover image by Linda MacFarlane, and with an additional interior color image by Mitchell Nolte, limited to two thousand copies, was released 24 February, 2025.

Scribæ Quo Mysterium Famulatur